The Bible in America

Essays in Cultural History

Edited by

NATHAN O. HATCH

MARK A. NOLL

New York   Oxford

OXFORD UNIVERSITY PRESS

1982

Copyright © 1982 by Oxford University Press, Inc.

Library of Congress Cataloging in Publication Data
Main entry under title:

The Bible in America.

1. Bible—Criticism, interpretation, etc.—
United States—Congresses.   2. United States—
Religion—Congresses.   I. Hatch, Nathan O.
II. Noll, Mark A., 1946–
BS540.B4453   220′.0973   81-18751
ISBN 0-19-503099-0   AACR2
ISBN 0-19-503100-8 (pbk.)

Printing (last digit): 9 8 7 6 5 4 3 2 1

Printed in the United States of America

TO

F.F. Bruce,
J.I. Packer,
John R.W. Stott,

who, though British,
have served the Bible in America
very well

Acknowledgments

Most of the essays which appear in this volume were presented as papers at a conference, "The Bible in American Culture: A Historical Inquiry," November 1–2, 1979, at Wheaton College, Wheaton, Illinois, under the sponsorship of The Lilly Endowment and Wheaton College. The editors would like to thank Dr. Robert Linn of the Lilly Endowment for his role in making both the conference and this book possible, and several individuals at Wheaton College who rendered valuable support for the conference: Dr. Hudson Armerding, president; Dr. David Johnston, vice president for finance; Dr. Donald Mitchell, now president of King College, Bristol, Tennessee; and Mrs. Jane Nelson, Administrative Assistant of the Billy Graham Center.

We would also like to acknowledge our indebtedness to those who attended the Wheaton conference. We are particularly grateful to the others who contributed papers and commentary during the conference and whose insights shaped the essays that appear here: Sydney Ahlstrom, Yale University; Donald Bloesch, University of Dubuque; Joel Carpenter, Trinity College, Deerfield, Illinois; C. C. Goen, Wesley Theological Seminary, Washington, D.C.; E. Brooks Holifield, Emory University; Donald Mathews, University of North Carolina, Chapel Hill; Bruce Metzger, Princeton Theological Seminary; J. I. Packer, Regent College, Vancouver; Ernest Sandeen, Macalaster College; Timothy Smith, The Johns Hopkins University; Keith Sprunger, Bethel College, North Newton, Kansas; David Wells,

Gordon-Conwell Theological Seminary; James White, Trinity Christian
College, Palos Heights, Illinois; and Mr. Kenneth Woodward, *Newsweek*
magazine.

Secretaries and research assistants are the unsung heroes in the production of books by academics. For this one, Mrs. Beatrice Horne provided excellent typing, and Mr. Robert Lackie, industrious research for
Mark Noll. Mrs. Catherine Box provided superb typing and proofreading
for Nathan Hatch.

N.O.H.
M.A.N.

A faculty development grant from Wheaton College helped with the final
preparation of the manuscript.

Contents

Introduction
Nathan O. Hatch and Mark A. Noll   3

I Word and Order in Colonial New England
   Harry S. Stout   19

II The Image of the United States as a Biblical Nation,
    1776–1865
    Mark A. Noll   39

III *Sola Scriptura* and *Novus Ordo Seclorum*
     Nathan O. Hatch   59

IV Everyone One's Own Interpreter?: The Bible, Science,
    and Authority in Mid-Nineteenth-Century America
    George M. Marsden   79

V The Two-Edged Sword: The Fundamentalist Use
   of the Bible
   Timothy P. Weber   101

VI The Demise of Biblical Civilization
    Grant Wacker   121

VII   The Bible in Twentieth-Century Protestantism:
       A Preliminary Taxonomy
       Richard J. Mouw   139

VIII   The Quest for a Catholic Vernacular Bible in America
       Gerald P. Fogarty, S.J.   163

       Index   181

THE BIBLE IN AMERICA

Introduction

NATHAN O. HATCH
MARK A. NOLL

It is impossible to proceed very far in the study of American history before encountering the Bible. For almost all varieties of Americans, the
Jewish-Christian Scriptures have provided a vast reservoir of themes,
phrases, meanings, and habits of thinking. During the early years of the
United States, Mason Weems, who would gain fame as Washington's biog-
rapher, earned his living as a traveling Bible salesman in Virginia. From
there he once made a rhapsodic report on business: "I tell you this is the
very season and age of the Bible. Bible Dictionaries, Bible tales, Bible stories—Bibles plan or paraphrased, Carey's Bibles, Collin's Bibles, Clarke's
Bibles, Kimptor's Bibles, no matter what or whose, all, all will go down—
so wide is the crater of public appetite at this time. God be thanked for
it."[1] The science of public polling gives more prosaic witness to the resil-
iency of the Bible's appeal even in contemporary America. A full 42 percent of the American population, as polled by George Gallup in 1978,
professed to believe that "the Bible is the word of God and is not mistaken
in its statements and teachings." Belief can be cheap, so it is even more
impressive that Gallup found 30 percent of the population actually reading the Bible at least once a week (12 percent at least once a day).[2] The
names American settlers gave to their communities, particularly in the
eastern half of the country, offer another testimony to the pervasive presence of Scripture: Zoar, Ohio (Genesis 13:10), Ruma, Illinois (II Kings
23:36), Mount Tirzah, North Carolina (Joshua 12:24), Zela, West Vir-

ginia (Joshua 18:28), as well as 47 variations on Bethel, 61 on Eden, and 95 on Salem.[3]

The Bible that has appealed to the masses is the same book opinion-makers and cultivated elites have also read. William Bradford, the early Pilgrim governor, wrote his *History of Plymouth Plantation* in a biblical idiom only slightly less pronounced than John Bunyan, his near-contemporary, used in the *Pilgrim's Progress.*[4] Noah Webster, creator of the American dictionary, thought he could teach the children of the new United States to read and write by giving them a distinctly American translation of the Bible.[5] The Scriptures have been the constant companion of many Presidents: the great (Abraham Lincoln), the near-great (Woodrow Wilson), the forgotten (Grover Cleveland), and the yet to be judged (Jimmy Carter).[6] They have colored the imaginative universes of some of America's best writers, from Herman Melville who wrote of Ishmael, Ahab, and Leviathan in *Moby-Dick,* to William Faulkner whose very titles—*Absalom, Absalom!, Go Down Moses*—reflect a biblical presence.[7] Even those who abandoned conventional religion did not always flee from Scripture. Thomas Jefferson, who desired a faith purified of all but sweet reasonableness, twice prepared abridged editions of the New Testament for his own use.[8] Henry Adams, who moved beyond conventional faith to embrace, alternately, science and despair, nonetheless began his intellectual autobiography with an extended biblical metaphor.[9]

An examination of either popular or literary culture leads to two general conclusions about the Bible in America. The first is that Scripture has been nearly omnipresent in the nation's past—a conclusion this book demonstrates indirectly. Its major concern, however, is with the second: that the actual use of the Bible in American life has been attended with considerable complexity and decided ambiguity.

The person with eyes to see knows that the Bible remains prominent in America. In recent years the mass media have highlighted several controversies which underscore that fact. Angry West Virginia parents attacked local school boards in 1974 for assigning literature textbooks that transgressed "biblical values."[10] In California, litigants arguing for the introduction of "Creationist" teachings into the state's science curriculum gained publicity and a modest judicial concession in 1981.[11] Major Protestant denominations, most recently the Luthern Church-Missouri Synod and the Southern Baptist Convention, have experienced well-publicized controversies over the Bible.[12] And in recent years, the presses serving the nation's theologically conservative Protestants have turned out an avalanche of books debating the nature and authority of Scripture.[13] Yet all this activity surrounding the Bible does not explain itself, nor have media pundits done a good job at linking modern concerns about the Bible to the biblical heritage of the country.

Historians have long recognized, at least in a general way, that the Bible has played a central role in the various forms of American religious life and in some aspects of the national history.[14] They have, for example, recorded the way that Americans use the Bible to express charged symbolic meanings at pivotal moments in their history. Grateful blacks from Baltimore in September 1864 presented President Lincoln with a pulpit Bible bound in violet-tinted velvet, furnished in gold, with a raised design depicting the emancipation of the slaves, which cost far more than the average per capita income of white Americans.[15] Hours after the death of President Kennedy his legislative liaison, Larry O'Brien, secured the slain President's own leather-bound Bible for the swearing in of Lyndon Johnson.[16] A few historians—Jews and the uncommitted as well as Christians—have even tried to talk specifically about the impact of the Scriptures on American life.[17]

Popular and scholarly interest in the Bible has, however, tended to concentrate on Scripture's importance for theological construction, on highly charged confrontations between biblicists and secularists, or on general connections between a supposedly biblical ethos and the American way of life. Much less attention has been paid to the ways in which the Bible has interacted with other cultural forces in American history. Yet to come at the Bible this way—not denying its special religious significance but concentrating on its activity in wider worlds—opens a fascinating range of subjects with nearly as much to offer those who hold no special convictions about Scripture as for those who do. The premise of this book is that students of American history need to be reminded how central the Bible has been in the development of national life just as much as believers in the Bible's divine authority need to recognize how its use has been shaped by events and forces in American history. Failure to consider Scripture as a cultural force has created two problems: it has left gaps and distortions in the recording of the American past, and it has encouraged artificial attitudes toward the Bible among those who read it as a sacred text.

To be sure, the attempt to chart the Bible's role in culture poses special problems for the historian, problems Perry Miller once highlighted in discussing the influence of the Old Testament during an earlier period: "The Old Testament is truly so omnipresent in the American culture of

1800 or 1820 that historians have as much difficulty taking cognizance of it as of the air people breathed."[18] Without making light of that difficulty, the authors of these essays believe that it is worth the effort to go beyond a mere recognition that the Bible has been ever present in American life. Our desire is to investigate what has happened to and with the Bible in wider dimensions of American history.

We feel that it is past time to consider the Bible's presence in social, intellectual, political, and even economic spheres as well as in its ecclesiastical relations. We proceed under the assumption that if the cultural history of America is unthinkable without the Bible, it is appropriate to think carefully and in some detail about the actual history of the Bible itself. We assume that nearly everyone has heard the Bible cited in defense of mutually exclusive arguments (e.g., to defeat godless communism in Vietnam, to repent for imperialistic atrocities in Vietnam). We assume that nearly everyone has at some time had the thought that anything can be proven from the Bible. We assume that even casual students of history would be quick to apply Herbert Butterfield's remark to the American situation: "The Bible has proved to be the most flexible of authorities and the most capable of progressive interpretation."[19] Yet these very ambiguities confirm our belief that it is a valuable enterprise to study the history that surrounds the many-faceted character of the Bible in America.

The essays that follow make a beginning on this topic, but they can only touch briefly on important aspects of the problem which deserve special attention in themselves. For example, the history of the printing and distribution of the Bible and biblical materials is an immense, yet vastly neglected subject. Americans have sustained an incredible rate of Bible publication and an even more stupendous appetite for literature about the Bible. Over 2500 different English-language editions of the Bible were published in the United States from 1777 to 1957.[20] Recent American translations of the Bible have sold in breathtaking numbers: the Revised Standard Version averaged a million copies annually for the first ten years after its publication in 1952; the Living Bible paraphrase of Kenneth Taylor had 25 million copies in print after its first eleven years; the New International Version and the Good News Bible have both been overnight million-sellers in the last decade.[21] The American Bible Society from its founding in 1816 through 1979 had distributed over three billion Bibles, testaments, portions, and selections, with nearly 110 million in the United States in 1979 alone.[22] Americans have also expended vast energies in translating Scripture into other tongues, from John Eliot's rendering of the

New Testament into "the Indian Language" (Natick) in 1661 to the work of the Wycliffe Bible Translators who in the twentieth century have translated at least portions of the Scriptures into nearly a thousand languages.[23] Yet the great quantity of printed Bibles constitutes but a fraction of the total publications concerning Scripture: fifty tightly packed pages in a recent listing of books in print, four great volumes in the Library of Congress's catalogue of books held by American libraries before 1956, many pages each year in annual surveys by religious periodicals.[24] These bare statistics sketch in broadest strokes the outlines of a story which contains many fascinating chapters—as, for instance, the publication of the very first English-language Bible in America, an event which took place in 1782 with the express authorization of the new United States Congress and which led, perhaps for the only time, to a serious financial loss for the publisher.[25] Study of the printing and distribution of biblical materials in order to gain an understanding of American mass culture is also a potentially fruitful enterprise, one we do not pursue directly.[26]

In addition, since the intent of this book is to look at the Bible in relationship to broad themes in American culture, we do not spend much time considering Scripture as an ancient text, honored for both its religious and literary significance. Yet American attention to the Bible from this perspective has been so consistent, thorough, and prolific that it has spawned at least four inter-related "industries" deserving brief mention. The first is discussion of the doctrine of the Bible. From the early days of settlement, Protestants—now lyrically, now learnedly, now viciously—have regaled each other and the broader world on the religious character of Scripture;[27] Catholics have striven among themselves and with Protestants on this same issue;[28] and Jews have also participated in the fray[29]—all to the end of defending, expounding, or maintaining dogmatic convictions about the religious authority of the Bible. The second is the related effort to discover how best to interpret the Scriptures. Historians have not done as well in addressing this hermeneutical question for America as they have for Europe.[30] But particularly as European ideas have gained acceptance on these shores, Americans too have expended vast energies in exploring the best ways to read and understand Scripture.[31] The third is the scholarly study of the Bible in its own linguistic, historical, and cultural settings. A host of technical publications, led by the *Journal of Biblical Literature,* regularly and learnedly dissect, analyze, and assess the worlds reflected in the words of Scripture.[32] The fourth is a more recent enterprise, which received a major boost from the Supreme Court's 1963 ruling on the Bible that prohibited its use in public schools as a religious text but encouraged its study as a literary influence. So far at least, American experience has failed to bear out C. S. Lewis's contention that the Bible is "a book so remorselessly and continuously sacred that it does not invite, it excludes or repels, the merely aesthetic approach."[33] American scholarship has, in fact, produced mountains of material devoted to describing the Bible's character as great literature[34] and tracing its influence on American writers.[35] It is as gratifying as it is fitting that the Society for Biblical Literature, to honor its 100th anniversary in 1980, began an ambitious publication program which will deal with these four areas of biblical scholarship.[36]

While the essayists in this book touch on different aspects of the Bible's publishing, doctrinal, and literary history, they are more interested in the Bible as a focus for cultural values. They endeavor to explain how Scripture, as a collection of meanings and explanations about the world, interacts with other centers of meaning and explanation in American life.

Several of the essays examine roles the Bible has played in American social history. These explore what it means for Scripture to have acted as both a conservative and a radical social force, to have provided a vocabulary for both traditional deference and innovative egalitarianism, and to have been a source for both stability in the face of anarchy and freedom in the face of tyranny. How is it, for example, that Scripture could have penetrated to such a profound level nationally that it became a bulwark for both sides during the country's most intense internal division? From an abolitionist one could hear the Bible used like this:

> The spirit of slavery never seeks refuge in the Bible of its own accord. . . . Goaded to phrenzy in its conflicts with conscience and common sense, denied all quarter, and hunted from every covert, it vaults over the sacred inclosure and courses up and down the Bible, "seeking rest, and finding none." . . . At last, it slides away under the types of the Mosaic system, and seeks to burrow out of sight among their shadows. Vain hope![37]

From a Georgian it was a different story:

> We assert, and we shall prove, that the system of slavery in the United States, in every feature and in every particular of every feature, is essentially the same as the system authorized by the Bible, and introduced into the church at the time of its organization, and continued to the present day.[38]

Until the triumph of Union arms made further debate pointless, Americans continued to assault each other with texts like Exodus 21:16[39] and

Leviticus 25:44–46[40] from the Book they both revered. Essays by Harry Stout, Mark Noll, and Richard Mouw explore similar, if less extreme, situations where the Bible has appeared to bolster both sides of divisive social arguments.

The Bible's role in the rhetoric of social values, the main theme of the essay by Harry Stout, testifies to its power to shape and express different cultural mentalities that have flourished in America. More than a century before the Civil War, for example, scriptural phraseology could inform a very traditional picture of society from Virginian William Byrd II: "like one of the Patriarchs, I have my Flocks and my Herds, my Bond-men and Bond-women, and every Soart of Trade amongst my own Servants, so that I live in a kind of Independence on every one but Providence."[41] It could also inspire an attack on the socially stabilizing hierarchies of the church from New Jersey's Gilbert Tennent: "We should mourn over those, that are destitute of faithful Ministers . . . *as Sheep having no Shepherd*. . . . And let those who live under the Ministry of dead Men, whether they have got the Form of Religion or not, repair to the Living, where they may be edified."[42]

The Bible has also been a charter of social liberty for many who have felt constrained by traditional rigidities or even dominating cultural fashions, as the essays by Nathan Hatch and Timothy Weber attest. But on other occasions it has fulfilled quite a different role in enforcing social conformity. When the Roman Catholic Bishop of Philadelphia, Francis Patrick Kenrick, petitioned city officials in 1842 to allow school children of his faith to hear readings from the Douay version of the Bible instead of the King James Version sacred to Protestants, strong protest followed. Evangelical ministers formed national anti-Catholic organizations and, eventually, Protestant laymen vented their spite by rioting against Philadelphia's Catholic churches.[43] The other side of this picture is explored in the essay by Gerald Fogarty, showing how the Bible has provided an index of both Americanization and ethnic autonomy in the history of American Roman Catholics.

If the Bible deserves special attention for its presence in society, it should receive no less when considering the life of the mind. The celebrated debate between William Jennings Bryan and Clarence Darrow at Dayton, Tennessee, in 1925 represents only the most extravagant instance of an ongoing effort to forge a unified field of knowledge with both Scripture and human learning in their proper places.[44] It is in theory possible to dismiss the acrimony between these forms of knowledge as the result of badly posed questions, as G. K. Chesterton once did with savage delight: "private theories about what the Bible ought to mean, and premature theories about what the world ought to mean, have met in loud and widely advertised controversy, especially in the Victorian time; and this clumsy collision of two very impatient forms of ignorance was known as the quarrel of Science and Religion."[45] In the contingencies of actual history, however, the issue will not go away. Essays by George Marsden and Grant Wacker address this matter directly—the first by examining the Christian effort to accommodate the dominant nineteenth-century view of science within a scriptural framework and the second by assessing the effort to make room within a biblical faith for twentieth-century conceptions of history. General reflections on American intellectual history serve only to heighten the piquancy of the relationship between scriptural and other forms of knowledge. The Bible has provided a staple intellectual diet for at least one of America's authentic geniuses (Jonathan Edwards),[46] for many of its organizational prodigies (e.g., Alexander Campbell, founder of the Disciples of Christ),[47] for more than a handful of its deadly psychopaths (e.g., "The Son of Sam," David Berkowitz),[48] and—surprising as it may be to Protestants—for its Catholic priests as well.[49] The history of American formal education could itself almost be written as a function of efforts to come to terms with the Bible. From the early seventeenth to the late nineteenth century faculty and students labored to integrate scriptural and other forms of truth; since then one concern of many American educators has been to overcome the effects of scriptural training.[50]

The Bible has also played an important role in efforts to define the character of the nation. Recent books by Professor Sacvan Bercovitch[51] have driven home the extent to which Americans have perceived their country in biblical terms. Particularly at moments of crisis, the themes of Scripture have become themes of national identity—apocalypse during the Revolutionary and Civil Wars,[52] judgment during natural disasters from the seventeenth to the twentieth century,[53] redemption during the Civil War by the one whom some called "Father Abraham" and in World War I by the Presbyterian minister's son whose vision of divine order inspired his effort to make the world safe for democracy.[54] It could be argued that the Bible's presence in political history has been more superficial than in social or intellectual history, yet it cannot be denied that messages in American politics have frequently depended upon the meanings of Scripture. How this general tendency has worked out specifically, for the colonial period and for the early national period, are the subjects of the essays by Stout and Noll.

Finally, this sort of book would err greatly if it did not pay considerable attention to how differences over interpreting Scripture have led Christians to dramatically different stances on social, intellectual, and political issues in the national arena, or—to phrase the matter differently—how differences over social, intellectual, and political issues have led Christians to dramatically different ways of interpreting the Bible. However one perceives the cause and effect relationship, it is obvious that the way people interpret the Bible is the most important variable affecting the interaction of Scripture with other cultural forces. Very early in American history the Puritan minister Thomas Shepard noted that "Men's wits in imagining types and allegories [from Scripture] are very sinfully luxuriant."[55] Sinners or not, Americans who have delved deeply in Scripture have returned to life in the world with a creative variety of applications. The essays by Hatch and Mouw treat this problem with special care; it is the umbilical connecting the private life of the churches with the public presence of the Bible.

These then are the themes of this book: the Bible as a multiform social, intellectual, and political force in American life, and the interpretation of the Bible as a crucial consideration for the nature of its influence. Although these themes inform the entire book, the essays with one exception proceed chronologically. The first (Stout) and last (Mouw) treat developments before the United States came into being and after that the United States had undergone a considerable degree of secularization. Three (Hatch, Noll, Marsden) focus on the first two-thirds of the nineteenth century, "the great time of evangelical triumph" in Sydney Ahlstrom's words,[56] when Protestant influence and values reached their widest extent. Two (Weber and Wacker) deal specifically with the traumatic period at the end of the nineteenth century when the evangelical consensus gave way to a divided culture in which fierce loyalty to the Bible coexisted alongside perplexity about the place of its message in the modern world and outright hostility to its continued influence. The one exception to the chronological presentation is Gerald Fogarty's treatment of the Bible among American Roman Catholics. This essay provides a counterpoint to the otherwise Protestant cast of the book. Were this a definitive volume, it would include substantially more material on the Orthodox, the Jews, and other religious minorities as they too have put the Bible to use in America.

Some who read these essays may conclude that the Bible in American culture is a meaningless topic since, as the book documents at length, Scripture has been used in so many, often contradictory ways. Others may feel that social, economic, or ideological explanations having nothing to do with religion can provide exhaustive accounts of the shape of Scripture in the American landscape. Still others may come to share the view of the authors, who concede that the Bible has been a flexible wax nose on the many faces of American life. They also grant that the Bible's significance for the nation's history demands assessment from all the varieties of secular explanation which the documentary record justifies. But they feel as well that the very survival of Scripture in America—often in the face of its defenders' best efforts to bring discredit upon it—suggests a reality about the Bible which goes beyond history to faith.

NOTES

1. Quoted in Garry Wills, "Mason Weems, Bibliopolist," *American Heritage,* February–March 1981, p. 68.
2. "Evangelical Christianity in the United States: National Parallel Surveys of General Public and Clergy," conducted for *Christianity Today* by the Gallup Organization, Inc., and the Princeton Religion Research Center (Princeton: Gallup, n.d.), pp. 94, 126. See Walter A. Elwell, "Belief and the Bible: A Crisis of Authority?" *Christianity Today,* March 21, 1980, pp. 20–23.
3. John Leighly, "Biblical Place-Names in the United States," *Names,* 27 (March 1979), 53, 56.
4. Jesper Rosenmeier, " 'With My owne Eyes': William Bradford's *Of Plymouth Plantation,*" in *Typology and Early American Literature,* ed. Sacvan Bercovitch (Amherst: University of Massachusetts Press, 1972), pp. 68–105.
5. Richard M. Rollins, *The Long Journey of Noah Webster* (Philadelphia: University of Pennsylvania Press, 1980), pp. 117–118.
6. William J. Wolf, *The Almost Chosen People: A Study in the Religion of Abraham Lincoln* (Garden City, N.Y.: Doubleday, 1959), chap. 7, "The Best Gift God Has Given to Man," pp. 131–42; John M. Mulder, *Woodrow Wilson: The Years of Preparation* (Princeton: Princeton University Press, 1978), pp. 49, 270, and *passim;* Robert Kelley, "Presbyterianism, Jacksonianism, and Grover Cleveland," *American Quarterly,* 18 (1966), 615–36; Welsey G. Pippert, *The Spiritual Journey of Jimmy Carter: In His Own Words* (New York: Macmillan, 1979).
7. On Melville, see Nathalia Wright, *Melville's Use of the Bible* (Durham: Duke University Press, 1949); and Lloyd N. Jeffrey, "A Concordance to the Biblical Allusions in *Moby Dick,*" *Bulletin of Bibliography,* 21 (1956), 223–29. On Faulkner, see Irving Mallin, *William Faulkner: An Interpretation* (Stanford: Stanford University Press, 1957), "Faulkner and the Bible," pp. 65–78; and Hyatt H. Waggoner, *William Faulkner* (Lexington: University of Kentucky Press, 1959), "Passion Week of the Heart," pp. 238–51.
8. Charles Mabee, "Thomas Jefferson's Anti-Clerical Bible," *The Historical Magazine of the Protestant Episcopal Church,* 48 (December 1979), 473–81; Francis

I. Fesperman, "Jefferson's Bible," *Ohio Journal of Religious Studies,* 4 (October 1976), 78–88; and Edgar J. Goodspeed, "Thomas Jefferson and the Bible," *Harvard Theological Review,* 40 (January 1947), 71–76.

9. Adams likened his birth to that of a scion in old Israel: "Had he been born in Jerusalem under the shadow of the Temple and circumcised in the Synagogue by his uncle the high priest, under the name of Israel Cohen, he would scarcely have been more distinctly branded." *The Education of Henry Adams,* ed. Ernest Samuels (Boston: Houghton Mifflin, 1974), p. 3.

10. "Battle of the Books: Kanawha County," *Time,* September 30, 1974, p. 81; "Book Burners Alive and Well: Kanawha and Boone Counties," *Christian Century,* October 9, 1974, p. 924; Barry Doyle, "West Virginia Uproar: Courting the Textbooks," *Christianity Today,* October 11, 1974, pp. 44–46.

11. "Creationism Battle," *Christian Century,* March 25, 1981, p. 320; "California Evolution Trial Raises Creationist Profile," *Christianity Today,* April 10, 1981, pp. 60–61.

12. For the Lutheran Church-Missouri Synod, see "The Lutherans: Fractured Fellowship," *Christianity Today,* November 5, 1976, pp. 81–84; and the 13 articles in the *New York Times* during 1976 bearing, at least to some extent, upon this controversy: April 3, p. 28; April 6, p. 26; April 11, p. 30; April 18, p. 36; May 30, p. 20; June 13, p. 26; July 2, sect. IV, p. 11; September 15, p. 17; September 19, sect. IV, p. 6; October 2, p. 17; October 10, p. 10; November 14, p. 22; and December 5, p. 26. For the Southern Baptists, see John Maust, "Feuding and Finessing in the Family: Inerrancy Commotion in the Southern Baptist Convention," *Christianity Today,* July 20, 1979, pp. 32–34; and Kenneth A. Briggs, "A Rift Appears Among Baptists Who Differ on Fundamentalism," *New York Times,* March 30, 1981, pp. 1, 11. See also, "Presbyterians and Biblical Authority," *Journal of Presbyterian History,* 59 (Summer 1981), 95–284.

13. For example, Harry R. Boer, *Above the Battle: The Bible and Its Critics* (Grand Rapids: Eerdmans, 1977); James M. Boice, ed., *The Foundations of Biblical Authority* (Grand Rapids: Zondervan, 1977); D. A. Carson and John D. Woodbridge, eds., *Scripture and Truth* (Grand Rapids: Zondervan, forthcoming); Richard J. Coleman, *Issues of Theological Conflict* (rev. ed., Grand Rapids: Eerdmans, 1979); Stephen T. Davis, *The Debate About the Bible: Inerrancy Versus Infallibility* (Philadelphia: Westminster, 1977); Norman L. Geisler, ed., *Inerrancy* (Grand Rapids: Zondervan, 1980); Harold Lindsell, *The Battle for the Bible* (Grand Rapids: Zondervan, 1976) and *The Bible in the Balance: A Further Look at the Battle for the Bible* (Grand Rapids: Zondervan, 1979); Roger R. Nicole and J. Ramsey Michaels, eds., *Inerrancy and Common Sense* (Grand Rapids: Baker, 1980); Jack Rogers, ed., *Biblical Authority* (Waco, Texas: Word, 1977); Jack Rogers and Donald McKim, *The Authority and Interpretation of the Bible: An Historical Approach* (San Francisco: Harper & Row, 1979); and J. I. Packer, *Beyond the Battle for the Bible* (Westchester, Ill.: Cornerstone, 1980).

14. For an excellent example of such a discussion, see Timothy L. Smith, "Righteousness and Hope: Christian Holiness and the Millennial Vision in America, 1800–1900," *American Quarterly,* 31 (Spring 1979), 21–45. Two works by theologians which point to the ambiguities of the biblical character of America are H. Richard Niebuhr, *The Kingdom of God in America* (New York: Harper & Row, 1937); and Reinhold Niebuhr, *The Irony of American History* (New York: Scribner's, 1952).

15. Benjamin Quarles, *The Negro in the Civil War* (New York: Russell & Russell, 1968; orig. 1953), pp. 254–55; the Bible cost $580.75, which is more than per capita income figure recorded by Stuart Bruchey, *The Roots of American Economic Growth 1607–1861* (New York: Harper & Row, 1968; orig. 1965), pp. 76–81.

16. William Manchester, *The Death of a President* (New York: Harper & Row, 1967), p. 324. Even November 22, 1963, testified to the sensitive place which the Bible holds in American culture. Manchester reports (*ibid.*, n.) that Judge Sarah Hughes, who swore in Lyndon Johnson as President, hesitated momentarily at using Kennedy's Bible because of a suspicion that it might be a "Catholic Bible," representing an unwarranted alteration of the Authorized Version.

17. The intellectual historian, John C. Greene, is unusual in his notice of the Bible. He has argued, for instance, that "the doctrine of the plenary inspiration of Scripture . . . has been insufficiently appreciated" as a factor in recent "conflict between science and religion." *Science, Ideology, and World View: Essays in the History of Evolutionary Ideas* (Berkeley: University of California Press, 1981), p. 19 (reprinted from "Objectives and Methods in Intellectual History," *The Mississippi Valley Historical Review*, 44 (1957), 58–74). The role of the Bible is also a prominent theme in the essays gathered in *Religious Perspectives in American Culture,* Volume II: *Religion in American Life,* eds. James Ward Smith and A. Leland Jamison (Princeton: Princeton University Press, 1961). See also, Lawrence E. Nelson, *Our Roving Bible: Tracking Its Influence Through English and American Life* (New York: Abingdon, 1945); and P. Marion Simms, *The Bible in America: Versions That Have Played Their Part in the Making of the Republic* (New York: Wilson-Ericson, 1936). For works from a Jewish perspective, see Joseph Gaer and Ben Siegel, *The Puritan Heritage: America's Roots in the Bible* (New York: Mentor, 1964); and Abraham I. Katsh, *The Biblical Heritage of American Democracy* (New York: KTAV, 1977).

18. Perry Miller, "The Garden of Eden and the Deacon's Meadow," *American Heritage,* December 1955, p. 54. Sydney E. Ahlstrom made virtually this same important point—that it is very difficult to disentangle biblical influences from other cultural forces in Western history—in an oral presentation at the conference where most of these essays were first presented, Wheaton College, Wheaton, Ill., November 2, 1979.

19. Herbert Butterfield, *The Whig Interpretation of History* (New York: Norton, 1965; orig. 1931), p. 79.

20. Margaret T. Hills, *The English Bible in America: A Bibliography of Editions of the Bible & the New Testament Published in America 1777–1957* (New York: American Bible Society and New York Public Library, 1961). For special consideration of Catholic versions, see "American Editions of the Catholic Bible," in Hugh Pope, O.P., *English Versions of the Bible* (St. Louis: B. Herder, 1952), pp. 719–46. It must be conceded, however, that Americans have not produced histories of the versions of the Bible in America that rival, for example, F. F. Bruce, *The English Bible: A History of Translations from the Earliest English Versions to the New English Bible* (3rd ed., New York: Oxford University Press, 1978); or *The Cambridge History of the Bible,* 3 vols. (Cambridge: Cambridge University Press, 1963).

21. "R.S.V.," *Christian Century,* September 24, 1952, pp. 1086–87; "Five Publishers To Issue RSV Bible in the Fall," *Publishers Weekly,* January 29, 1962, pp. 78–80; Kathleen Maloney, "Tyndale: An Industry Built on the Good Book," *ibid.*,

June 21, 1976, pp. 38–40; a phone conversation with Tyndale, February 24, 1981, obtained the 25 million figure for the Living Bible; Chandler B. Grannis, "The Holy Bible, New International Version," *Publishers Weekly,* November 20, 1978, p. 39; plus letter from N. David Hill of the NIV's publisher, Zonderan, April 27, 1981; "Good News Bible," *ibid.,* March 14, 1977, p. 78. Richard N. Ostling, "Rivals to the King James Throne," *Time,* April 20, 1981, pp. 62–63, provides up-to-date figures on the Bible trade: $150 million annual sales; sales to 1981 of 50 million for the Revised Standard Version, 14 million for the New American Standard Bible, 12 million for the New English Bible, 12 million for the Good News Bible, and 3 million for the New International Version. It also mentions the most important recent non-Protestant translations: the Catholic New American Bible (1970) and Jerusalem Bible (1966) and the Jewish Publication Society's Holy Scriptures (forthcoming 1982).

22. *One Hundred and Sixty-fourth Annual Report of the American Bible Society* (New York: American Bible Society, n.d.), pp. 44, 51.

23. Edmund Bailey O'Callaghan, *A List of Editions of the Holy Scriptures and Parts Thereof Printed in America Previous to 1860* (Detroit: Gale, 1966; orig. 1861), pp. 1–6. Ruth M. Brend and Kenneth L. Pike, eds., *The Summer Institute of Linguistics: Its Works and Contributions* (The Hague: Mouton, 1977) offers a good survey of the work of the Wycliffe Bible Translators.

24. *Subject Guide to Books in Print 1980–1981, Volume I: A-J* (New York: R. R. Bowker, 1980), pp. 496–545; *The National Union Catalogue Pre-1956 Imprints, Volumes 53–56* (London: Mansell, 1980), with 63,000 entries in 700 languages and dialects. *Christianity Today,* for example, runs an annual review of biblical literature (in February, for vols. 1–16, 1957–72, and in March thereafter) which extends to 10 tightly packed pages or more.

25. Two popular treatments of that publisher, Robert Aitken, are Laton E. Holmgren, "A 'Pious and Laudable Undertaking'," *American History Illustrated,* 10:6, 1975, pp. 12–17; and Frederick E. Maser, "The Day America Needed Bibles," *Religion in Life,* 45 (Summer 1976), 138–45.

26. American historians have begun to pursue this approach quite effectively, but not yet for the distribution of Scripture; see Robert Darnton, *The Business of Enlightenment: A Publishing History of the Encyclopedie* (Cambridge: Harvard University Press, 1979); David D. Hall, "The World of Print and Collective Mentality in Seventeenth-Century New England," in *New Directions in American Intellectual History,* eds. John Higham and Paul K. Conkin (Baltimore: Johns Hopkins University Press, 1979), pp. 166–180; and the conference on "Print and Society in Early America," American Antiquarian Society, Worcester, Mass., October 1980.

27. See note 13 for modern debates among theologically conservative Protestants and the appropriate sections of the many systematic theologies that have come from all points on the American theological compass. A good study of important nineteenth-century debates on the Bible is Jerry Wayne Brown, *The Rise of Biblical Criticism in America, 1800–1870: The New England Scholars* (Middletown, Conn.: Wesleyan University Press, 1969). Americans in general, however, lack the sensitive work on the history of the doctrine of the Bible that exists for Great Britain and the Continent; see, for example, James T. Burtchaell, *Catholic Theories of Biblical Inspiration since 1810* (Cambridge: Cambridge University Press, 1969); and H. D. McDonald, *Ideas of Revelation, An Historical Study, A.D. 1700 to A.D. 1860* (London: Macmillan, 1959), and *Theories of Revelation,*

An Historical Study, 1860–1960 (London: G. Allen & Unwin, 1963), now published together as *Theories of Revelation: An Historical Study 1700–1960* (Grand Rapids: Baker, 1979).

28. For recent comment, see Raymond E. Brown, S.S., " 'And the Lord Said'? Biblical Reflections on Scripture as the Word of God," *Theological Studies,* 42 (March 1981), 3–19; and Roland E. Murphy and Carl L. Peter, "The Role of the Bible in Roman Catholic Theology," *Interpretation,* 25 (January 1971), 81–94.

29. For example, Isaac Wise, *Pronaos to Holy Writ Establishing, on Documentary Evidence, the Authorship, Date, Form, and Content of Its Books and the Authenticity of the Pentateuch* (Cincinnati, 1891). This book and many other similar efforts are discussed learnedly in a wide-ranging collection of papers by Harry M. Orlinsky, *Essays in Biblical Culture and Bible Translation* (New York: KTAV, 1974).

30. For example, the work by Hans W. Frei, *The Eclipse of Biblical Narrative: A Study in Eighteenth and Nineteenth Century Hermeneutics* (New Haven: Yale University Press, 1974); and David H. Kelsey, *The Uses of Scripture in Recent Theology* (Philadelphia: Fortress, 1975), which refer only tangentially to things American.

31. See, for example, the many citations under "Bible–Hermeneutics" and "Hermeneutics" in *Religion Index One: Periodicals, Volume 13: January 1977–December 1978* (Chicago: American Theological Library Association), pp. 24, 142.

32. The periodic index volumes of the *Journal of Biblical Literature* provide bird's-eye views of the sweep of this scholarship.

33. C. S. Lewis, *The Literary Impact of the Authorized Version* (Philadelphia: Fortress, 1963), p. 33.

34. Examples are cited in John H. Gottcent, *The Bible as Literature: A Selective Bibliography* (Boston: G. K. Hall, 1979); and Thayer S. Warshaw, *et al., Bible-Related Curriculum Materials: A Bibliography* (Nashville: Abingdon, 1976).

35. For citations, consult Roland Bartel *et al., Biblical Images in Literature* (Nashville: Abingdon, 1975); Robert A. Rees, "Toward a Bibliography of the Bible in American Literature," *Bulletin of Bibliography,* 29 (July–September 1972), 101–8; Nelson Burr, *Religion in American Life* (Arlington Heights, Ill.: AHM, 1971), pp. 129–41, especially "Biblical Influence," pp. 132–33; and Nicholas Ayo, "A Check-List of the Principal Book Length Studies in the Field of English and American Literature Directed to a Single Author's Use of the Bible," *Bulletin of Bibliography,* 25 (1967), 7–8. A good example of work which traces scriptural influence is Carlos Baker, "The Place of the Bible in American Fiction," in *Religious Perspectives in American Culture,* eds. Smith and Jamison, pp. 243–72.

36. The Centennial Publications Editorial Board of the Society of Biblical Literature has planned an ambitious and learned library of volumes on the history of biblical scholarship in America. It includes series on "The Bible and American Culture," eds. Edwin S. Gaustad and Walter Harrelson; "Biblical Scholarship in North America," eds. Paul J. Achtemeier, Eldon Jay Epp, E. Brooks Holifield, and Kent Harold Richards; "The Bible and Its Modern Interpreters," ed. Douglas A. Knight; and "Biblical Scholarship in Confessional Perspective," eds. Adela Yarbro Collins and George W. McRae.

37. Theodore Dwight Weld, *The Bible Against Slavery . . .* (4th ed., New York: Anti-Slavery Society, 1838), p. 5.

38. Howell Cobb, *A Scriptural Examination of the Institution of Slavery in the United States, with Its Objects and Purposes* (Georgia: by the author, 1856), p. 9.

39. "And he that stealeth a man, and selleth him, or if he be found in his hand, he shall surely be put to death." This text was one of Nat Turner's favorites; see Stephen B. Oates, *The Fires of Jubilee: Nat Turner's Fierce Rebellion* (New York: Harper & Row, 1975).

40. "Both thy bondmen, and thy bondmaids, which thou shalt have, shall be of the heathen that are round about you; of them shall ye buy bondmen and bondmaids. Moreover of the children of the strangers that do sojourn among you, of them ye shall buy, and of their families that are with you, which they begat in your land: and they shall be your possession. And ye shall take them as an inheritance for your children after you, to inherit them for a possession; they shall be your bondmen for ever." For an excellent discussion of the role of this text in debates over slavery during the antebellum period, see David Brion Davis, *The Problem of Slavery in the Age of Revolution* (Ithaca: Cornell University Press, 1975), pp. 531ff.

41. Quoted by T. H. Breen, "Horses and Gentlemen: The Cultural Significance of Gambling among the Gentry of Virginia," *William and Mary Quarterly,* 3rd ser., 34 (April 1977), 244.

42. Gilbert Tennent, "The Danger of an Unconverted Ministry" (1740), in Alan Heimert and Perry Miller, eds., *The Great Awakening* (Indianapolis: Bobbs-Merrill, 1967), pp. 84, 97.

43. John Tracy Ellis, *American Catholicism* (2nd ed., Chicago: University of Chicago Press, 1969), pp. 63–67. For similar controversies in Canada and Wisconsin, see, respectively, Ian Ross Robertson, "The Bible Question in Prince Edward Island from 1856 to 1860," *Acadiensis,* 5 (1976), 3–25; and Thomas C. Hunt, "The Reformed Tradition, Bible Reading and Education in Wisconsin," *Journal of Presbyterian History,* 59 (Spring 1981), 73–89. For an older, general treatment of this subject, see Donald E. Boles *The Bible, Religion, and the Public Schools* (2nd ed., Ames: Iowa State University Press, 1963).

44. Ray Ginger, *Six Days or Forever? Tennessee vs. John Thomas Scopes* (New York: Oxford University Press, 1974).

45. G. K. Chesterton, *St. Thomas Aquinas: "The Dumb Ox"* (New York: Doubleday, 1956; orig. 1933), p. 88.

46. Stephen J. Stein, "The Quest for the Spiritual Sense: The Biblical Hermeneutics of Jonathan Edwards," *Harvard Theological Review,* 70 (January–April 1977), 99–113.

47. John L. Morrison, "The Centrality of the Bible in Alexander Campbell's Thought and Life," *West Virginia History,* 35 (1974), 185–204.

48. On the Bible reading of the New York City mass murderer, David Berkowitz, see "Son of Sam Child of God," *Christianity Today,* September 23, 1977, pp. 45–46.

49. See the essay below by Gerald Fogarty.

50. On the greatly reduced role of the Bible in modern American higher education, see Laurence R. Veysey, *The Emergence of the American University* (Chicago: University of Chicago Press, 1965), pp. 374–75; John Bernard, *From Evangelicalism to Progressivism at Oberlin College, 1866–1917* (Columbus: Ohio State University Press), pp. 25, 112, 121; and three essays from *The Organization of Knowledge in Modern America, 1860–1920,* eds. Alexandra Oleson and John Voss (Baltimore: Johns Hopkins University Press, 1979): Edward Shils, "The Order of Learning in the United States: The Ascendancy of the University," pp.

31, 35–36; Laurence Veysey, "The Plural Organized Worlds of the Humanities," p. 52; and Dorothy Ross, "The Development of the Social Sciences," p. 115.

51. Sacvan Bercovitch, *The Puritan Origins of the American Self* (New Haven: Yale University Press, 1975); and *The American Jeremiad* (Madison: University of Wisconsin Press, 1978).

52. Nathan Orr Hatch, *The Sacred Cause of Liberty: Republican Thought and the Millennium in Revolutionary New England* (New Haven: Yale University Press, 1977); James H. Moorehead, *American Apocalypse: Yankee Protestants and the Civil War 1860–1869* (New Haven: Yale University Press, 1978); and John F. Berens, *Providence and Patriotism in Early America* (Charlottesville: University Press of Virginia, 1978).

53. Perry Miller, "Errand into the Wilderness," in *Errand into the Wilderness* (Cambridge: Harvard University Press, 1956), pp. 1–15; Bercovitch, *The American Jeremiad.*

54. Elton Trueblood, *Abraham Lincoln: Theologian of American Anguish* (New York: Harper & Row, 1973); Mulder, *Woodrow Wilson;* and Arthur S. Link, "Woodrow Wilson: Presbyterian in Government," in *Calvinism and the Political Order,* ed. George L. Hunt (Philadelphia: Westminster, 1965).

55. Quoted by Andrew Delbanco, "Thomas Shepard's America: The Biography of an Idea," in Daniel Aaron, ed., *Studies in Biography* (Cambridge: Harvard University Press, 1978), p. 177.

56. Sydney E. Ahlstrom, *A Religious History of the American People* (New Haven: Yale University Press, 1972), p. 387. Martin E. Marty has styled roughly this same period "The Evangelical Empire," in *Righteous Empire: The Protestant Experience in America* (New York: Harper & Row, 1977; orig. 1970).

I

Word and Order
in Colonial New England

HARRY S. STOUT
University of Connecticut

Many scholars see in American Puritanism the first statement of America's self-consciousness as a divinely appointed "redeemer nation." Most recently, and in greatest detail, Sacvan Bercovitch describes how the Puritans' enduring sense of millennial expectancy and special calling came to represent a national "ritual of consensus" that helped to bring the new nation together around a common messianic identity.[1] The role of the Bible for personal faith and social order is central to such understanding of the Puritans' identity. Whether as the "covenanted society," "theocracy," "Bibliocracy," "new Israel," or "Bible Commonwealth," the Puritan experiment depended on the Bible. It was the Puritans' commitment to reading and comprehending the Bible, after all, that wrought in New England an educational system that made Yankees, on the eve of the American Revolution, one of the most literate peoples in the world.[2]

except in South [handwritten annotation in right margin]

It is surprising then, that with all of the attention to Puritan Biblicism, the actual translation used in New England has not come under very close scrutiny. Entire histories of Puritanism in Old and New England have been written which do not even consider the possibility that a crucial element may have been the particular translation employed. And this failure is symptomatic of an even greater omission that skims over the Bible generally in accounting for the rise of Puritanism and moves directly to landmark theological statements circulated among the civil and ecclesiastical hierarchy.[3] To the extent that students of English and American

Puritanism ignore this most basic of all texts in reconstructing the popular wellsprings of the movement they overlook the basic life work of an entire people whose *sole* reading habit was the vernacular Bible. In this essay we shall see that Puritanism was actually the product of two Bible translations, each of which dominated at different stages in the movement's history, and each of which served different needs and purposes. In its infant stage, English Puritanism was organized around the Genevan translation of 1560. As the movement grew in power and influence, clerical loyalties switched to the Authorized or "King James" version of 1611. This later version furnished the primary text on which New England's Bible Commonwealth would rest.[4]

The roots of the earlier Genevan translation go back to the age of religious persecution under the reign of Mary Tudor (1553–58), when a group of committed Protestants fled the homeland eventually to settle in Geneva.[5] By 1556, two of these exiles, the Hebrew scholar Anthony Gilby and William Whittingham, later Dean of Durham, conceived a plan to publish a new translation of the English Bible that would be aimed primarily at a common lay audience.[6] At that time vernacular Bibles were still in their infancy, and ordinary people had no ready access to the Word of God in an intelligible and affordable edition. Until that need was met, the Reformation ideal of *sola Scriptura* would remain just that: an ideal with no realistic prospect of implementation in a living society. The exiles' proposed translation, then, represented the necessary precondition for a biblically-based culture organized solely on God's ordinances.

The exiled translators could not have been better situated for their ambitious undertaking. In addition to the earlier translations of Martin Luther's German edition (the prototype of all vernacular Bibles), and the earlier English translations of William Tyndale (1494–1536) and Myles Coverdale's "Great Bible" (1550 edition), they had direct access to the cultural milieu of Geneva, then the leading center of print and biblical scholarship in the Reformed Protestant world.[7] Under the theological leadership of John Calvin, the textual criticism of Theodore Beza, particularly his Latin translation of the New Testament (1556), and the printing presses of Robert Estienne, vernacular translations of the Bible were simultaneously undertaken in French, Italian, Spanish, and English. Diverse scholars willingly collaborated on the various translations and shared textual explanations, woodcuts, maps, and commentaries that could be included in each translation.[8] By means of "suche diversities of translations in diverse tongues," the English translators were able to incorporate innumerable improvements in their translation, making it one of the finest vernacular editions of its day.

The "great and wonderful worke" was completed in 1560 and copies were available in England almost immediately. Despite the fact that the "Bishop's Bible" was sanctioned by ecclesiastical authority for use in public worship, the Geneva Bible circumvented official channels and found its way into common dwellings throughout the realm. Within a generation it had outstripped all other versions in circulation and came to stand as the unchallenged emblem of popular piety in the English realm.[9] Biblical scholar F. F. Bruce points out that the Genevan version "became the household Bible of English-speaking Protestants . . . its excellence as a translation was acknowledged even by those who disagreed with the theology of the translators."[10] When presented with their own copies of the Geneva Bible common English readers encountered a document that was directed to their convenience and comprehension in every way. Physically, the work was issued in a relatively inexpensive single volume, Roman type edition that was conveniently organized into sentence units of "verses" and "chapters." Substantively, they enjoyed a "plainly rendered" translation expressed in the language of their own idiomatic speech. As the Bible's preface to the reader made plain, the translation was not aimed at learned scholars but at common readers throughout the realm. Textual decisions were governed by the needs of "simple readers" to understand the "hard places" of Scripture. Like the "plain style" sermons that flowed from it, the translation was devoid of circumlocutions and Latinisms which would only distract the reader from a text "which is the light to our paths, the keye of the kingdome of heaven, our comfort in affliction, our shielde and sworde against Satan, the schoole of all wisdome, the glasse wherein we beholde God's face, the testimonie of his favour, and the only food and nourishment of our soules." The Geneva Bible was, in brief, the first English translation that could legitimately be characterized as a people's Bible.

To enhance the Bible's popular intelligibility the translators included a massive body of marginal commentary, which was drawn largely from Olivetan's French translation revised and commented on by Calvin and published in Geneva in 1558.[11] In all, the commentary exceeded 300,000 words in length and constituted, in effect, a self-contained theological library for common readers. The marginal notes immediately excited comment from friends and foes alike, and they have continued to intrigue historians. It would be difficult to overstate their influence in molding lay perceptions of godly living and Christian faith. Aside from the Bible itself, the Genevan commentary was the only literary product all people shared in common and it exerted a far more direct influence on the popular religious imagination than the less widely circulated sermons, devotionals, and spiritual autobiographies.[12] The physical linkage of text and commentary on every page gave added weight to the notes and gave them the appearance of a direct extension of sacred writ. When we view the contents of these notes we are observing the symbolic universe of popular piety at its most direct and formative level.

The inclusion of theological commentary was not original with the Geneva Bible. Martin Luther's German translation included it as did Calvin's French. Indeed, what would have been novel in the sixteenth century would have been the preparation of a popular translation *without* comment. Protestant churchmen believed they were already taking risks simply in making Bibles available to the masses and encouraging their active use. Such an endeavor was unprecedented and its effects were unpredictable. To provide this Word raw, with no interpretive guidance, would be socially and spiritually reprehensible. It would encourage readers to think they were also their own interpreters of Scripture when, in fact, they lacked the linguistic tools necessary to interpret the "real" Scriptures preserved in the original tongues and ancient manuscripts.[13] While the people could and must read their Bibles, they could not interpret them independent of ministerial guidance. The commentary, together with the sermon, was responsible for leading Bible readers into true spiritual awareness.

Like its Lutheran and Calvinist prototypes, the Geneva Bible's commentary largely ignored peripheral theological issues of interest to the specialist, and concentrated instead on the central meaning of Scripture as recently articulated by Martin Luther. Both in time and circumstance the Geneva Bible was a *popular* Reformation document. It ignored technical disputes common among English and Continental Churchmen and focused singlemindedly on the signal rediscovery of justification by faith in Christ alone. At every point in the commentary the reader's attention is focused unblinkingly on the person and work of Jesus Christ. This was particularly evident in the Old Testament marginal notes in which, as Luther insisted, Christ must be the sole object of contemplation. If he is not explicitly mentioned in texts then the reader must go beyond the "grammar" or literal meaning, to the inner spiritual meaning visible only through the eyes of faith. In Luther's words, "Grammar is necessary for declension, conjugation and construction of sentences, but in speech the [Christocentric] meaning and subject matter must be considered[,] not the grammar, for the grammar shall not rule over the meaning."[14] Throughout their commentary the Genevan translators retained this perspective. There is, they repeatedly insisted, "no joye no consolacion, no peace or quietnes, no felicitie nor salvation, but in Jesus Christ, who is the very substance of the Gospel, and in whome all the promises are yea and amen."[15]

The single term which recurred most frequently in the marginal notes and best captures their central interpretive thrust, is *promise*.[16] Phrases such as "the faithful keeping of his promises," or the "just performances of his promise," saturate the commentary. All competing themes were subordinated to the proclamation of a deliverance freely promised and freely bestowed upon an undeserving humanity. The emphasis was on personal salvation and eternal life. The meaning of Old Testament laws, rituals, objects, and historical covenants was to be sought uniformly as precursors, representations, and "types," of the deliverance fully manifest in the Cross and the open sepulcher. There was not one preface to an Old Testament book that did not explicitly focus on the life and person of Christ. Indeed, so conscious were the translators of the actual presence of Christ in the Old Testament that references to the "Angel of the Lord" were routinely identified as the pre-existent Christ who lay at the core of both Old and New Testament.[17] In this interpretive framework, the Old Testament language of national covenant, judicial laws, or temporal rewards and punishments was uniformly spiritualized and interpreted as "signs" or "figures" of the Messiah.

The spiritualized quality of the commentary and popular faith did not keep pace with the main body of Puritan thought emanating from the universities at Cambridge and Oxford. Here the primary issues came to be *covenant theology* centered on "covenant theology" and the related exegetical question of "national election." Not surprisingly, covenant themes dominate the intellectual history of the period.[18] But they were not representative of the popular piety centered on the Geneva Bible and its notes. Contained within the marginalia was a structure of symbols that stood outside of the issues raised by most intellectual historians. It was a world severely circumscribed in literary range and theological implication. This is most apparent when we examine the treatment given to covenant in the Genevan commentary. There was no effort to elevate the term to unifying theological significance. Where the term appeared in the biblical text it was seldom elaborated on except to point out that the "ark of the covenant" was a type of Christ. Where explicit references to covenant appeared in the

Bible text they were identified solely with the "covenant of grace" which, in the translators' usage, stood as a synonym or metaphor for God's redemptive promises to His people completed in Christ. There was no extension of this individual and personal covenant of grace to a national ("federal") covenant between God and an entire people (including both saved and unsaved) which, as with Israel of old, would be premised on mutual obligations and temporal rewards and punishments. Indeed the commentary did not even refer to the nation of Israel, but instead to the "people of God" or the "heirs of the promise," or the "true seed of Abraham," who always constituted a redeemed minority within the larger nation. Israel itself was a type of the invisible church of Christ. Lest the reader be misled by the Old Testament language of covenant and duty into thinking that it implied some sort of literal "conditions" or works that might "prepare" the way to personal salvation or national preeminence, the translators insisted that the covenant was personal and "grounded upon [God's] free grace: therefore in recompensing their obedience he hath respect to his mercie and not to their merites."

Signal events and personalities in the history of Israel were appreciated less for their national, historical significance, than for the gospel truths they prefigured. Israel, Canaan, or Jerusalem were all understood as "temporal" signs of the invisible "Kingdom of Christ." Thus, for example, in explaining Psalm 49:36 the commentators pointed out that "under the temporal promises of the land of canaan he comprehendeth the promises of life everlasting to the faithful and their posterity." Important personages were similarly spiritualized as Christ-types. Readers learned that Joshua was important to them not as a conquering soldier of the Lord but because he "doth represent Jesus Christ the true Joshua, who leadeth us into eternal felicitie, which is signified unto us by this land of Canaan." Place and personality frequently came together in Christic unity as in the commentary on Isaiah 11:1 where the readers learned that "because the captivitie of Babylon was a figure of the spiritual captivitie under sinne, he sheweth that our true deliverance must come by Christ for as David came out of Ishai a man without dignitie: so Christ shulde come of a poore carpenters house. . . ." Throughout, the effect was never to deny the historicity of the Old Testament nation of Israel, but rather to subordinate that history to the fuller spiritual meaning embodied in the Gospel.

Given the strong identification of the Genevan translation with the rise of Puritan preaching and popular piety, scholars have hypothesized that the translation—particularly the commentary—constituted an implicit political or economic manifesto compatible with the new social ethic of middle-class Puritanism.[19] This view unfortunately will not do. It takes isolated statements of social teaching and expands them into full-blown interpretive themes.[20] Social commentary appears, of course, but only in grammatical explanations where it is explicitly mentioned in the text. In fact, what made the Geneva Bible distinctive was not its radical social commentary, but rather the very *absence* of any particular social or political platform. The detached, apolitical vantage point of the commentators grew naturally from the Bible's origins in exile and abandonment. The translators assumed no official social or political responsibility in the home country and were free to fashion a translation which was not responsible for upholding social order. They could concentrate with singleminded attention on the spiritual claims of the Bible, leaving concrete social applications to others. In tracing the history of the English Bible, the nineteenth-century churchman Brooke Foss Westcott pointed out, rightly, that "the Genevan revision was the work of exiles whose action was unfettered by considerations of national policy. A work was comparatively easy for them which was not possible in the English Church."[21]

As the Puritan movement continued to grow, and as the prospect of New World settlement began to dawn, questions of national policy and social order increasingly received attention from the learned divines. Taking seriously their own insistence that Scripture speaks to all of life completely and infallibly, the ministers found it increasingly necessary to apply biblical doctrines to questions of a temporal and political nature. The changed social situation together with numerous advances in biblical scholarship since 1560 convinced many of the need for a new vernacular edition of the Bible better suited to the needs of the new century. The resultant *King James* Authorized Version of 1611 was soon adopted by most Puritan clergymen and inaugurated a new era in Puritan history. Unlike the earlier Genevan translation, the Authorized Version lacked marginal comment and was, in every sense, an establishment Bible of impeccable social and intellectual credentials. The forty-seven translators included the finest Anglican and Puritan scholars in the realm and were supported by royal and ecclesiastical preferment.[22] The new version of the Bible coincided with a period of new beginnings for the Puritan clergy. Now that the people had been indoctrinated in the truths of Holy Writ, it was possible to begin moving to the second, and more ambitious, phase of building an entire social order according to scriptural blueprint.

Where the Geneva Bible and its marginalia served well the purpose of an embattled religious minority with thoughts fixed firmly on martyrdom and the world to come, it was less useful in fashioning binding principles of social organization and order in this world. It is not coincidental that the Puritan leaders' preference for the Authorized Version grew in direct proportion to their growth in numbers and influence. Before the New World settlement English Puritans had gradually moved beyond the Reformation emphases of the Geneva Bible and spoke increasingly of a special national covenant that existed alongside of a personal covenant of grace. In a study of the changes wrought in seventeenth-century Puritanism Leonard Trinterud points out that:

> As early as 1572 [Thomas] Cartwright had noted that disinterest in the Geneva Bible was growing. A federalist Puritan, John Reynolds, at the Hampden Court conference had urged the preparation of a new translation of the Bible, and the edition of 1611 had been due to his suggestion. Although numerous editions of Calvin's works had been issued during the Elizabethan era, it is significant that from 1603 to 1700 only eight printings of any and all of Calvin's works were made in England and Scotland combined. Moreover, even before the Civil War well-known Puritans were cool toward, and quite independent of, Calvin's theology. The covenant theology had won its brief struggle for supremacy with the Geneva Bible and Calvin's theology.[23]

Nowhere was the movement beyond the Geneva Bible more evident than in the Puritan-sponsored migration to Massachusetts Bay in 1630. This migration had as its overarching mission nothing less than the carving out of a new world order solely according to biblical precept. Theirs would be a society governed in every detail according to the Word of God as interpreted by his ministers. Elements of the population could, and no doubt did, demur from this official policy privately, but they could not introduce their grievances publicly. In public settings, the only allowable voice was the Word of God as channeled through his personal ambassadors, the clergy.

Other New World colonies and cultures, of course, had their own regenerative hopes for the New World, but only in New England were messianic themes and biblical texts fused with an official public mission that bound an entire populace to its terms. William Penn, the Quaker, for example, was certainly no less biblical when he dreamed of planting a "Holy Experiment" yet he came to despair of ever seeing his vision of brotherly love widely shared or deeply held by Pennsylvania's citizens. For one thing, the Quakers placed the Bible in a secondary role, lest it supplant the initiative of God's Spirit and the need of obeying the Light within. "Friends conceded that the Bible was authoritative," Hugh Barbour has written, "and then talked about the Spirit."[24] In addition, the Quakers refused to ordain a regular clergy to ensure a definitive interpretation of Scripture, failed to pursue comprehensive education as a religious mission, and welcomed rather than resisted religious dissent and ethnic pluralism.[25]

The result was a surprisingly unstable mix of anti-authoritarianism, ethnic tension, and factionalism—a world of competing visions over which no single one could claim hegemony. As this pluralism intensified during the eighteenth century, the Quakers lost all hope of subduing the province they had created. Withdrawing from politics entirely, they moved toward purity rather than providence and nourished modest aims rather than cosmic errands. The vision of a redeemer nation, which the American republic would in time come to own, was the manifestation of a sense of history that had its primary roots in Puritan Boston rather than Quaker Philadelphia.[26]

The Puritans' new order was given classic formulation in the first New World sermon of their governor John Winthrop, preached while still on board the flagship *Arbella*. In words familiar to pastors, school children, song writers, and civic leaders since, he proceeded to inform his fellow travelers that they were different from all other peoples on earth; not because of their own righteousness, but because God had singled them out, like Israel of old, to be the instruments of his redemptive plan for mankind. Other colonists could worry about profit and worldly advancement; the business of New England would be the carrying out of a divine "commission" from God to establish His Word in the midst of a professing, "peculiar" people.[27] Borrowing a metaphor from Christ's Sermon on the Mount he informed the people that they would be as a "City upon a Hill" entrusted with enacting a "modell of Christian charity" that would flow from their special covenant with God. The stakes were high: "soe that if wee shall deale falsely with our God in this worke wee have undertaken and soe cause him to withdrawe his present helpe from us, wee shall be made a story and a by-word through the world . . . wee [shall] be consumed out of the good land whether wee are goeing."

It is important to remember that in delivering his platform Winthrop was not simply expressing a private opinion which he would *like* to see implemented. He was articulating the official, public ideology of the land. Henceforth New England society would go on public record as a special covenant people who would be regulated in every regard by Scripture.

The vernacular Word, particularly the Old Testament, provided them with the "articles of our Covenant with him." Along with the performance of those articles or "duties" came an eternal promise: if they performed them in a proper spirit of humility and dependence they would be blessed, and if they failed to perform them, then as surely as Israel met its Babylon, even so would He "make us knowe the price of the breache of such a Covenant." Everything would hinge on the faithful proclamation and application of the Word in every community throughout the land.

Winthrop's sermon vividly illustrates how Scripture was bound indissolubly to the New England Way. The platform was delivered in the form of a sermon rather than a constitution and scriptural citations underscored every point. The citations themselves were drawn, deliberately or not, from both Genevan and Authorized translations and indicate how the Puritan leaders fused the original concern with personal salvation to the novel task of model society building.[28] For Winthrop and his clerical peers the interpretive framework of the Geneva Bible was not so much wrong as it was anachronistic. It continued to speak authoritatively to questions of justification, and was even used in some regular preaching. But two generations of Christians nourished on the vernacular Word now faced more ambitious challenges which placed new demands on scriptural interpretation. The New World realities of community formation, social containment, and survival shifted the interpretive concerns from personal to corporate piety, and from the saint's progress to heaven to his life on earth.

For the model Bible Commonwealth to survive in the "howling wilderness" of the New World and not splinter off in a hundred different directions, the highest sanctions would have to be invoked. The populace had to be convinced that their personal salvation depended in some measure on their collective behavior in the New World. As Winthrop had warned, they would have to "be knitt together in this worke as one man . . . alwayes having before our eyes our Commission and Community." Questions of personal and corporate regeneration could not be separated and the leaders could ignore questions of corporate duty and national covenant only at the expense of undermining all social order. For the first time Puritan leaders experienced the responsibility of power. And this responsibility placed them on the horns of a dilemma they would never entirely escape.[29] Their personal faith rested firmly on the doctrine of *sola Fides,* while their social doctrine was modeled directly after the Old Testament theocracy. The Puritans' separatist "Pilgrim" neighbors

avoided the dilemma by retaining the original message of free grace uncontaminated by notions of special errand or national covenant. Not surprisingly, the Geneva Bible remained the preferred version in Plymouth
Colony.[30] But as Plymouth itself revealed, such doctrinal purity provided
no cultural glue for a world-redeeming mission. It was a view that led ultimately to withdrawal and separation from the world.

As Perry Miller first demonstrated, the more culturally aggressive Puritans responded to the dilemma by affirming *both* an absolute and a conditional covenant.[31] This was articulated in the vocabulary of a national
covenant involving both personal and historical redemption. The individual could not earn his salvation, but he could "prepare" for it by attending
to the preaching of the Word and by being a loyal citizen in the society. He
could find assurance in the realization that New England was God's
chosen nation. If the leaders could not resolve the dilemma, they could
hold it in balance by simultaneously affirming a personal salvation dependent solely upon free grace and a collective covenant premised on
works and duties.

With respect to biblical interpretation, the revamped and expanded covenant theology meant that the leaders must read the Old Testament with
a closer eye to historical and literal implementation. The only historical
model directly relevant to their enterprise was ancient Israel. Of all the
peoples who preceded them, only Israel stood as they in a special redemptive covenant with God. For that reason, the "Jewish Commonwealth"
enjoyed a normative status even greater than that ascribed to classical
Greece and Rome. The spiritualization of the Old Testament which dominated the Geneva Bible must now accommodate an increasing literaliza-
tion or actualization of Old Testament practices, including the judicial
law. Because the American Puritans identified themselves as a peculiar
people, historical covenants stated in the conditional language of corporate duties, mutual obligations, and temporal rewards and punishments
were reactivated. If presented in the form of a syllogism, the American
Puritans' reasoning would go something like this:

Major premise: God's promises of blessing and judgment recorded in
Scripture apply to professing peoples as well as to individuals.

Minor Premise: New England is a professing people bound in public
submission to the Word of God.

Conclusion: Therefore New England is a peculiar people of God.

As we have already seen, a precondition of the minor premise was that a prospective people of God actually have access to the Word, together with the requisite literacy skills to understand it, and a faithful ministry to apply it in local settings. On all counts the New England Puritans believed themselves uniquely fitted to the work at hand. They had at least one and often two university-trained ministers in every community throughout the land. Bibles existed in virtually every household, and the regional literacy rates were perhaps the highest in the world.[32] When all of these factors were read into biblical exegesis the simple and irresistible conclusion was that the meaning of America could be found *specifically* in biblical prophecies. Sacvan Bercovitch describes the new exegesis in the following words:

> Unmistakably the New World, like Canaan of old, belonged wholly to the history of salvation. Other peoples, the colonists explained, had their land by providence; *they* had it by promise. Others must seek their national origins in secular records and chronicles; the story of America was enclosed in the scriptures, its past postdated and its future antedated in prophecy.[33]

The identification of America with the New Israel was understood by the leaders not as a repudiation of the earlier evangelical message of free grace, but as its culmination. The new exegesis was engrafted onto the existing message of free grace and Puritan ministers would preach unconditional individual election and conditional corporate rewards and punishments at the same time and with equal enthusiasm. In local contexts Puritan preaching included some of the most searching, heartfelt evangelical sentiments in all of Protestant history.[34] At the same time, the official printed literature of the colonies reflectively scrutinized colonial settlements from the standpoint of a people collectively bound in a special covenant with God.[35] Although formal syllogisms seldom appeared in printed sermons, they were ubiquitous in abbreviated form and invariably pressed home the point that New England was a special people. In his Election Sermon of 1673 Urian Oakes, president of Harvard College, reiterated the ancient litany of special mission:

> You have been as a City upon a hill (though in a remote and obscure Wilderness) as a Candle in the Candlestick that gives light to the whole House. You have, to a considerable Degree, enlightened the whole House (world I mean) as to the pattern of God's House; the Form and Fashion and Outgoings and Incomings thereof: convinced and helped many, and left others, that shut their eyes against the Light of your Profession and Practice, without excuse. God hath been doing (in my Apprehension) the

same thing for the substance of it here, that shall be done more universally and gloriously, when *Israel shall blossom and bud and fill the face of the world with fruit:* Isaiah 27:6. You have been though a handfull of people separated from the greatest part of the Christian World (as it is prophesied of Jacobs remnant that it should be in the midst of many people. Mic. 5.7) *as a Dew from the Lord, and as the flowers upon the grass.* God hath priviledged and honoured you greatly in this respect.[36]

In sermon after sermon the point was pressed home that New England's covenant people were God's special instruments and stood in a unique relationship to church history and revelation.

Although the synthesis of absolute and conditional covenant was largely the creation of the Puritan ministers, many common people such as the Woburn joiner and militia captain Edward Johnson embraced the new orthodoxy as a harbinger of the millennium. In his manuscript history of the first generation settlers he extolled the Bible Commonwealth and its covenant theology as nothing less than a "new Heaven, and a new Earth in, New Churches, and a new Common-wealth." In words that would resound through the following decades he issued the following challenge to posterity: "Then judge all you . . . whether these poore New England People, be not the forerunners of Christ's Army."[37]

Others however were less certain and were unwilling to grant the major premise that God's promises extended to nations as well as individuals. Their spiritual consciousness and reading world continued to be informed by the otherworldly perspective of the Geneva Bible commentary, where they could find no justification for a conditional covenant in personal or national terms. Believing that the national covenant had ended with Christ, they could only understand New England's public corporate identity as a "covenant of works" that jeopardized one's personal relationship with Christ. We do not know how many people throughout the colonies shared misgivings about the new orthodoxy. We do know they were particularly strong in Boston where, under the "prophesyings" of Anne Hutchinson and her brother-in-law the Rev. John Wheelwright, a dissenting party emerged in opposition to the official ideology of the Bay colony.[38] The complex theological issues which surrounded the ensuing "Antinomian Crisis" have tended to obscure the fact that the two sides of the controversy drew their inspiration and proofs from different translations of Scripture. The Hutchinsonian party spoke from the Geneva Bible, while the leaders accused them from the Authorized. At stake in the controversy was who could speak for God in public settings. For the New England

Way to survive intact there could be only one official voice of God articulated by His Prophet, the settled minister. Alternative interpretations and applications of Scripture threatened an exegetical anarchy where everyone became his or her own interpreter of Scripture. If competing voices such as Anne Hutchinson's were allowed public expression, they would rend the fabric of colonial society and jettison the special status and mission of the land.[39]

The first skirmish in the battle for public authority took place in 1637 when Wheelwright preached an inflammatory Fast Day sermon from the Genevan translation of Matthew 9:15.[40] From start to finish the sermon was characteristically Christocentric in theme and disdainful of all efforts to impute adherence to corporate duty as a preparation for personal salvation. Wheelwright responded to the covenant theology by saying, "No, no, this is a covenant of works, for in the covenant of grace, nothing is revealed but Christ for our righteousness . . . not by the works of righteousness, they are layd aside, and the Lord revealeth only to them the righteousness of himselfe given freely to the soul. . . ."[41] In the precarious New World settlements such a sentiment threatened to undermine the credibility of the entire society. In spite of popular protest, Wheelwright was convicted of sedition and banished from the colony.

Wheelwright's battle was continued on a more sophisticated level by Anne Hutchinson who, in the course of her trial, evidenced a nearly verbatim memory of long portions of the Geneva Bible.[42] Throughout her defense she focused singlemindedly on the person of Christ and the actual moment of spiritual union when the soul is infused with divine grace. Her scriptural supports were drawn particularly from the Epistle to the Galatians which, according to Governor Winthrop's account, she termed "the rule of the new creature. . . ."[43] Something of the flavor of the Genevan gloss on Galatians can be captured from the commentary on Galatians 1:7 which posits an unbridgeable gulf between grace and works, free promise and conditional covenant: "For what is more contrarie to our fre[e] justification by faith, then the justification by the Law, of our workes? Therefore to joyne these two together, is to joyne light with darkness, death with life, and doeth utterly overthrow the Gospel."

Anne Hutchinson never fully comprehended the new mission of American Puritan orthodoxy and its eschatological vision. Nor could she accept its conditional terms and unique construction of biblical prophecies in national terms. She and her followers came from an older language and, like foreigners, spoke past their clerical opponents. The language issue was settled abruptly and decisively in favor of the new orthodoxy and its world-redeeming vocabulary. In March 1637 Anne was excommunicated from the Boston Church and one month later banished to Rhode Island. Other exiles from the Puritan experiment would join her there, dissenters such as the Baptist John Clarke, who founded Newport in 1639. Clarke's Bible, one is not surprised to learn, was a 1608 edition of the Geneva Bible—a book that survives today in the possession of the Rhode Island Historical Society.[44]

With the removal of Anne Hutchinson the issue of who spoke for God was settled finally and irrevocably, and the Puritan clergy proceeded to construct their own unique meaning of America on the foundation of their own interpretation of Scripture. Throughout the colonial period the vernacular Bible interpreted by a learned ministry remained the mainstay of New England culture. Amidst disappointments, defeats, and periodic failures of nerve, the faith in God's promise of ultimate triumph for his covenant people remained fixed and unchanged. As with Israel of old, failures and judgments were incentives for renewal, and defeats merely temporary reverses on a larger battlefield in which victory was ultimately assured. Despite divisions between the people and their ministers and, in the "Great Awakening," divisions among the clergy themselves, all shared in an unbroken allegiance to the Bible as the inspired Word of God and infallible rule for all issues of life. The terms "Liberal" and "Evangelical" taken to distinguish the eighteenth-century clergy did not extend to differences over the authority and sufficiency of Scripture. This remained a common legacy.

When Revolution came in 1776 it was greeted with the same unswerving faith in scriptural promises that had animated the first generation founders. As Winthrop's sermon marked the beginning of one epoch in 1630 so did the Rev. Samuel West inaugurate a new beginning for the ages in his Election Sermon of 1776.[45] The two sermons were separated by more than 150 years of social change and adaptation to the realities of New World settlement. No longer did ministers alone speak for God (that right was now bestowed on the people-as-a-whole), and New England's special status was now extended to include America. But the biblically-based sermon remained the primary ritual of social order and the institution entrusted with interpreting life's meaning to God's special New World inhabitants. That meaning, as West made plain, had not changed. Repeating words that had been internalized over six generations, he observed that God had "planted a vine in this American wilderness which he has caused to take deep root, and it has filled the land, and will never be plucked up or destroyed." The bedrock of West's doctrine of resistance and revolution remained the Bible. To underscore its importance to the American cause, he devoted no less than eleven pages of his sermon text to an exegesis of the Apostle Paul's injunction in Romans 13:1–6 to "be subject to the higher powers." This command, he makes plain, applies only to legitimate rulers and not to tyrants who subvert the purposes and ends of government and good order. Indeed, from scriptural warrant, he concludes that it is a sin *not* to resist tyranny. Rebellion against false leaders who jeopardized Americans' special relationship with God was not merely a right but "a duty so sacred that it cannot justly be dispensed with for the sake of our secular concerns."

Like Winthrop, West concluded that the success of the American cause "depends upon our being firmly united together in the bonds of love to one another. . . ." If such love and obedience to divine authority is maintained then by the terms of God's covenant Americans can lay hold of his promise of both temporal and spiritual deliverance: "he will not forsake us if we do not forsake him. Our cause is so just and good that nothing can prevent our success but only our sins. . . . I cannot help hoping, and even believing, that Providence has designed this continent for to be the asylum of liberty and true religion. . . ."

Other colonists might celebrate "the rights of man," and justify their rebellion solely with reference to the libertarian thought of the age. But New England people bred on the Word could never accept such a man-centered, optimistic ideological platform. Their world, like that of their fathers before them, was entirely suffused with the Word of God. It furnished the terms and vocabulary with which they instinctively confronted life's meaning, and interpreted the significance of their collective presence in the New World. As ministers never tired of pointing out, there was not one week nor one town in the colony's history in which the Word was not faithfully proclaimed. And on that basis of direct dependence on divine Providence, they would march forth to war strong in the conviction that they remained God's special Bible-believing people. And if God was for them, then who could be against them?

NOTES

1. Sacvan Bercovitch, *The American Jeremiad* (Madison, Wis., 1978).
2. Kenneth A. Lockridge has argued that male literacy in eighteenth-century Anglo-America hovered around 60 percent, except in Scotland and New England, where, by the end of the century, rates approached universal male literacy. Apparently

the only force sufficient to generate a significant change in literacy in this period was the intense biblicism and associated schools of these Calvinists. See Lockridge, *Literacy in Colonial New England: An Enquiry into the Social Context of Literacy in the Early Modern West* (New York, 1974), pp. 72–101.

3. George M. Marsden has suggested that Perry Miller under-estimated the extent to which the Puritan thought was biblically oriented. See Marsden, "Perry Miller's Rehabilitation of the Puritans: A Critique," *Church History* 39 (1970), 91–105.

4. The use of the Authorized Version in New England printed sermons is well known. In addition I have discovered that unpublished sermon manuscripts throughout the colonial period rely upon the Authorized Version or free renderings of Greek and Hebrew texts. At the same time, sufficient numbers of Genevan Bible translations survive in historical archives to indicate continued popular usage of the Geneva Bible in New England. I am indebted to Rebecca Guild for cataloguing the Bible holdings of the following archives: Harvard University Libraries, Episcopal Theological Seminary Library, Massachusetts Historical Society, and the Congregational Historical Society. The condition of colonial Bibles reflects the lack of attention given them in historical research. For the most part they are haphazardly maintained and poorly indexed.

5. The Genevan exiles who would prepare the English Translation of the Bible were a splinter group from the English community in Frankfurt. For a contemporary account of the differences that led to the Genevan removal, see William Whittingham, *A Brief Discourse of the Troubles at Frankfurt 1554–1558 AD* (privately printed, London, 1907).

6. Others thought to be involved in the translation at various stages include John Knox, Myles Coverdale, Christopher Goodman, Thomas Sampson, John Bodley, and William Cole.

7. Lewis Lupton, *A History of the Geneva Bible,* 7 vols. (London, 1966), I, p. 67.

8. For descriptions of the textual and exegetical aspects of the Genevan translation see: Lewis Lupton, *A History of the Geneva Bible;* Brooke Foss Westcott, *A General View of the History of the English Bible,* 3d ed. (reprinted New York, 1972), pp. 90–95; Basil Hall, *The Genevan Version of the English Bible* (London, 1957); S. L. Greenslade, ed., *The Cambridge History of the Bible,* 3 vols. (Cambridge, Eng., 1963), III, pp. 155–59; and F. F. Bruce, *The English Bible: A History of Translations* (New York, 1970), pp. 86–92.

9. Between 1560 and 1640 the Geneva Bible went through more than 160 editions from presses in Geneva, London, and Amsterdam. See Charles Eason, *The Genevan Bible: Notes on Its Production and Distribution* (Dublin, 1937).

10. F. F. Bruce, *The English Bible,* p. 91.

11. S. L. Greenslade, ed., *Cambridge History,* III, pp. 158–59.

12. The only rival of the Geneva Bible in popularity was John Foxe's *Book of Martyrs.* See William Haller, *The Elect Nation: The Meaning and Relevance of Foxe's Book of Martyrs* (New York, 1963).

13. See W. Schwarz, *Principles and Problems of Biblical Translation: Some Reformation Controversies and Their Background* (Cambridge, Eng., 1955), pp. 211–12: "Like the humanists, [Luther] believed that only the original could be used for the interpretation of Holy Writ, for no human endeavor could produce a translation which would replace God's Word. Yet he wanted the Bible to be read by the public in the vernacular German. The resolution of the apparent logical contradiction between these two views is of some delicacy, since of necessity it

creates Bibles of different values; the original for the learned theologian who is able to interpret the text, and the translation for the congregation, who cannot arrive at an exegesis without the help of the theologian."

14. Quoted in Schwarz, *Principles and Problems of Biblical Translation,* p. 211.

15. Lloyd E. Berry, ed., *The Geneva Bible: A Facsimile of the 1560 Edition* (Madison, Wis., 1969), New Testament, p. 2. All references to the Geneva Bible will be to the Berry edition.

16. This too reflects a Reformation perspective. Jaroslav Pelikan observes in *Luther the Expositor: Introduction to the Reformer's Exegetical Writings* (St. Louis, 1954), p. 59, that "Luther often equated the Old Testament term 'Word of God' with 'promise'; for when God spoke His redemptive Word to Israel, the redemption which the Word wrought and brought was the redemption ultimately accomplished in Christ. By this profound insight Luther was able to go beyond the 'Messianic prophecies' *of* the Old Testament to a recognition of the Word of God *in* the Old Testament even in the passages where the Messiah was not mentioned." The theme of promise is developed more fully in James S. Preus, *From Shadow to Promise: Old Testament Interpretation from Augustine to the Young Luther* (Cambridge, 1969).

17. See, for example, *The Geneva Bible,* Old Testament, pp. 15, 23, 111, 115.

18. On the development of covenant theology, see Jens G. Møller, "The Beginnings of Puritan Covenant Theology," *Journal of Ecclesiastical History* 14 (1963), 46–67; and J. Wayne Baker, *Heinrich Bullinger and the Covenant: The Other Reformed Tradition* (Athens, Ohio, 1980).

19. On the identification of the Geneva Bible with nonconformity see Paul Christianson, *Reformers and Babylon: English Apocalyptic Visions from the Reformation to the Eve of the Civil War* (Toronto, 1978), pp. 36–39; Christopher Hill, *Society and Puritanism in Pre-Revolutionary England* (London, 1964), pp. 32–49; and Patrick Collinson, *The Elizabethan Puritan Movement* (Berkeley, 1967), p. 175. Explicit identifications of the Geneva Bible as a radical document can be found in Harding Craig, "The Geneva Bible as a Political Document," *Pacific Historical Review,* 7 (1938), 40–49; Richard Greaves, "Traditionalism and the Seeds of Revolution in the Social Principles of the Geneva Bible," *Sixteenth Century Journal,* 7 (1976), 94–109; and Christopher Hill, *The World Turned Upside Down: Radical Ideas During the English Revolution* (New York, 1972), pp. 129–30.

20. It is significant that, in an age known for its censorship and suppression of the press, neither Elizabeth nor the Star Chamber prohibited the publication and sale of the Genevan translation. Most editions of the Geneva Bible were issued by the Queen's printer, Christopher Barker.

21. Westcott, *A General View,* p. 95.

22. The instructions to the translators can be found in Westcott, *A General View,* pp. 115–16. One significant effort to base a new translation on the Genevan text rather than the Bishop's Bible was undertaken by the Hebraist, Hugh Broughton. Broughton died before bringing his work to completion, but of the Authorized Version he had the following comments: "The cockles of the sea shores and the leaves of the forest, and the grains of the poppy, may as well be numbered as the gross errors of this Bible. . . ." Quoted in F. F. Bruce, *The English Bible,* p. 107.

23. Leonard J. Trinterud, "The Origins of Puritanism" *Church History,* 20 (1951), 50. On the shift away from Calvin toward a "conditional" or "Preparationist"

covenant theology see also Jens G. Møller, "The Beginnings of Puritan Covenant Theology," p. 64; John von Rohr, "Covenant and Assurance in Early English Puritanism," *Church History*, 34 (1965), 195–203; Everett H. Emerson, "Calvin and Covenant Theology," *Church History*, 25 (1956), 134–44; and Perry Miller, *Errand into the Wilderness* (New York, 1956).

24. Hugh Barbour, *The Quakers in Puritan England* (New Haven, 1964), p. 158.

25. The Keithian Schism, early Pennsylvania's most volatile crisis, concerned, ironically, the attempt of the dissenter George Keith to place more emphasis on the Bible and less on "the light within." The Quaker majority, however, developed no mechanism for expelling such malcontents and thus could only learn to put up with antagonistic factions. For excellent discussions of this religious and political instability, see Gary B. Nash, *Quakers and Politics: Pennsylvania, 1681–1726* (Princeton, 1968), pp. 127–80; and Jon Butler, "Gospel Order Improved: The Keithian Schism and the Exercise of Quaker Ministerial Authority in Pennsylvania," *William and Mary Quarterly*, 3d ser., 31 (1974), 430–52.

26. For two provocative statements about the contrasting cultural legacies of Pennsylvania and New England, see Daniel T. Rodgers, "Democracy, Mediocrity, and the Spirit of Max Weber," *Reviews in American History*, 8 (1980), 465–70; and Mary Maples Dunn, "Saints and Sisters: Congregational and Quaker Women in the Early Colonial Period," *American Quarterly*, 30 (1978), 582–601.

27. Quotations from Winthrop's sermon are taken from Michael McGiffert, ed., *Puritanism and the American Experience* (Reading, Mass., 1969).

28. I am indebted to Professor McGiffert for pointing out Winthrop's variant Bible usage to me in private correspondence.

29. The Puritan dilemmas of power in the New World are treated from a slightly different perspective in Edmund Morgan's *The Puritan Dilemma: The Story of John Winthrop* (Boston, 1958).

30. Lloyd Berry, ed., *The Geneva Bible*, introduction, 22. Samuel Eliot Morison described the use of the Geneva Bible in Plymouth in his edition of William Bradford's *Of Plymouth Plantation 1620–1647* (New York, 1963).

31. See especially, "The Marrow of Puritan Divinity," reprinted in *Errand into the Wilderness*, pp. 48–98; and *The New England Mind: The Seventeenth Century* (New York, 1939), Book IV, pp. 365–492.

32. See Lockridge, *Literacy in Colonial New England*.

33. Sacvan Bercovitch, ed., *The American Puritan Imagination: Essays in Revaluation* (Cambridge, Eng., 1974), p. 9.

34. See especially the collected sermons of Thomas Shepard, Richard Mather, and John Cotton.

35. The classic formulation was Peter Bulkeley's *The Gospel-Covenant: or The Covenant of Grace Opened* (London, 1646).

36. Urian Oakes, *New England Pleaded With* (Cambridge, 1673), p. 9.

37. J. Franklin Jameson, ed., *Johnson's Wonder-Working Providence 1628–1651* (New York, 1910), pp. 25, 60.

38. The fullest account of the Antinomian crisis is found in Emery Battis, *Saints and Sectaries: Anne Hutchinson and the Antinomian Controversy in the Massachusetts Bay Colony* (Chapel Hill, N.C., 1962).

39. For an interpretation which discusses Antinomianism in feminist terms, see Lyle Koehler, "The Case of the American Jezebels: Anne Hutchinson and Female Agitation during the Years of Antinomian Turmoil, 1636–1640," *William and Mary Quarterly*, 3d ser., 31 (1974), 55–78. Mary Maples Dunn also discusses Hutchinson's biblical defenses of her rights as a woman in "Saints and Sisters:

Congregational and Quaker Women in the Early Colonial Period," *American Quarterly,* 30 (1978), 582–601.

40. Wheelwright's sermon is reprinted in David D. Hall, ed., *The Antinomian Controversy, 1636–1638: A Documentary History* (Middletown, Conn., 1968), pp. 152–72. Throughout the sermon biblical references are to the Genevan version.

41. *Ibid.,* p. 269.

42. See Patricia Caldwell, "The Antinomian Language Controversy," *Harvard Theological Review,* 69 (1976), 345–67.

43. Quoted in Hall, ed., *The Antinomian Controversy,* p. 269.

44. Edwin S. Gaustad has suggested that Baptists in early New England were most familiar with the Geneva Bible. See Gaustad, ed., *Baptist Piety: The Last Will and Testimony of Obadiah Holmes* (Grand Rapids, Mich., 1978), pp. 113, 158.

45. Samuel West, *A Sermon Preached . . .* (Boston, 1776). Quotations are from a reprinting of this sermon in John Wingate Thornton, ed., *The Pulpit of the American Revolution* (New York, 1970; orig. 1860), pp. 267–322.

II

The Image of the United States as a Biblical Nation, 1776-1865

MARK A. NOLL
Wheaton College

"Both read the same Bible."

Abraham Lincoln, Second Inaugural

"What a sermon! The preacher stirred my blood. . . . A red-hot glow of patriotism passed through me. . . . There was more exhortation to fight and die, à la Joshua, than meek Christianity."

Mary Boykin Chesnut, after a sermon
by the Confederate Presbyterian Benjamin Palmer[1]

On the face of it, it would be hard to imagine a nation more thoroughly biblical than the United States between the American Revolution and the Civil War. The cadences of the Authorized Version informed the writing of the elite and the speech of the humble.[2] One of the ways that Noah Webster, premier wordsmith of the new nation, attempted to reform the country's educational system was to organize early schooling around the reading of his own distinctly American translation of the Bible.[3] For their part, denominational bodies took steps to preserve the integrity of published Bibles, as when Massachusetts Congregationalists and Baptists petitioned Congress in 1790 to regulate the accuracy of printed Bibles.[4] Many Americans also took pains to defend the divine authority of the Bible's message.[5]

This was the period in which Bible societies arose to place a copy of the Scriptures in the hands of every citizen, an effort which even so un-evangelical a figure as Thomas Jefferson supported in 1814 with a $50 contribution.[6] The Monroe County (New York) Bible Society illustrated the thoroughness with which such groups could work by giving a Bible to each of the county's 1200 households that an 1824 census had shown to be without the Scriptures.[7] It was an age when public leaders unabashedly proclaimed their devotion to Scripture. John Adams could call the Bible "the best book in the World."[8] Henry Clay referred to it as "the only book to give us hope in darkness."[9] Daniel Webster asserted that it was "the book of all others for lawyers as well as for divines."[10] And Abraham Lincoln named it "the best gift God has given to man."[11] To be sure, the practice of naming children for biblical characters did begin to decline between the Revolution and the Civil War.[12] Yet the people who influenced public opinion throughout the period were named for biblical figures more often than not. Of the nation's first seventeen Presidents, for example, twelve wore biblical first names.[13] Over 49 percent of the people who published books in 1831 were similarly named.[14]

As had been the case in the colonial period, national leaders proclaimed days of fasting and thanksgiving, at which ministers regularly expounded texts of Scripture. During the Civil War, for example, Jefferson Davis called for nine national days of fasting in the Confederacy, and Abraham Lincoln proclaimed four days of thanksgiving for the Union.[15] The widespread practice of printing sermons prepared for these and other notable public occasions continued. Not only ministers but politicians and other leaders used biblical images to quicken public spirit. Benjamin Franklin proposed in 1776 that the Continental Congress make the national seal an image of Moses leading Israel to safety through the Red Sea. Thomas Jefferson's suggestion was for a depiction of Israel led by the pillar of cloud and fire through the wilderness.[16] At the other end of the period, during the 1850s, public leaders, as well as "chiliastic sects," expressed their vision for the nation in millennial terms borrowed from the pages of the Bible.[17] The great reform movements of the day sought to inculcate a biblical righteousness into the social fabric.[18] And stories continued to circulate about the extraordinary consolation of Scripture (e.g., the family engulfed in a New Hampshire avalanche which devoted its last hours to a perusal of the Bible[19]) and even its talismanic value (e.g., the Confederate soldier whose pocket Bible stopped a bullet to the heart at the battle of Manassas[20]).

Nothing, in short, could be more obvious than the biblical character of the United States during its early years.

Once past the obvious fact that the Bible was a ubiquitous presence, however, we discover that the country's biblical character was not simple at all. This is particularly so if we set aside the ways in which Christians used Scripture for private spiritual nourishment and concentrate instead on the public use of the Bible, particularly the ways in which ministers employed Holy Writ to explain the character and destiny of the United States.[21] The problem appears most clearly in sermons preached at times of great national crisis, where even the most superficial sampling leads to a troubling question. Did ministers, preaching from the Bible as public spokesmen, really use Scripture as a primary source for the convictions they expressed? Or did they in fact merely exploit Scripture to sanctify convictions—whether nationalistic, political, social, or racial—which had little to do with biblical themes? The following examples, drawn almost at random from sermons preached at crisis periods in the country's early years, illustrate the seriousness of the difficulty.

In 1773 we find a Connecticut Congregationalist basing a discourse concerning the virtues of home rule and the folly of government by a foreign power on Exodus 1:8—"Now there arose up a new king over Egypt, which knew not Joseph."[22] A year later a Presbyterian *Sermon on Tea* took Colossians 2:21 for its text—"Touch not; taste not; handle not."[23] During the years of the war itself, a Boston minister inveighed against the "curse" of inflation in a sermon constructed around the story of Achan's deceit at Ai. His text was Joshua 7:13—"Up, sanctify the people . . . There is an accursed thing in the midst of thee, O Israel: thou canst not stand before thine enemies, until ye take away the accursed thing from among you."[24] When George Washington died in December 1799, the country responded with an outpouring of eulogies, discourses, memorials, and sermons to mark his passing. Of the more than 200 such speeches published in 1800, over 100 were sermons, and of those a full twenty-one used David's lament for Abner in II Samuel 3:38 to mourn the father of his country: "Know ye not that there is a prince and a great man fallen this day in Israel?"[25] During the War of 1812 a New York minister employed the handwriting on the wall at Belshazzar's feast (Daniel 5:27) to weigh the moral character of Great Britain in the balances and find it wanting.[26]

Two generations later, ministers had lost none of their skill at putting biblical texts to use for public purposes. Early in the Civil War a southern

Presbyterian teased II Chronicles 6:34–35, King Solomon's prayer for success in battle for Israel, into a biblically worded analysis of the current crisis: "Eleven tribes sought to go forth in peace from the house of political bondage, but the heart of our modern Pharoah is hardened, that he will not let Israel go."[27] In the North, one of the more than 400 sermons published after the assassination of Lincoln was an exposition of II Samuel 18:32, in which David learns about the treacherous slaying of his son Absalom. After an examination of the text, the minister could conclude that no one "will be able to separate in thought the murder of the president, from [Jefferson] Davis' persistent effort to murder the Union."[28]

These examples, which could be multiplied virtually without limit, leave the impression that although the Bible may have been the nation's *vade mecum* in times of crisis, it was not in fact the source of the deepest sentiments expressed on those occasions. Rather, ministers seem to have introduced the Bible fairly late into the process of preparing sermonic responses to momentous public events. All too often during the two great wars of the period, a minister's identification with his nation—whether Great Britain or a newly independent United States, whether the Confederacy of the South or the Union of the North—became the fundamental conviction behind the preparation and delivery of sermons.[29] The same pattern was present only slightly less frequently during other crises between the great wars.[30] Public events occurred which seemed to call for sermonic commentary. Ministers prepared and delivered sermons on a text of Scripture. But this text of Scripture became a gateway not for the proclamation of essentially biblical messages but for the minister's social, political, or cultural convictions, which had been securely in place long before he had turned to the Bible.

Modern students noting this state of affairs will be chagrined or pleased depending on their own convictions. Those for whom the Bible remains in principle the infallible guide to faith and practice will rue the prostitution of Scripture before alien ideologies. On the other hand, those who with Marx, Durkheim, or Freud regard religion as a function of some other more fundamental reality will find ample confirmation for their views in the public use of the Bible during this earlier period.[31] In the process of making these judgments, however, it is possible for modern Christians and secularists alike to miss the historical significance of the nation's biblical style in its early period. Only by examining concrete examples of this style is it possible to appreciate the ironies which characterized America's use of the Bible during the early years of the republic.

To come at the public use of Scripture from the inside is to recognize at once that the Bible represented two very different books. It was first a compendium of instruction for faith and practice, a source of universally valid insight about the human condition.[32] At the deaths of Washington and Lincoln, for example, several ministers turned to the wisdom literature of the Old Testament to remind their congregations of verities ordained by God: that the Lord reigned sovereignly over the affairs of men and nations (Psalm 93:1),[33] that a people will long remember its "righteous" men (Psalm 112:6),[34] or that even godlike rulers must succumb to death with all humanity (Psalm 82:6-7).[35] Used in this way the Bible that spoke to Americans was much the same as that which had spoken to Christians of all times and places.

Much more frequently, however, the Bible was not so much the truth above all truth as it was the story above all stories. On public occasions Scripture appeared regularly as a typical narrative imparting significance to the antitypical events, people, and situations of United States history.[36] That is, ministers preached as if the stories of Scripture were being repeated, or could be repeated, in the unfolding life of the United States. This was as true for white Congregationalists and Presbyterians, decision-makers in American society, as it was for black Baptists and Methodists, who could express their opinions on public affairs only by indirection. Elite whites and slave blacks both looked, for instance, to the Pentateuch as a paradigm for American experience. Whites, at different times and places, saw the Exodus as the model for liberation from Great Britain or from the North; they regarded Moses as the archetype for the United State's own great lawgivers and friends of God.[37] Blacks proclaimed Moses' cry to let his people go with entirely different intentions.[38]

Two convictions were at work in this use of the Bible as the controlling myth for American experience: the belief that Scripture was most useful on public occasions if it was treated as a storehouse of types, and the belief that the United States was an antitype which fulfilled biblical types. These convictions never showed more clearly than when ministers throughout the period invested current events with significance drawn from the history of the ancient Hebrews.

In this activity the only limits upon a preacher's treatment of "our American Israel"[39] were the limits of his imagination. During the Revolution, the patriot victory at Saratoga became the triumph of Hezekiah over the Assyrians.[40] The ones who leaped to the aid of the colonies were like "the children of Issachar . . . that had understanding of the times, to know what Israel ought to do" (I Chronicles 12:32).[41] Those who hesitated received the Curse of Meroz for not coming "to the help of the Lord against the mighty" (Judges 5:23).[42] At the death of Washington, ministers emptied the catalogue of Old Testament worthies and likened the fallen General to Abel, Jacob, Moses, Joshua, Othniel, Samuel, Abner, Elijah, David, Josiah, Jehoiada, Mordecai, Cyrus, and Daniel.[43] Sixty-five years later most of these figures appeared again at metaphors for another fallen President who, perhaps because of the season of his assassination, was also likened cautiously to Christ.[44] Northern ministers lacked nothing when reading current events through the lens of Scripture, but Southerners excelled in this exercise. Lincoln was Pharaoh, Jefferson Davis, Moses, and the Yankees in general, Judas.[45] Victories at Fort Sumter and in the first Peninsula campaign repeated the conquest of Midian and the defeat of Sennacherib.[46] And during the dark days of 1864, a minister could ask his congregation with great feeling: "were not the victorious Hebrews vastly outnumbered by the Yankees of the desert?"[47] Although many ministers undoubtedly used such metaphors as self-conscious literary devices, the frequency of their appearance suggests that at least some had blurred the line between simile and reality.

The clearest Revolutionary statement concerning the congruence of Old Testament Israel and modern America came from Ezra Stiles, president of Yale College. In a sermon of 1783 on Deuteronomy 26:19, a passage detailing God's exaltation of Israel, Stiles concluded that the verse was "allusively prophetic of the future prosperity and splendor of the United States."[48] By the time of the Civil War, Northern ministers subscribed to an even more ardent millennialism, and they had begun to place greater weight on the New Testament.[49] This resulted, however, in little more than a shift in emphasis for traditional themes, as the title of a work published in 1854 suggests: *Armageddon: or the . . . existence of the United States Foretold in the Bible, its . . . expansion into the millennial republic, and its dominion over the whole world.*[50] At Lincoln's death ministers could still ask rhetorically whether Psalm 147:20 ("He hath not dealt so with any nation") "is . . . not as true of us as of ancient Israel?"[51] They still could affirm that "the Hebrew Commonwealth, 'in which all the families of the earth were to be blest,' was not more of the whole world's concern than is this Republic."[52] Even Isaac Wise, a rabbi, could use the language of the Old Testament in an appeal for the American "Israel" to repent of its sins and to obey God's law.[53]

This predisposition to read Scripture typically and to regard the United States as a new Israel naturally led ministers to stress the grand narratives of the Old Testament. Well into the national period, the public Bible of the United States was for all intents the Old Testament. During the Revolution just about the only ministers who preached consistently from the New Testament were pacifists and loyalists, trying—in vain—to overcome the power of Old Testament narratives about setting captive Israel free with straight-forward exposition of New Testament injunctions to honor the king and love one's enemies.[54] When Washington died, only seven of the 120 texts used in published discourses came from the New Testament. And of those seven, four were references to Old Testament characters.[55] A sampling of sermons preached after Lincoln's assassination shows that while the Old Testament was used less frequently than at Washington's death, it still supplied over 70 percent of the texts, and this in spite of the fact that Lincoln died at the end of Holy Week.[56]

The reasons why ministers used the Bible as they did on public occasions in this period are found in a combination of historical influences and of prevailing beliefs about the character of the United States. Historians have frequently noted the importance of the Bible for the English since the Reformation,[57] and the particular importance of the Old Testament for Puritans in Old and New England.[58] They have recognized that although Puritanism had collapsed as a total way of life by the eighteenth century, it continued to exert a powerful influence on the public life of the new United States.[59] They have also described a long English tradition of reading Scripture typologically, a tradition which Cotton Mather brought to a peak in his *Magnalia Christi Americana*.[60] And they have noted the deeply entrenched conviction that the English people were God's elect nation.[61] During the early national period these religious traditions combined with convictions about the United States to create the context for public Bible reading. As many historians have pointed out, heterodox Americans as much as the consistent evangelicals shared convictions about the sacred character and the cosmic destiny of this "first new nation."[62] It is not at all unexpected, then, that the Bible should come to be read in terms dictated by the development of American nationalism.

Once having recognized the lengthy typological tradition and the widely shared beliefs in the special character of the United States, it is not so easy to regard the use of the Bible in the country's early history as simple ideological prostitution or a mere illustration of religious functionalism. It appears, rather, that the Bible was woven into the warp and woof of American culture—that especially its Old Testament images and the flow of its Old Testament narrative had become common coinage for the realm.

There was little self-conscious deception, and hence little deliberate ma-
nipulation of Scripture for ulterior purposes. Still, in becoming common
coinage a certain debasement of the Bible's message did take place. A
quantity of bad money—nationalistic particularism, presumptuous self-
righteousness, gratuitous assumptions about national election—drove out
the good—universal standards of righteousness and grace, intimations of a
hope in Christ transcending loyalties to earthly powers. The result was
that although the Bible had worked itself into the foundation of national
consciousness, it contributed little to the shape of the structures built upon
that foundation—except for the conviction that the structures were as sac-
rosanct as the biblical foundation itself.

The image of the United States as a biblical nation was, thus, based upon
a union of biblical typology and American nationalism. But this was not
the whole story, for there were also Americans for whom the Bible and
American nationalism were at odds. And from these individuals came an
entirely different image of the United States as a biblical country. Two
quite different groups illustrate this second way in which Scripture acted
as a public force between the Revolution and the Civil War.

The first group was made up of the immediate theological heirs of Jonathan Edwards. In the early days of the Great Awakening, Edwards had
made much of the colonies' place in God's eschatological designs. Yet unlike most American students of prophecy, he came to emphasize the spiritual, supra-national character of the millennium.[63] In addition, the dispute
over church purity which cost him the Northampton pulpit in 1750 provided him with an occasion to distinguish God's covenant of grace from
national covenants.[64] Even more important, that same dispute forced him
to reconsider the application of biblical typology to the American situation. He did not abandon the idea that Israel and its history were types to
be fulfilled in later years. But he did insist that these were types of spiritual realities having little or nothing to do with later nations as such. Israel, he wrote,

> was a *typical nation*. There was there literally a *land*, which was a type of
> heaven, the true dwelling-place of God; and an *external city*, which was
> a type of the spiritual city of God; an *external temple of God*, which was a
> type of his spiritual temple. So there was an *external people and family of
> God*, by carnal generation, which was a type of his spiritual progeny. And
> the covenant by which they were made a people of God, was a type of the
> covenant of grace.[65]

This spiritual typology would become important for some of Edwards's heirs as they sought to use ethical injunctions from the Bible as a counterweight to the nationalistic use of its types.

Yet only a handful of Edwards's closest followers succeeded in using his theological insights to liberate Scripture in the national arena. Many who bore the title New Light in the Revolutionary years or the name Edwardsean in the early national period set aside Edwards's teaching on biblical types and joined their fellow Americans in regarding the nation itself as the antitype of biblical patterns.[66] Those who did preserve Edwards's convictions included his closest theological pupil, Joseph Bellamy. This Connecticut Congregationalist resisted, even during the alarms of the Revolutionary period, the widespread practice of uniting the types of Scripture with the aspirations of American patriotism and continued to use the Bible to speak of the individual's spiritual needs before God.[67] Another, more obscure follower of Edwards in Connecticut, Israel Holley, also disdained the use of Scripture as type and employed it instead to call for the reform of Connecticut's church-state establishment.[68] Also during the Revolution, Edwardseans Levi Hart of Connecticut and Jacob Green of New Jersey set aside typological identifications of Israel and the emerging United States long enough to direct biblical injunctions against the practice of slavery.[69]

Green and Hart were joined in their anti-slave efforts by the Edwardsean whose use of Scripture broke most clearly with prevailing patterns, Samuel Hopkins of Newport. Early in the war, Hopkins published *A Dialogue, concerning the Slavery of the Africans,* the burden of which was to show "the inconsistence of promoting the slavery of the Africans, at the same time we are asserting our own civil liberty, at the risque of our fortunes and lives."[70] Although Hopkins made free use of the patriots' political theory in attacking slavery, a good portion of his pamphlet was frankly biblical. In clearing the way for the injunctions of Scripture, however, Hopkins first had to deal with a set of widespread assumptions. Scriptural Israel, so the argument ran, held slaves; America is at least a Bible-honoring land and at most an antitype of Israel itself; therefore, slavery cannot be censured as anti-biblical. Hopkins responded that slavery was "condemned by the whole of divine revelation." Israel could enslave Canaanites because of God's express permission. But this was one of those "many directions and laws to the *Jews* which had no respect to mankind in general.' Now things are different: "the distinction [of Israel] is . . . at an end, and all nations are put upon a level; and Christ . . . has taught us to look on all nations as our neighbors and brethren."[71] Hopkins realized that the Bible nowhere explicitly condemned slavery itself, but having cleared away national typology and the American recapitulation of Israel, he could let biblical teaching advance as far as it could: in attacking the slavers' use of liquor to capture Africans (Habakkuk 2:15), in pointing out the differences between modern slavery and that of the first century (I Timothy 6:1), in showing the inconsistency between the slave trade and New Testament injunctions against harsh treatment of servants (Ephesians 6:9), in echoing biblical demands to plead the cause of the poor and oppressed (Proverbs 31:9), to love our neighbors as ourselves (Matthew 22:39), and to care for the stranger and fatherless (Jeremiah 7:6).[72] For Hopkins, to read the Bible as he had been taught by Edwards was to find a very different public book than that which many of his contemporaries opened to illuminate the Revolutionary era.

The other group which resembled this small band of Edwardseans in its use of Scripture differed from the scholarly New England clergymen in nearly every other way. The nation's very significant numbers of enslaved Christians included many for whom Scripture was not bound by American nationalism. It included many who, while believing wholeheartedly in biblical typology, did not find its fulfillment in the legendary events of United States history.

Only recently have historians, searching for ante-bellum black religious consciousness in general, cast light on the slaves' use of Scripture in particular.[73] They have found that slaves discriminated between the Bible which their masters presented and the Bible they found for themselves. The sterilized message of the master's Scriptures rarely went beyond expositions of Exodus 20:15 ("Thou shalt not steal"), Ephesians 6:5–6 ("Servants, be obedient to them that are your masters according to the flesh, with fear and trembling, in singleness of your heart, as unto Christ; Not with eyeservice, as men-pleasers, but as the servants of Christ, doing the will of God from the heart"), or I Peter 2:18 ("Servants, be subject to your masters with all fear; not only to the good and gentle, but also to the froward").[74] One former slave, unimpressed, presented this summary of such preaching: " 'Serve your masters. Don't steal your master's turkey. Don't steal your master's chickens. Don't steal your master's hogs. Don't steal your master's meat. Do whatsomeever your master tell you to do.' Same old thing all de time."[75]

To this use of the Bible, slaves responded by napping during white services, by refusing opportunities for Bible reading organized by whites, or—most frequently—by simply remaining indifferent.[76] A few whites admitted frankly that it was not safe to let slaves see any further into the Bible than these passages. South Carolinian Whitemarsh Seabrook, for example, suggested in 1833 that anyone who urged the slaves to read the entire Bible should be committed to a "room in the Lunatic Asylum."[77]

Some masters, it is true, encouraged or permitted Bible reading among their slaves. But with permission or not, slaves went to great lengths to possess Scriptures for themselves. Sometimes this involved strenuous and perilous efforts to learn to read.[78] More frequently it meant gathering to hear a black preacher—"Stealing away to Jesus," as the spiritual put it. From these preachers they heard a message from a different Bible.[79] One slave left a striking record of the contrast: "A yellow [light-complexioned] man preached to us. She [the slave owner] had him preach how we ought to obey our master and missy if we want to go to heaven, but when she wasn't there, he came out with straight preachin' from the Bible."[80] Another slave, Anthony Dawson, spoke even more succinctly: "Mostly we had white preachers, but when we had a black preacher, that was heaven."[81]

The biblical messages of these preachers, as well as the biblical themes that informed the great body of slave songs, did share some common features with white use of Scripture. It was the Bible-as-story which captured the imagination of slaves just as it did the whites who put Scripture to work on public occasions. Blacks sang and preached about Adam and Eve and the Fall, about "wrestlin' Jacob" who "would not let [God] go," about Moses and the Exodus from Egypt, about Joshua possessing the Promised Land, about Daniel in the lions' den and Daniel's three friends in the fiery furnace, about Jonah in the whale and preaching before Nineveh, about the birth of Jesus, his death, and future return.[82] Unlike all but a few whites, however, the slaves did not consider the Bible's narratives to be foreshadowings of national realities. Or if they did, they reversed the analogy: *America* was Egypt, escape *from* American institutions was the Exodus.[83]

If whites saw future political realities in Scriptural narrative, and Edwardseans discerned spiritual ones, slaves saw a combination of social and spiritual truths. The narratives of the Old Testament in particular lent slave use of the Bible its special social dimension. Lawrence Levine has summarized this well: "The essence of slave religion cannot be fully grasped without understanding this Old Testament bias. It is important that Daniel and David and Joshua and Jonah and Moses and Noah, all of

whom fill the lines of the spirituals, were delivered in *this* world and delivered in ways which struck the imagination of the slaves. . . . The simi-
larity of these tales to the situation of the slaves was too clear for them
not to see it; too clear for us to believe that the songs had no worldly content for blacks in bondage. 'O my Lord delivered Daniel,' the slaves observed, and responded logically: 'O why not deliver me, too?' "[84]

For slaves, the figure of Moses assumed a special importance as the one
whom God had raised up to free his people. A Union soldier commented
somewhat disparagingly on this fixation in 1864: "There is no part of the
Bible with which they are so familiar as the story of the deliverance of the
children of Israel. Moses is their *ideal* of all that is high, and noble, and
perfect, in man. I think they have been accustomed to regard Christ not so
much in the light of a *spiritual* Deliverer, as that of a second Moses who
could eventually lead *them* out of their prison-house of bondage."[85] The
soldier was only part right. The figure of Jesus—who suffered innocently,
who ministered particularly to the oppressed—added a distinctly spiritual
dimension to the hope of social liberation. As Eugene Genovese puts it:
"Moses had become Jesus, and Jesus, Moses; and with their union the two
aspects of the slaves' religious quest—collective deliverance as a people
and redemption from their terrible personal sufferings—had become one
through the mediation of that imaginative power so beautifully manifested
in the spirituals."[86] In sum, deliverance from Egypt, the suffering of the
Saviour, and the final Day of the Lord had very little to do with the fate
of the United States. Nor did they foreshadow an exclusively spiritual
transaction between God and the individual. Rather, they provided the
framework for a social hope, for communal aspirations, in which the
power of God would break in pieces the fetters of slavery and the bonds of
sin together.

More fundamentally than even the Edwardseans, black slaves also employed the injunctions of Scripture to counter the nationalistic typology of
whites. Some of the favorite texts of slaves were verses that heralded the
universality of the gospel's message: Malachi 2:10 ("Have we not all one
father? hath not one God created us?"[87]), Acts 10:34 ("Of a truth I perceive that God is no respecter of persons"[88]), and Acts 17:26 ("And
[God] hath made of one blood all nations of men"[89]). Fortified by such
texts blacks had no trouble setting aside white beliefs about the recapitulation of Israelite history in North America. God's chosen people did not
constitute a nation among nations, but those who suffered unjustly among
all peoples. The story of Israel was not the prototype of God's gracious

call of a modern nation, but of all who would hunger and thirst after righteousness.[90]

If the blacks were similar to the Edwardseans in combining biblical types and scriptural injunctions to break the nationalistic use of Scripture, it is less readily apparent that their employment of Scripture constituted a public statement about the character of the United States. Samuel Hopkins set out to reform an evil which he pictured as a distinctly *national* blight. At first glance, he seems to have had few imitators among slave Bible-readers who were prohibited from making formal declarations about national character or national policy.[91] In fact, however, black biblical consciousness was probably as intensely public, as vitally concerned about the national future, as was the Edwardsean. To recognize that blacks—because of their African heritage and their particular Christian sensibilities—made little distinction between the sacred and the secular, is to recognize that their religious activities were, as Donald Mathews suggests, "political because they were the means by which blacks created a public life for themselves."[92] And that public life was one shaped by both biblical narrative and biblical propositions.

Only rarely did slaves pause to indulge the fanciful nationalistic exegesis so characteristic of whites. Such an occasion occurred during the Civil War when slaves in Richmond delighted in Daniel 11:13 which speaks of "the king of the north" with his "great army and . . . much riches."[93] For the most part, however, slaves showed little interest in applying biblical categories to the United States as a special entity. This was no mere oversight. Preoccupied as they were with the Bible's unfathomable mysteries, with its message of hope for those who despaired, and with its offer of a reality more fundamental than even the scourge of slavery, the slaves' silence on the fate of the nation as such may have been the most authentically scriptural comment on the national destiny of the entire period.

In the years between the American Revolution and the Civil War, the Bible offered to many Americans a key for understanding not only private religious reality but also the public life of the country. The Scriptures were so widely used that it is not inaccurate to call the country a biblical nation during this period. The image of the United States as a biblical nation, however, is an ironic one. Those who applied the Bible's teachings to the nation's destiny most directly seemed to have understood its message least. Those, on the other hand, for whom the country itself was least important seemed to have understood it best.

NOTES

1. Quoted in James W. Silver, *Confederate Morale and Church Propaganda* (Gloucester, Mass.: Peter Smith, 1964; orig. 1957), p. 54.

2. Recent studies have begun to document the prevalence of biblical themes and vocabulary among the "common" people. See especially Lewis O. Saum, *The Popular Mood of Pre-Civil War America* (Westport, Conn.: Greenwood Press, 1980), pp. 3–104; also Anne C. Loveland, *Southern Evangelicals and the Social Order 1800–1860* (Baton Rouge: Louisiana State University Press, 1980), pp. 34, 36, 104–5, and *passim*.

3. Harry R. Warfel, *Noah Webster: Schoolmaster to America* (New York: Macmillan, 1936), pp. 11, 13, 20, 66, 401–15; and Richard M. Rollins, *The Long Journey of Noah Webster* (Philadelphia: University of Pennsylvania Press, 1980), pp. 117–18. William J. Wolf, *The Almost Chosen People: A Study of the Religion of Abraham Lincoln* (New York: Doubleday, 1959), pp. 133–34, relates Lincoln's humorous reminiscences on the difficulty some students in his "blab school" encountered when attempting to pronounce the Bible's proper names.

4. William G. McLoughlin, *New England Dissent, 1630–1833* (Cambridge: Harvard University Press, 1971), 2:711.

5. This concern is illustrated in the inaugural sermon by Archibald Alexander, first professor of Princeton Theological Seminary, *The Sermon, Delivered at the Inauguration of the Rev. Archibald Alexander . . .* (New York: J. Seymour, 1812), pp. 69–77. On the general effort to defend Scripture during this period, see E. Brooks Holifield, *The Gentlemen Theologians: American Theology in Southern Culture 1795–1860* (Durham: Duke University Press, 1978), pp. 85–96; and Herbert Hovenkamp, *Science and Religion in America 1800–1860* (Philadelphia: University of Pennsylvania Press, 1978), pp. 57–78.

6. Jefferson to Samuel Greenhow, Jan. 31, 1814, *The Writings of Thomas Jefferson*, ed. A. A. Lipscomb (Washington: Thomas Jefferson Memorial Association, 1905–1907), 14:81.

7. Whitney R. Cross, *The Burned-Over District: The Social and Intellectual History of Enthusiastic Religion in Western New York, 1800–1850* (New York: Harper & Row, 1965; orig. 1950), p. 127. Robert Baird offers a comprehensive contemporary view of the wide dispersion of Bibles in *Religion in the United States of America* (New York: Arno Press & New York Times, 1969; orig. 1844), pp. 372–74.

8. Adams to Thomas Jefferson, Dec. 25, 1813, L. J. Capon, ed., *The Adams-Jefferson Letters* (Chapel Hill: University of North Carolina Press, 1959), 2:412.

9. C. Colton, ed., *The Works of Henry Clay* (New York: G. P. Putnam's Sons, 1904), 3:55.

10. Charles Lanman, *The Private Life of Daniel Webster* (New York: Harper & Bros., 1856), p. 104.

11. Lincoln, "Reply to Loyal Colored People of Baltimore upon Presentation of a Bible," Sept. 7, 1864, *The Collected Works of Abraham Lincoln*, ed. R. P. Basler (New Brunswick: Rutgers University Press, 1953), 7:542.

12. See David W. Dumas, "The Naming of Children in New England, 1780–1850," *New England Historical and Genealogical Record*, 132 (July 1978), 196–210, for a detailed study of names given to children in Charlemont, Massachusetts. Dumas shows a decline in the number of boys given biblical names from 76 per-

cent (1780–89) to 25 percent (1840–49) and of girls from 55 percent (1780–89) to 31 percent (1840–49).

13. By contrast, of the next twenty-three Presidents (Grant through Reagan), only three had biblical first names. In these tallies, Zachary is counted as a biblical name (a form of Zacharias), but Jimmy is not.

14. This figure is from a tabulation of the authors whose last names began with the letters A, L, and S in *A Checklist of American Imprints for 1831,* comp. S. Bruntjen and C. Bruntjen (Metuchen, N.J.: Scarecrow, 1975). The same tabulation for 1801 yielded 62.2 percent biblical first names, *American Bibliography: A Preliminary Checklist for 1801,* comp. R. R. Shaw and R. H. Shoemaker (New York: Scarecrow, 1958).

15. Silver, *Confederate Morale,* p. 64; *Collected Works of Abraham Lincoln,* 5:185–86; 6:332–33, 496–97; 8:55–56.

16. John F. Berens, *Providence and Patriotism in Early America 1640–1815* (Charlottesville: University Press of Virginia, 1978), p. 107.

17. George M. Fredrickson, *The Inner Civil War: Northern Intellectuals and the Crisis of the Union* (New York: Harper & Row, 1965), p. 7. These millennial themes had been securely wedded to American nationalism by the events of the Revolution; see Nathan O. Hatch, *The Sacred Cause of Liberty: Republican Thought and the Millennium in Revolutionary New England* (New Haven: Yale University Press, 1977).

18. Two recent essays recognize more clearly than do earlier efforts the strength of religious convictions flowing from the Second Great Awakening into the various reform movements: Donald G. Mathews, "The Second Great Awakening as an Organizing Process, 1780–1830," *American Quarterly,* 21 (1969), 23–43; Lois W. Banner, "Religious Benevolence as Social Control: A Critique of an Interpretation," *Journal of American History,* 60 (June 1973), 23–41; both essays are reprinted in J. M. Mulder and J. F. Wilson, eds., *Religion in American History* (Englewood Cliffs, N.J.: Prentice-Hall, 1978). A positive argument for the distinctly biblical character of reform aspirations is offered by Timothy L. Smith, "Righteousness and Hope: Christian Holiness and the Millennial Vision in America, 1800–1900," *American Quarterly,* 31 (Spring 1979), 21–45.

19. Saum, *Popular Mood of Pre-Civil War America,* p. 85.

20. Silver, *Confederate Morale,* p. 14.

21. Setting the issue up this way does, admittedly, skew the analysis by overemphasizing the publishing ministers, who tended to be concentrated in New England. For example, more than one-third of the published sermons commemorating the death of Washington, which receive attention below, came from the state of Massachusetts alone.

22. Benjamin Trumbull, *A Discourse* (New Haven: Thomas & Samuel Green, 1773).

23. The sermon was by David Ramsay of Charleston, S.C.; "David Ramsay," James McLachlan, ed., *Princetonians 1748–1768: A Biographical Dictionary* (Princeton: Princeton University Press, 1976), p. 518.

24. Charles Chauncy, *The accursed thing must be taken away from among a People* (Boston: Thomas & John Fleet, 1778).

25. A full listing of Washington eulogies is found in Clifford K. Shipton, *The American Bibliography of Charles Evans, Vol. 13: 1799–1800* (Worcester, Mass.: American Antiquarian Society, 1955), pp. 347–79. For helpful discussions of the Washington eulogies, see Robert P. Hay, "George Washington: American Moses," *American Quarterly,* 21 (Winter 1969), 780–91; Michael T. Gilmore, "Eulogy

as Symbolic Biography: in *Studies in Biography,* ed. Daniel Aaron (Cambridge: Harvard University Press, 1978), pp. 147–48; and James H. Smylie, "The President as Republican Prophet and King: Clerical Reflections on the Death of Washington," *Journal of Church and State,* 18 (Spring 1976), 233–52.

26. Alexander McLeod, *A Scriptural View of the Character, Causes, and Ends of the Present War* (New York: Eastburn *et al.,* 1815), second sermon.

27. Benjamin M. Palmer, *National Responsibility Before God* (New Orleans, 1861), p. 5; cited in Silver, *Confederate Morale,* p. 27.

28. Henry A. Nelson, *The Divinely Prepared Ruler, and the Fit End of Treason* (Springfield, Ill., 1865), p. 32. Jay Monaghan describes 404 sermons commemorating Lincoln in "An Analysis of Lincoln's Funeral Sermons," pamphlet at the Chicago Historical Society, reprinted from *Indiana Magazine of History,* 41 (March 1945).

29. For just a sampling of the secondary literature on this phenomenon, see Hatch, *The Sacred Cause of Liberty,* pp. 55–96; Mark A. Noll, *Christians in the American Revolution* (Grand Rapids, Mich.: Eerdmans, 1977), pp. 49–77, 103–22; Silver, *Confederate Morale;* James H. Moorhead, *American Apocalypse: Yankee Protestants and the Civil War 1860–1869* (New Haven: Yale University Press, 1978), pp. xi, 19, 21, and *passim;* and George M. Marsden, *The Evangelical Mind and the New School Presbyterian Experience* (New Haven: Yale University Press, 1970), pp. 182–98. Berens, *Providence and Patriotism in Early America,* shows a similar process at work as political leaders appropriated biblical themes for American nationalism.

30. See, for example, William Gribbin, *The Churches Militant: The War of 1812 and American Religion* (New Haven: Yale University Press, 1973), especially pp. 78–103; Clayton Sumner Ellsworth, "The American Churches and the Mexican War," *American Historical Review,* 45 (January 1940), 301–26. I have not in this essay tried to sort out the creative uses of Scripture in the ante-bellum arguments about slavery, however similar those uses may have been to what took place in times of war. For a sensitive treatment of that subject and an introduction to the critical literature, see David Brion Davis, "The Good Book," in *The Problem of Slavery in the Age of Revolution* (Ithaca: Cornell University Press, 1975), pp. 523–56.

31. Karl Marx (with Friedrich Engels), *The Holy Family, or A Critique of Critical Criticism;* Emile Durkheim, *The Elementary Forms of the Religious Life;* Sigmund Freud, *Moses and Monotheism* and *The Future of an Illusion* are classic texts.

32. This usage resembles the private devotional use of the Bible documented by Saum, *Popular Mood of Pre-Civil War America,* in chapters entitled "Providence," "Religion," "Conversion, Revival, and Millennium," and "Death"; and it reflects the religiosity of Southern evangelicals described by Donald G. Mathews, *Religion in the Old South* (Chicago: University of Chicago Press, 1977), pp. 1–80.

33. John E. Todd, in *Sermons Preached in Boston on the Death of Abraham Lincoln* (Boston: J. E. Tilton, 1865).

34. Solomon Blakeslee, *An Oration* (Hartford, 1800); Nathaniel Fisher, *A Sermon* (Salem, Mass., 1800).

35. Caleb Alexander, *A Sermon* (Boston, 1800); Benjamin Trumbull, *The Majesty and Mortality of Created Gods Illustrated and Improved* (New Haven, 1800).

36. For typology in America, see Sacvan Bercovitch, "Introduction," and Thomas

M. Davis, "The Traditions of American Typology," in *Typology and Early American Literature* (Amherst: University of Massachusetts Press, 1972).

37. Numerous illustrations may be found in the sources cited in note 26 above.

38. See James Weldon Johnson, *The Book of American Negro Spirituals* (New York: Viking, 1925), p. 21, as quoted by Benjamin E. Mays, *The Negro's God as Reflected in His Literature* (New York: Atheneum, 1973, orig. 1938), p. 27: "It is not possible to estimate the sustaining influence that the story of the trials and tribulations of the Jews as related in the Old Testament exerted upon the Negro. This story at once caught and fired the imaginations of Negro bards, and they sang, sang their hungry listeners into a firm faith that . . . as God delivered Israel out of bondage in Egypt, so would He deliver them." On this same theme, see also the last section of this essay.

39. For this phrase, see David Osgood, *A Discourse* (Boston, 1800), p. 5; and Abiel Abbot, *Thanksgiving Sermon* (1799), as quoted by Conrad Cherry, ed., *God's New Israel: Religious Interpretations of American Destiny* (Englewood Cliffs, Prentice-Hall, 1971), p. [v].

40. Timothy Dwight, *Sermon upon the General Thanksgiving* (Hartford, 1778), p. 16; as quoted in James West Davidson, *The Logic of Millennial Thought: Eighteenth-Century New England* (New Haven: Yale University Press, 1977), p. 20.

41. This was the text of a sermon preached by Isaac Backus in 1775 on the first Sunday after Lexington and Concord; McLoughlin, *New England Dissent,* 1: 586–87; McLoughlin, *Isaac Backus and the American Pietistic Tradition* (Boston: Little, Brown, 1967), p. 134.

42. Nathaniel Whitaker of Salem, Massachusetts, used this text twice, *An Antidote against Toryism* (Newbury-Port: John Mycall, 1777) and *The Reward of Toryism* (Newbury-Port: John Mycall, 1783). For an excellent discussion of these sermons and the entire "Curse of Meroz" tradition, see Alan Heimert, *Religion and the American Mind from the Great Awakening to the Revolution* (Cambridge: Harvard University Press, 1966), pp. 332–34, 500–509.

43. To be fair, it must be noted that one minister took Stephen from the New Testament as a model for Washington, but not without also adding Jacob and Josiah from the Old; Peleg Burroughs, *An Oration* (Newport, R.I., 1800).

44. In the 77 sermons I sampled, Lincoln was likened to Abraham (only once), Joseph, Moses, Abner, David, Solomon, and Abel.

45. Silver, *Confederate Morale*, pp. 30, 97.

46. *Ibid.,* pp. 31, 33.

47. Joseph Cross, *Camp and Field* (Macon, 1864), quoted in *ibid.,* p. 40.

48. Ezra Stiles, *The United States Elevated to Glory and Honor* [1783], in John Wingate Thornton, ed., *The Pulpit of the American Revolution* (Boston: Gould & Lincoln, 1860), p. 403.

49. On the shift to the New Testament, see Donald M. Scott, *From Office to Profession: The New England Ministry 1750–1850* (Philadelphia: University of Pennsylvania Press, 1978), pp. 138–39. On the millennial spirit of the Civil War era, see Marsden, *The Evangelical Mind and the New School Presbyterian Experience,* pp. 182–98; and Moorhead, *American Apocalypse,* pp. 42, 54–65.

50. Cited in Bercovitch, ed., *Typology,* p. 301.

51. T. R. Howlett, *The Dealings of God with Our Nation* (Washington, D.C., 1865), p. 1.

52. Treadwell Walden, *The National Sacrifice* (Philadelphia, 1865), p. 17.

53. Emmanuel Hertz, ed., *Abraham Lincoln: The Tribute of the Synagogue* (New York: Bloch, 1927), p. 93.

54. See loyalist Jonathan Boucher, *A View of the Causes and Consequences of the American Revolution* (London: G. G. and J. Robinson, 1797), pp. 503–6; and pacifist Anthony Benezet, *Serious Reflections* (n.p., 1778), p. 3. For an overview of loyalist and pacifist arguments from Scripture, see Noll, *Christians in the American Revolution,* pp. 113–14, 126, 141–42.

55. The only two memorial sermons for Washington exclusively derived from New Testament texts were James Madison, *A Discourse* (Richmond, 1800), on II Timothy 4:7; and John Prince, *Part of a Discourse* (Salem, Mass., 1800), on Revelation 10:5–6.

56. The 77 sermons I sampled used 45 Old Testament texts 60 times, and 24 New Testament texts each once.

57. See, for example, A. G. Dickens, *The English Reformation* (New York: Schocken, 1964), pp. 189–91 and elsewhere; Philip Edgcumbe Hughes, *Theology of the English Reformers* (Grand Rapids, Mich.: Eerdmans, 1965), pp. 9–53; and, a more popular account, Derek Wilson, *The People & the Book: The Revolutionary Impact of the English Bible 1380–1611* (London: Barrie & Jenkins, 1976).

58. See, for example, William Haller, *Liberty and Reformation in the Puritan Revolution* (New York: Columbia University Press, 1955), pp. 26–27; Perry Miller, "The Garden of Eden and the Deacon's Meadow," *American Heritage,* December 1955, pp. 54–61, 102.

59. See, for example, Edmund S. Morgan, "The Puritan Ethic and the American Revolution," *William and Mary Quarterly,* 3d ser., 24 (January 1967), 3–43.

60. See Sacvan Bercovitch, *The Puritan Origins of the American Self* (New Haven: Yale University Press, 1975), especially the chapter "The Elect Nation in New England."

61. See William Haller, *The Elect Nation: The Meaning and Relevance of Foxe's "Book of Martyrs"* (New York: Harper & Row, 1963).

62. See, for examples, Cherry, *God's New Israel,* pp. 25–153; Paul C. Nagel, *This Sacred Trust: American Nationality 1798–1898* (New York: Oxford University Press, 1971), pp. 3–128; J. F. Maclear, "The Republic and the Millennium," in *The Religion of the Republic,* ed. E. A. Smith (Philadelphia: Fortress, 1971); and Ernest Lee Tuveson, *Redeemer Nation: The Idea of America's Millennial Role* (Chicago: University of Chicago Press, 1968).

63. On Edwards's gradual retreat from the idea that the millennium would begin in New England, see Stephen J. Stein, ed., *The Works of Jonathan Edwards: Apocalyptic Writings* (New Haven: Yale University Press, 1977), pp. 26–28, 48.

64. Patricia J. Tracy, *Jonathan Edwards, Pastor: Religion and Society in Eighteenth-Century Northampton* (New York: Hill and Wang, 1979), relates the social setting for the dismissal of Edwards.

65. Jonathan Edwards, *An Humble Inquiry into . . . Qualifications Requisite to . . . Full Communion* (1749), in *The Works of President Edwards* (New York: Burt Franklin, 1968; orig. London, 1817), 7:102.

66. A discussion of Edwardseans who do not follow Edwards is developed in Mark A. Noll, "Moses Mather (Old Light) and the Evolution of Edwardseanism," *Church History,* 49 (September 1980), 273–85.

67. See Mark A. Noll, "Church Membership and the American Revolution: An

THE UNITED STATES AS A BIBLICAL NATION

Aspect of Religion and Society in New England from the Revival to the War for Independence" (Ph.D. dissertation, Vanderbilt University, 1975), pp. 192–227.

68. Israel Holley, *God brings about his holy and wise Purpose . . . by using . . . the wicked Dispositions of Mankind . . . illustrated in a Sermon, Preached . . . the next Sabbath after the Report arrived, that the People at Boston had destroyed A Large Quantity of Tea* (Hartford: Eben. Watson, 1774); and *An Appeal to the Impartial* (Norwich: Green & Spooner, 1778), arguing against the taxing of Separates.

69. See Levi Hart, *Liberty Described and Recommended* (Hartford: Eben. Watson, 1775); and Mark A. Noll, "Observations on the Reconciliation of Politics and Religion in Revolutionary New Jersey: The Case of Jacob Green," *Journal of Presbyterian History,* 54 (Summer 1976), 217–37.

70. Samuel Hopkins, *A Dialogue, concerning the Slavery of the Africans* (Norwich, Conn.: Judah P. Spooner, 1776), p. iii. For an excellent discussion of Hopkins's religiously motivated reform, see David S. Lovejoy, "Samuel Hopkins: Religion, Slavery, and the Revolution," *New England Quarterly,* 40 (June 1967), 227–43.

71. Hopkins, *Dialogue,* pp. 19, 20, 21.

72. *Ibid.,* pp. 8, 23, 24–25, 30, 34, and 58.

73. Excellent accounts of slave religion, all of which include consideration of the Bible, include Eugene D. Genovese, *Roll, Jordan, Roll: The World the Slaves Made* (New York: Vintage, 1976; orig. 1972), pp. 159–284; Timothy L. Smith, "Slavery and Theology: The Emergence of Black Christian Consciousness in Nineteenth-Century America," *Church History,* 46 (December 1972), 497–512; Lawrence W. Levine, *Black Culture and Black Consciousness: Afro-American Folk Thought from Slavery to Freedom* (New York: Oxford University Press, 1977), pp. 3–189; Donald G. Mathews, *Religion in the Old South* (Chicago: University of Chicago Press, 1977), pp. 185–236; and Albert J. Raboteau, *Slave Religion: The "Invisible Institution" in the Antebellum South* (New York: Oxford University Press, 1978).

74. The phrase "sterilized message" paraphrases Genovese, *Roll, Jordan, Roll,* p. 166. For a discussion of these texts, see *ibid.,* pp. 208, 264; Levine, *Black Culture,* pp. 44–46; and Paul D. Escott, *Slavery Remembered: A Record of Twentieth-Century Slave Narratives* (Chapel Hill: University of North Carolina Press, 1979), p. 114.

75. Quoted in Charles V. Hamilton, *The Black Preacher in America* (New York: William Morrow, 1972), pp. 38–39.

76. Genovese, *Roll, Jordan, Roll,* p. 204; Escott, *Slavery Remembered,* p. 114; Mathews, *Religion in the Old South,* p. 142; Loveland, *Southern Evangelicals,* p. 236.

77. Quoted in William W. Freehling, *Prelude to Civil War: The Nullification Controversy in South Carolina, 1816–1836* (New York: Harper & Row, 1965), p. 335. On the same tie between the Bible and white fear of black literacy, see Genovese, *Roll, Jordan, Roll,* p. 725 n 4, which tells of a Memphis school superintendent who in 1870 forbade blacks to read the Bible; E. Franklin Frazier, *The Negro Church in America,* with C. Eric Lincoln, *The Black Church Since Frazier* (New York: Schocken, 1974; orig. 1963), pp. 17–18; and Levine, *Black Culture,* p. 46: "The dilemma that white ministers faced was simple to grasp but hard to resolve: the doctrine [of Christianity] that they were attempting to inculcate could easily subvert the institution of slavery—and both they and the slaves realized it."

78. For examples, see Genovese, *Roll, Jordan Roll*, pp. 169, 186, 191; Raboteau, *Slave Religion*, pp. 234, 239; and *A Narrative of the Life and Labors of the Rev. G. W. Offley, A Colored Man, and Local Preacher* (Hartford, 1850), in *Five Black Lives*, intro. Arna Bontemps (Middletown, Conn.: Wesleyan University Press, 1971), p. 133.

79. On the crucial relationship between the Bible and black preachers, see Hamilton, *The Black Preacher*, pp. 38–45; Genovese, *Roll, Jordan, Roll*, p. 256; Frazier, *The Negro Church*, pp. 18, 24; Henry H. Mitchell, *Black Preaching* (Philadelphia: J. B. Lippincott, 1970), p. 113; and Raboteau, *Slave Religion*, pp. 234–39.

80. Quoted in Hamilton, *The Black Preacher*, p. 39.

81. Quoted in Genovese, *Roll, Jordan, Roll*, p. 261.

82. Mathews, *Religion in the Old South*, pp. 203, 214, 217, 218, 220, 234; Smith, "Slavery and Theology," pp. 501, 502, 508; Genovese, *Roll, Jordan, Roll*, pp. 213, 242, 244, 249–54; Mays, *The Negro's God*, pp. 21–27; Levine, *Black Culture*, pp. 23, 37, 43, 50–51, 136; Raboteau *Slave Religion*, pp. 250–51, 311–12, 320; and Dena J. Epstein, *Sinful Tunes and Spirituals: Black Folk Music to the Civil War* (Urbana: University of Illinois Press, 1977), pp. 217–37.

83. Raboteau, *Slave Religion*, p. 251.

84. Levine, *Black Culture*, pp. 50–51.

85. Quoted in Raboteau, *Slave Religion*, pp. 311–12.

86. Genovese, *Roll, Jordan, Roll*, p. 253.

87. *Ibid.*, p. 264.

88. Matthews, *Religion in the Old South*, p. 219; *Narrative of the Rev. G. W. Offley*, p. 137.

89. Smith, "Slavery and Theology," p. 504; Mays, *The Negro's God*, pp. 41–42; Raboteau, *Slave Religion*, p. 232.

90. See Smith, "Slavery and Theology," p. 504.

91. To be sure, free blacks in the North did make extensive use of the Bible as Hopkins had done. See, for example, the many direct quotations of Scripture in the famous address by Frederick Douglass, "The Meaning of the Fourth of July for the Negro, speech at Rochester, New York, July 5, 1852," in Philip S. Foner, ed., *The Life and Writings of Frederick Douglas*, Volume II: *Pre-Civil War Decade 1850–1860* (New York: International, 1950), pp. 189, 196–200. See also Monroe Fordham, *Major Themes in Northern Black Religious Thought, 1800–1860* (Hicksville, N.Y.: Exposition, 1975), pp. 111–37.

92. Mathews, *Religion in the Old South*, p. 198.

93. Raboteau, *Slave Religion*, p. 312.

III

Sola Scriptura and
Novus Ordo Seclorum

NATHAN O. HATCH

University of Notre Dame

In a profound sense Abraham Lincoln was a man of the Book. He never
assumed responsibility for teaching the Bible, as did a more recent President, Jimmy Carter, and could not rival the theological expertise of the
Presbyterian minister's son, Woodrow Wilson, but Lincoln's character did
manifest a dominant strand of biblical thought and rhythm. Something of
a skeptic as a young man, he came in maturity to defend the Bible as absolutely true—"God's best gift to man." He possessed a rare command of biblical detail, searched its pages for personal strength, displayed its characters and settings even in his humor, and, in time of national crisis,
drew upon its themes to explain the meaning of slavery, civil war, and
emancipation.[1]

Lincoln defended the Bible, used it, and allowed its categories to frame
his expression. Yet his biblicism went even a step farther. He called for a
Christianity exclusively biblical that had no place for clergy, denominations, confessions, or creeds. What he came to affirm was a faith drawn
from the Scriptures without human mediation. Having come to religious
certainty by studying the Bible for himself, Lincoln had little use for "man-
made creeds and dogmas." He confessed in 1846: "I am not a member of
any Christian church, but I have never denied the truth of the Scriptures."
Lincoln believed that the Bible alone offered the high road to the knowledge of God and his world—the Bible without historical, theological, or institutional signposts.[2]

Lincoln's own faith was too personal for us to know exactly how he came to this starkly individual view of *sola scriptura*. But we do know that as a boy his family belonged to a Separatist Baptist Church which tolerated "No creed but the Bible"; that he could not abide the rage of competing sects in frontier Illinois; and that he was hardly willing to subject his own independence of thought in matters religious to the will of another. What we also know is that Lincoln grew up in a culture where the maxim "No creed but the Bible" held powerful sway. Any number of denominations, sects, movements, and individuals between 1800 and 1850 claimed to be restoring a pristine biblical Christianity free from all human devices. In this sense, Lincoln, that most biblical of Presidents, was also as American as apple pie in the way he went about extracting meaning from the Bible.

That certainly would have been the conclusion of John W. Nevin, who in 1848 surmised, after reading the statements of faith of 53 American denominations, that an exclusively biblical form of Christianity was the distinctive feature of American religion. Nevin argued that this emphasis stemmed from a popular demand for "private judgment," involved a wholesale dismissal of historical and systematic theology, and stripped the institutional church of all mystery and authority. Americans, he said, had caricatured the meaning of *sola scriptura*—that Magna Charta of Protestantism—by interpreting it through lenses of individualism and democracy. Nevin, a German Reformed theologian of high church sympathy, inveighed against this hermeneutic because it encouraged every man to approach Scripture "in a direct way for himself, through the medium simply of his own mind." In his view, the American Republic, the *Novus Ordo Seclorum,* threatened to reduce *sola scriptura* into a new kind of charter that would encourage reveling in private opinion more than submitting to a common authority.[3]

In this essay, I would like to explain the rise in American culture of the notion "no creed but the Bible" and to elaborate some of its implications for popular religion in the early nineteenth century. First, I shall make some general observations on Protestant concepts of biblical authority; second, discuss the renewed biblicism of ministers who reinterpreted Christianity according to norms of the Enlightenment; third, sketch the crisis of authority within popular culture in America, 1780–1820; fourth, explain the unsettling effects of this ferment within popular religion and the pilgrimage by which many people came to reject every source of authority outside the uninstructed conscience of the individual and the open pages of Scripture—what I shall call the individualization of conscience; and, fifth, suggest the legacy of this populist hermeneutic for American religion and American culture.

To What Extent Shall We Carry This Principle?

Protestants from Luther to Wesley had been forced to define very carefully what they meant by *sola scriptura*. They found it an effective banner to unfurl when attacking Catholics on the right, but always a bit troublesome when common people began to take the teaching seriously. For the Reformers, popular translations of the Bible did not imply that people were to understand the Scriptures apart from ministerial guidance, as Harry Stout notes above (p. 22) in his discussion of the Geneva Bible. Thus when dealing with a scholar such as Erasmus, Luther could champion boldly the perspicuity of Scripture, its clarity for all:

> Who will maintain that the public fountain does not stand in the light, because some people in a back alley cannot see it, when every boy in the market place sees it quite plainly?

Yet when confronted with headstrong sectarians, he withdrew such democratic interpretations and admitted the danger of proving anything by Scripture:

> I learn now that it is enough to throw many passages together helter-skelter, whether they are fit or not. If this is to be the way, then I can easily prove from the Scriptures that beer is better than wine.[4]

Calvin, similarly, charted a careful middle course in defining what biblical authority should mean: "I acknowledge that Scripture is a most rich and inexhaustible fountain of all wisdom; but I deny that its fertility consists in the various meanings which any man, at his pleasure, may assign." In the same vein, the Westminster Divines defended their flank against the Anglicans by arguing in the 1640s that on matters of church government and forms of worship the Scriptures contained all that a person needed to know. With the sectarians of the English Civil War in mind, however, they included in the Confessions the statement that the whole counsel of God was "either expressly set down in Scriptures, or by good and necessary consequence may be deduced from Scriptures."[5]

It is equally clear that eighteenth-century evangelicals like John Wesley and George Whitefield, Jonathan Edwards and Isaac Backus did not think of viewing the Bible absolutely alone, a source of authority independent of theology and of the mediations of clergymen trained formally or informally to explain the full counsel of God. Wesley called himself a *homo unius libri,* a man of one book, and Whitefield repeatedly exhorted his charges to return to the simplicity of Scripture. Yet they came to verbal blows and saw the Methodists divided over abstract theology—the Calvinist-Arminian debate. Similarly, even the "high flying New Lights" of New England and the South never sustained a convincing case that theology *per se,* the good and the bad, should be discarded for a new plateau based exclusively on Scripture. Jonathan Edwards lauded the spiritual perception of common folk, but he also noted the danger that "the less knowing and considerate sort of people" could easily be deceived in the very process of studying the Bible.[6] The Great Awakening, then, failed to unleash a movement to set the Bible over against theology, history, and tradition. In the middle of the eighteenth century, however, rumblings of this description came from a surprisingly unexpected quarter.

The Enlightenment and Rational Biblicism

The first Americans to underscore the right of private judgment in handling Scripture were, oddly enough, ministers who opposed the evangelical tenets of the First Great Awakening. As New Lights in New England worked to make people more theologically self-conscious, in many cases rewriting church covenants to include strict doctrinal standards, theological liberals became increasingly restive with strict creedal definitions of Christianity. The future President of the United States, John Adams, like many of his generation, came to despise theological argumentation, reporting in his diary in 1756: "Where do we find a precept in the Gospel requiring Ecclesiastical Synods? Convocations? Councils? Decrees? Creeds? Confessions? Oaths? Subscriptions? and whole cart-loads of other trumpery that we find religion encumbered with in these days?"[7]

To gain leverage against the entrenched Calvinism of the Awakening, theological liberals redoubled their appeal to the Scriptures alone. "Why may not I go to the Bible to learn the doctrines of Christianity as well as the Assembly of Divines?" the prominent Boston clergyman Jeremy Belknap remarked in 1784. Exhorting ministers to "keep close to the Bible," and to "avoid metaphysical additions," another minister of a more liberal persuasion, Simeon Howard, advised clergymen to "lay aside all attachment to human systems, all partiality to names, councils and churches, and honestly inquire, 'what saith the scriptures?' "[8]

Charles Chauncy, the pastor of Boston's First Church for over half a century (1727–87), stands as the most prominent example of the unraveling of theological orthodoxy by an exclusive appeal to biblical authority. Chauncy came to his new emphasis on Bible study by reading such works of English divines as Samuel Clarke's *The Scripture-Doctrine of the Trinity* (London, 1712) and John Taylor's *The Scripture-Doctrine of Original Sin* (London, 1740). Both of these had used a "free, impartial and diligent" method of examining Scripture, to jettison, respectively, the doctrines of the Trinity and of Original Sin and to espouse a Christianity more attuned to the Age of Reason.[9]

In the 1750s, in the wake of the Great Awakening, Charles Chauncy spent seven years engaged in the kind of Bible study which he had found so appealing in the work of these English authors. He appears to have started the project early in 1752, for by the spring of 1754 he wrote to a friend, "I have made the Scriptures my sole study for about two years; and I think I have attained to a clearer understanding of them than I ever had before." The fruit of these labors led Chauncy to draft a lengthy manuscript rejecting the idea of eternal punishment and embracing universalism. This *magnum opus* remained in Chauncy's desk for over a quarter-century, its conclusions, he confessed, too controversial "to admit of publication in this country."[10] He was almost eighty years old when he finally allowed a London publisher in 1784 to bring out *The Mystery Hid from Ages and Generations . . . or, The Salvation of All Men.* To justify his conclusions, Chauncy relied on the biblical force of his argument—"a long and diligent comparing of *scripture with scripture*"—explaining to Ezra Stiles: "The whole is written from the scripture account of the thing and not from any human scheme."[11] This unorthodox biblicist would have been gratified indeed by the reaction of one minister who wrote, after finding the book's arguments convincing: "He has placed many texts and passages of Scripture in a light altogether new to me, and I cannot help thinking his system not only rational, but Scriptural."[12]

Well into the nineteenth century, rational Christians, many of whom swelled the ranks of denominations such as the Unitarians and the Universalists, argued against evangelical orthodoxy by appealing to the Bible. Typical were the arguments of the prominent Unitarian Noah Worcester who challenged people to think for themselves, to slough off a "passive state of mind" that deferred to great names in theology. "The scriptures," he declared, "were designed for the great mass of mankind and are in general adapted to their capacities." Worcester assumed that mysteries such as the Trinity would collapse before a disbelieving public if people would learn to explore the Bible for themselves. He recounted his own conversion to the Unitarians in a book appropriately entitled *Bible News of the Father, Son, and Holy Spirit* (Concord, N.H., 1810).[13] In the same vein, Charles Beecher defended his rejection of his father Lyman's orthodoxy by renouncing "creed-power" and raising the banner of "the Bible, the whole Bible, and nothing but the Bible."[14] By the 1840s however, when Beecher had moved beyond the pale of orthodoxy, it was a different and decidedly more evangelical notion of biblicism that had taken deep root within American culture. How was it that, in the Age of Jackson, revivalists of almost every stripe, came to defend the same right of private judgment and the same argument about the Bible's exclusive authority that the liberal Charles Chauncy had employed to discredit the Great Awakening and its theological underpinnings?

The Right To Think for Oneself

Between 1780 and 1820 the notion of the sovereignty of the people captured the imagination of the American people—common people—and wrought a serious crisis of authority within popular culture. From the debate over the Constitution to the election of Jefferson, a second and explicitly democratic revolution united many who suspected power and many who were powerless in a common effort to pull down the cultural hegemony of a gentlemenly few. In a complex cultural process that historians have just begun to unravel, people on a number of fronts began to speak, write, and organize against the authority of mediating elites, of social distinctions, and of any human tie that did not spring from volitional allegiance.[15] This raising of popular consciousness gained momentum from a variety of sources: the conflict and confusion over establishing republican governments, the social implications of the French Revolution, the growth of overt electioneering, the formation of democratic clubs and popular organizations, and the explosive growth and popularization of American newspapers.[16]

This crisis of confidence in a hierarchic and ordered society led to demands for root and branch reform: in politics, in law, and in religion. In each of these areas, radical Jeffersonians, seizing upon issues close to the hearts of the people, resurrected "the spirit of 1776" to protest the control of elites and the force of tradition. Rhetoric which had once unified people across the social spectrum now drove a powerful wedge between rich and poor, elite and commoner, privileged classes and the people. Federalists, members of the bar, and the professional clergy also heard the wisdom of the ages ridiculed as a mere connivance of the powerful to maintain the status quo.

These repeated attacks on the capacity of a conspicuous few to speak for the whole struck at the root of traditional conceptions of society, as Gordon S. Wood has argued.[17] Extending the logic of Antifederalists, radical Jeffersonians came to ridicule the assumption that society was an organic hierarchy of ranks and degrees; they argued, rather, that it was a heterogeneous mixture of many different classes, orders, interest groups, and occupations. In such a society the elites could no longer claim to be adequate spokesmen for people in general. As the implications of these views were worked out, it took little creativity for some to begin to re-examine the social function of the clergy and to question the right of any order of men to claim authority to interpret God's Word. An egalitarian agenda could easily call into question any set of men in the habit of mediating truth for another's conscience. If opinions about politics and society were no longer the monopoly of the few, why could not all begin to think for themselves in matters of religion?

The parallel demands that people come to their own convictions about politics, law, and religion converge strikingly in the career of the Boston radical Benjamin Austin, Jr. As successor to Samuel Adams as the leader and favorite of the Boston crowd, Austin held various town offices during the 1780s, contributed to the popular press, and opposed the Federal Constitution. During the 1790s, this "Democratic enragee" incurred the wrath of Federalists more than any other man in Massachusetts for his talents as a writer—probably the ablest polemicist in the state. Austin also gained national reputation in 1786 for a series of articles attacking the elitism of the legal profession.[18]

By the late 1790s, however, Austin had come to identify another threat to democracy. He redirected his fire to take in the Congregationalist clergy of New England who regularly aligned the cause of God with that of high-toned Federalism. Austin called for common people to throw off the yoke of "proud priests" who attempted to enslave their conscience:

> It is degrading to an American to take every thing on trust, and even the young farmer and tradesmen should scorn to surrender their right of judging either to *lawyers* or to *priests*.

In an exegesis of Scripture that bordered on a class analysis of society, Austin insisted that the people had always had an instinct for truth and virtue. The multitude had received Christ with great acclaim, with shouts of hosanna, while "the monarchical, aristocratical and priestly authorities cried crucify him." The scribes and Pharisees would have killed Jesus sooner, "but they feared the people." What Austin clearly advocated was the application of popular sovereignty to the sphere of the church and for common people to assert the right to think for themselves.[19]

The Individualization of Conscience

Amidst the volatile electioneering of the presidential campaign of 1800, one reader of Benjamin Austin's column in Boston's *Independent Chronicle* took to heart what he had to say. Elias Smith, a rising star among Calvinist Baptists in New England and pastor of a church in Woburn, Massachusetts, began to imbibe Austin's heady wine. Under his influence, Smith underwent a personal crisis of authority, a conversion to Jeffersonian politics, and a wholesale rejection of teachings such as election, the Trinity, the distinction between clergy and laity, and the power of discipline which a congregation held over its members. Resigning from his own church and from the Warren Association altogether—as a manifesto of his own liberty—Smith set about to translate the sovereignty of the people to the sphere of religion.[20] "Let us be republicans indeed," he declared. "Many are republicans as to government, and yet are but half republicans, being in matters of religion still bound to a catechism, creed, covenant or a superstitious priest. Venture to be as independent in things of religion, as those which respect the government in which you live."[21] Having lost his religious bearings, Smith spent several years in mental turmoil, struggling not only to find assurance but to determine the means by which truth could be known. "My mind was ensnared," he confessed, "and I felt myself in a situation from which it was not in my power to extricate myself." He finally resolved his dilemma one day as he pitted the claims of Calvinism against those of Universalism:

> While meditating upon these doctrines [Calvinism and Universalism] and my own situation, and saying what shall I do? there was a gentle whisper to my understanding in these words: *Drop them both and search the scriptures*. This command was immediately consented to; and instantly my mind was free from the entanglement before experienced.

"Having lost all my system," Smith continued, "my mind was prepared to search the Scriptures."[22]

Within months Smith began barnstorming through New England proclaiming his new discovery, a kind of populist hermeneutic. Discomfitting respectable Christians with harsh language and lively pamphlets, he demanded the absolute right of all persons to explain the New Testament for themselves. The central plank of Smith's message called for the "unalienable right" of the common person to follow Scripture wherever it led, "even an equal right with Bishops and Pastors of the church . . . even though his principles may, in many things, be contrary to what the Reverend D. D.'s call Orthodoxy." "Truth is no man's private property," Smith proclaimed, accusing clergymen of hoodwinking the people. "I further protest against that unrighteous and ungodly pretense of making the writings of the fathers, the decrees of councils, and synods, or the sense of the church, the rule and standard of judging of the sense of Scriptures, as Popish, Anti-Christian, and dangerous to the church of God."[23] In Salem, Massachusetts, where Smith regularly held meetings among the common folk, the staid diarist William Bentley groaned that "the rabble" had begun to do theology for themselves.[24]

The experience of Elias Smith illustrates well the pervasive crisis of authority within popular religion in America, 1780–1820. His experience suggests a three-stage pilgrimage that confronted, in one way or another, many Christians during this period. First, Smith came to find traditional religious systems no longer credible and to experience deep intellectual turmoil in groping for new verities. Second, he denied that his own interpretation of Scripture should be mediated by any other authority, historical or ecclesiastical—a conviction steeled by the competing claims of rival denominations. Third, he resolved his struggle for assurance by insisting that the unfettered conscience must encounter for itself the *ipse dixit* of the New Testament. This new hermeneutic relieved a cognitive dissonance that had been building and fired him with the hope that a new day had dawned— a *novus ordo seclorum*—that would set in place a New Testament form of Christianity.

Let me offer four other illustrations of this process—what I would like to call the individualization of conscience.

ELHANAN WINCHESTER (1751–1797)

A man with little formal schooling but near photographic memory, Elhanan Winchester by 1780 was reputed to be one of the best Baptist preachers in America. He served several churches in his native Massachusetts, a congregation in Welch Neck, South Carolina, and, after 1780, a large Baptist church in Philadelphia. The largest church building in the city was crowded by those who came to hear him preach.[25]

Upon his arrival in Philadelphia, Winchester began to waver on his commitment to Calvinism. What he found alluring was the idea advocated by Universalists that all persons would eventually be saved. His ambivalence on this issue brought on a crisis in his church in 1781 and forced him to defend or deny the idea of a universal restoration. Winchester chose to resolve his conflict in the following manner:

> I shut myself up chiefly in my chamber, read the Scriptures, and prayed to God to lead me into all truth, and not suffer me to embrace any error; and I think with an upright mind, I laid myself open to believe whatsoever the Lord had revealed. It would be too long to tell all the Teaching I had on this head; let it suffice, in short, to say, that I became so well persuaded of the truth of Universal Restoration, that I determined never to deny it.[26]

Like Elias Smith, Winchester expressed great emotional release after this experience and set out to champion the cause of Universalism. What is significant for our purposes is his method of resolving theological perplexity: locking the door and coming to grips with Scripture for himself.

WILLIAM SMYTHE BABCOCK (1764–1839)

In one nine-month stretch in 1802 and 1803, William Smythe Babcock estimated he traveled 1500 miles and preached 297 sermons as an itinerant minister in the hill country of New Hampshire and Vermont. History would have entirely swallowed the memory of this folk preacher had he not kept an extensive journal of his travels and preaching between 1801 and 1809—now preserved at the American Antiquarian Society. Babcock founded a Free-Will Baptist Church in Springfield, Vermont, in 1801 and from there launched extensive preaching forays throughout upper New England.[27]

Babcock proclaimed a message that revolved around the issue of bondage and liberty. The sentiments of this man are aptly summarized in a poem which he attributed to a nine-year-old girl in his congregation:

> Know then that every soul is free
> To choose his life and what he'll be
> For this eternal truth is given
> That god will force no man to heaven

He'll draw persuade direct him right
Bless him with wisdom love and light
In nameless ways be good and kind
But never force the human mind[28]

The Free-Will Baptist Connection exercised no real authority over Babcock, yet he repeatedly expressed the fear of relying too much on other men or of being coerced by them. By 1809 even the slight contact that he did have with other churches became unbearable. He unilaterally severed all ties with the Monthly Meeting of the Free-Will Baptists. "I told them that I now stood alone, unconnected to or with any one." The members of Babcock's congregation followed his lead and agreed to renounce all denominations and set up a church "independent in itself, free from control or of domination of any other churches whatever."[29] They agreed to defer to only one authority, the rule and guide of the Scriptures. Pressing the notion of Christian freedom to its logical conclusion, Babcock could not abide anyone having the right to suggest to him the parameters of biblical teaching.

LUCY MACK SMITH (1776–?)

Lucy Mack Smith, mother of Joseph Smith who founded the Mormons, also grew up in the hill country of New Hampshire and Vermont at the end of the eighteenth century. Lucy married Joseph Smith, Sr., in 1802 and they struggled to make a living and raise a family in Randolph, New Hampshire. Lucy wrestled interminably with the problems of competing denominations, each of which seemed to invalidate the claims of the others. "If I remain a member of no church," she confessed, "all religious people will say I am of the world; and if I join some one of the different denominations, all the rest will say I am in error." After one disillusioning experience in a Presbyterian church, Lucy Smith returned home and came to the following conviction:

> I said in my heart that there was not then upon earth the religion which I sought. I therefore determined to examine my Bible, and taking Jesus and the disciples as my guide, to endeavor to obtain from God that which man could neither give nor take away. . . . The Bible I intended should be my guide to life and salvation.

Lucy Smith sealed this individualization of conscience by finding a minister who would agree to baptize her as a solitary Christian—without attachment to any congregation.[30]

JOHN HUMPHREY NOYES (1811–1886)

John Humphrey Noyes, perfectionist, communitarian religious leader, and founder of the Oneida Community actually began his quest for innovative religion from within the mecca of orthodoxy. A graduate of Dartmouth in 1830, and then a student at Andover and Yale, Noyes found himself unable to square the tenets of Calvinism with the disposition of his own soul.[31] Warned as a student about the less-than-orthodox expressions that regularly slipped from his tongue, Noyes responded: "Never will I be compelled by ministers or anyone else to accept any doctrine that does not commend itself to my mind and conscience." He later recounted the actual experience in New Haven that pushed him beyond the boundaries of orthodoxy:

> I first advanced into actual heresy in the early part of the summer of 1833 while still a student at the New Haven Seminary. In the course of my Bible studies my attention was arrested by Christ's expression in John 21:22: "If I will that he [John] tarry till I come, what is that to thee." This seemed to imply that Jesus expected his disciple John to live until his second coming, and the disciples so construed it. The church on the contrary taught that Christ's second coming was still far in the future. I had long been in the belief that the Bible was not a book of inexplicable riddles, and I determined to solve this mystery. Accordingly, I read the New Testament ten times with an eye on the question as to the time of Christ's second coming, and my heart struggling in prayer for full access to the truth.[32]

What was Noyes's conclusion? Not unexpectedly, he discovered in the New Testament clear teaching that Christ's second coming had already occurred and had already opened the possibility for human perfection. Searching the Bible for answers convinced Noyes of sinless perfection and set his mind concocting various plans to implement a perfect society—the first such experiment called, interestingly enough, Bible Communism.

Change in Christian thought, as Edmund S. Morgan suggests, has usually been a matter of emphasis, of giving certain ideas greater weight than was previously accorded them, or of carrying one idea to its logical conclusion at the expense of others. "One age slides into the next," he says, "and an intellectual revolution may be achieved by the expression of ideas that everyone had always professed to accept."[33] What strikes one in studying the use of the Bible in the early years of the American Republic, is how much weight becomes placed on private judgment and how little on the role of history, theology, and the collective will of the church. In a culture that mounted a frontal assault upon the authority of tradition, of mediating elites, and of organizations that were perpetual rather than volitional, the Bible very easily became, as John W. Nevin complained, "a book dropped from the skies for all sorts of men to use in their own way."[34] This shift occurred gradually and without fanfare, concealed, I think, because innovators could exploit arguments as old and as trusted as Protestantism itself. Luther, Calvin, Wesley and Backus had all argued for the principle of *sola scriptura;* Elias Smith, Elhanan Winchester, William Smyth Babcock, Lucy Smith, and John Humphrey Noyes all argued that they were merely fulfilling that same mandate. Yet somewhere along the line, I would argue, a revolution had taken place that made private judgment the ultimate tribunal for the exposition of Scripture.

"The Bible Is Good Enough for Me"

What kind of legacy can one attribute to the popular sentiment, "everyman his own interpreter?" What were the implications for American religion of the voices on every hand challenging common people to open the Bible and think for themselves? Let me suggest, however tentatively, three ways that a populist hermeneutic colored subsequent American religion and American culture.

THE CHRISTIAN MOVEMENT

The Christian, or Disciples of Christ, Movement stands as the institutional embodiment of this new approach to Scripture. The central figures in this reform movement—Elias Smith in New England, James O'Kelly in Virginia, Barton Stone in Kentucky, and Alexander Campbell in Pennsylvania—are a diverse crew indeed with few common characteristics but that they all moved independently to similar conclusions within a fifteen-year span. A Congregationalist, a Methodist, and two Presbyterians all found traditional sources of authority anachronistic and found themselves groping toward similar definitions of egalitarian religion.[35] Starting from the premise "No creed but the Bible," the Christians formulated into specific tenets certain widely held assumptions.

First, they swore allegiance only to the New Testament and, while not flatly denying the authority of the Old, impugned most of the ways it had been used. Elias Smith divorced the testaments with even less qualification than did others:

> I still believed that all I am required to believe and do is contained in the New Testament, and that there is no command or ordinance in the Old

Testament binding on a Christian, unless it is in the New Testament, any more than though it had never been commanded.[36]

Second, the Christians attempted to dismiss the history of the church as a sordid tale of corruption and to return to New Testament simplicity. According to Barton Stone, the past should be "consigned to the rubbish heap upon which Christ was crucified." Alexander Campbell put it more positively: "Open the New Testament as if mortal man had never seen it before."[37]

In a shrewd move to ward off systematic theology, the Christians also demanded that religious discourse use only New Testament language. They dismissed as unscriptural any theological abstraction—concepts such as the Trinity, foreordination, or original sin—and insisted upon proving "every particular from plain declarations recorded in the Bible."[38] Finally, the Christians defined liberty of conscience as the right of any person to follow the teachings of the New Testament without having his views judged by anyone else. One Christian elder put it this way:

> Every member shall be considered as possessing in himself or herself an original right to believe and speak as their own conscience, between themselves and God, may determine; without being called into question by man.[39]

Two Presbyterian ministers in Kentucky who dabbled in the Christian movement but then returned to their confessional roots complained about this vacuum of authority:

> The Bible was the only Confession of our Faith, without any statement of the manner in which we understood even its first principles; therefore no man could be tried, or judged heretic, who professed faith in the scriptures, however heterodox he might be in his sentiments.[40]

The hermeneutic of the Christian Movement had considerable appeal early in nineteenth century for at least two reasons. It proclaimed a new ground of certainty for a generation perplexed by sectarian rivalry. If people would only abandon the husks of theological abstraction and return to the Bible, the truth would become plain for all to see. A second appeal was that common folk using this method could easily confound the most erudite clergymen. Any Christian using New Testament words could fend off the most brilliant theological argument by the simple retort that he was using God's word against human opinion. All the weight of church history could not begin to tip the scale against the Christian's simple declaration, say, that the New Testament did not contain the word "Trinity."

Yet the Christian approach to truth, making no man the judge of another's conscience, had little holding power and sent many early advocates scrambling for surer footing. What would keep the notion of private interpretation from degenerating into each defining a law for oneself?

THE SPLINTERING OF AMERICAN PROTESTANTISM

The heavy emphasis upon private judgment in biblical interpretation also served to promote and justify the splintering of the American church. For some such as Joseph Smith, the promise of a Scripture democratically interpreted seemed false from the beginning. Like his mother Lucy, he was dismayed by sectarian wrangling, but saw no answer to the problem in some new approach to the Bible:

> In the midst of this war of words and tumult of opinions, I often said to myself, What is to be done? Who of all these parties are right? Or, are they all wrong together? If one of them is right, which is it, and how shall I know? The teachers of religion of the different sects destroy all confidence in settling the question by an appeal to the Bible. At length I came to the conclusion that I must remain in darkness or confusion, or else I must do as James directs, that is ask of God.[41]

Smith immediately began to seek direct revelation and found his hopes fulfilled in a series of visions. He found bankrupt his mother's high hopes for a biblical Christianity and began exploring well beyond the pale of orthodoxy.

For others, the hope of a democratic authority provided a temporary way station before they too moved on to lay hold of more certain moorings. Richard McNemar, an early colleague of Barton Stone, came to ridicule Stone's position on the Bible after he found absolute certainty in the direct revelations which the Shakers claimed to enjoy. McNemar found that exclusive reliance on the Bible actually drove people apart rather than bringing them together:

> Ten thousand Reformers like so many moles
> Have plowed all the Bible and cut it [in] holes
> And each has his church at the end of his trace
> Built up as he thinks of the subjects of grace.[42]

It was this ironic quality of American appeals to the Bible that so baffled John W. Nevin. Instead of calming sectarian strife, trying to follow the Bible alone seemed to multiply denominations endlessly.

> But what are we to think of it when we find such a motley mass of protesting systems, all laying claim so vigorously here to one and the same

watchword? If the Bible be at once so clear and full as a formulary of Christian doctrine and practice, how does it come to pass that where men are left most free and to use it in this way, and have the greatest mind to do so, according to their own profession, they are flung assunder so perpetually in their religious faith, instead of being brought together, by its influence.[43]

In the first half of the nineteenth century people staked out religious systems convinced that their own configurations were, in Nevin's words, "self-sprung from the Bible, or through the Bible from the skies."[44] What few ever considered was that without a backdrop of history and theology, they would have difficulty assessing the very historical process which drove them apart at the very moment they were convinced that biblical unity could be achieved.

THE CHRISTIANIZATION OF POPULAR CULTURE

After 1800, one has difficulty assessing whether Americans were more adept at reading cultural values into the Bible or at reading biblical values into the culture. No matter: what is important is that democratic values and patterns of biblical interpretation were moving in the same direction, mutually reinforcing ideas of volitional allegiance, self-reliance, and private judgment. Both cultural values and hermeneutics balked at vested interests, symbols of hierarchy and timeless authorities. Both addressed the common man without condescension and dismissed, out of hand, theories that would not square with common sense. Both reinforced the importance of the individual as beholden to no one and master of one's own fate. At one level, then, the Enlightenment in America was not repudiated but popularized. Revivalists of the Second Great Awakening championed a Bible unencumbered by theological systems and authoritative interpreters. The rhetoric of rights which the Enlightenment had nurtured came to resonate as powerfully within American popular religion as it did within the democratic politics of the young republic.

One cannot overestimate the importance of this correlation in explaining the christianization of popular culture in the early republic—the phenomenal growth that evangelical churches experienced among common people. What plain people had available were value systems that endowed them with dignity and responsibility—as Barton Stone said about the lively response to his message:

> When we began first to preach these things, the people appeared as just awakened from the sleep of ages—they seemed to see for the first time that they were responsible beings.[45]

It is also not surprising that the right of private judgment with respect to Scripture became deeply embedded in American democratic culture. The innovations that Elias Smith and Barton Stone struggled to implement had become taken-for-granted assumptions by the 1840s—the heydey of William Miller and Charles G. Finney.

A Vermont freethinker and immigrant to New York, William Miller, the Adventist, could not abide New England Calvinism, "a system of craft rather than truth" that had "clothed the Scriptures in a mantle of mysticism," and in which "the common people were the greatest sufferers." When he finally did become a religious seeker, Miller, by his own confession, "laid by all commentaries, former views and pre-possessions, and determined to read and try to understand for myself. I then began reading the Bible in a methodical manner." Describing his fervent biblicism, Miller says, "I lost all taste for other reading and applied my heart to get wisdom from God." Miller argued that his millennial scheme sprang naturally from Holy Writ and was clear and plain in the New Testament for all to see; and the clarion call of his Adventist Movement was that people acknowledge their right to interpret Scripture for themselves.[46]

Despite very different circumstances, the Presbyterian evangelist Charles G. Finney experienced a similar hermeneutical awakening, when, after being ordained in the Presbyterian church, he finally took the time to study and soundly reject the Westminster Confession. "I found myself utterly unable to accept doctrine on the ground of authority . . ." he announced, "I had nowhere to go but directly to the Bible, and to the philosophy or workings of my own mind. I gradually formed a view of my own . . . which appeared to me to be unequivocally taught in the Bible."[47]

Whatever else may be said about the approach that Miller and Finney exemplify, it certainly sheds light upon the process by which an America that had been largely Presbyterian, Congregational, and Anglican became a bastion of Baptists, Methodists, and Disciples—and of Millerites, Mormons, Cumberland Presbyterians, Universalists, Free Communion, "Two-Seed," and Primitive Baptists, Methodist Protestants, and Christian Unionists, to name a few. Amidst all this diversity, oddly enough, there was much less a crisis of authority than there had been a generation before. Ears were now attuned to the voice of the people in politics and religion; and in matters religious the tide of public opinion clearly favored literal notions of *sola scriptura*. Abraham Lincoln certainly reflected this trend in his own use of the Bible—as did another Chief Executive, the Presbyterian minister's son Grover Cleveland, whom a friend overheard saying,

The Bible is good enough for me: just the old book under which I was brought up. I do not want notes or criticism, or explanations about authorship or origin, or even cross-references. I do not need them, and they confuse me.[48]

A republic dedicated to the proposition that all are created equal unleashed a powerful wave of biblicism within popular culture, a current borne along by the self-evident maxim: "the Bible—and the Bible alone—is good enough for me."

NOTES

1. For Lincoln's reliance on the Bible, see William J. Wolf, *The Almost Chosen People: A Study in the Religion of Abraham Lincoln* (Garden City, N.Y., 1969), pp. 131–42; and Elton Trueblood, *Abraham Lincoln, Theologian of American Anguish* (New York, 1973), pp. 48–71.

2. Wolf, *Almost Chosen People,* pp. 51, 73.

3. John W. Nevin, "Antichrist and the Sect System," in James Hastings Nichols, ed., *The Mercersburg Theology* (New York, 1966), pp. 93–119.

4. E. G. Rupp, "The Bible in the Age of the Reformation," in D. E. Nineham, ed., *The Church's Use of the Bible Past and Present* (London, 1963), p. 84; Martin Luther, *Works* (Weimar Edition), 6:301.

5. A. Skevington Wood, *The Principles of Biblical Interpretation: As Enunciated by Irenaeus, Origin, Augustine, Luther, and Calvin* (Grand Rapids, 1967), p. 92. Jack Bartlett Rogers, *Scripture in the Westminster Confession* (Grand Rapids, 1967); and John H. Leith, *Assembly at Westminster: Reformed Theology in the Making* (Richmond, 1973).

6. For Wesley's use of Scripture, see Mack B. Stokes, *The Bible in the Wesleyan Heritage* (Nashville, 1979), pp. 19–26. Edwards discusses this danger in John E. Smith, ed., *The Works of Jonathan Edwards: Religious Affections* (New Haven, 1964), pp. 143–44.

7. John Adams, *The Works of John Adams* (Boston, 1850), II, pp. 5–6; quoted in Conrad Wright, *The Beginnings of Unitarianism in America* (Boston, 1955), p. 231.

8. Wright, *Beginnings of Unitarianism,* p. 235.

9. Edward M. Griffin, *Old Brick: Charles Chauncy of Boston, 1705–1787* (Minneapolis, 1980), pp. 109–25. Henry May suggests that the Arian Samuel Clarke was one of the three most read and quoted divines in eighteenth-century America; Henry May, *The Enlightenment in America* (New York, 1976), p. 38. Chauncy acknowledged his debt to John Taylor for a method of examining the Bible in *The Mystery Hid from Ages and Generations . . . or, the Salvation of All Men* (London, 1784), pp. xi–xii. See Wright, *Beginnings of Unitarianism,* p. 78.

10. Griffin, *Old Brick,* p. 111.

11. Chauncy, *The Mystery Hid from Ages,* p. 359; Griffin, *Old Brick,* p. 11.

12. Griffin, *Old Brick,* p. 176.

13. See Worcester's article "On Humility in the Investigation of Christian Truth," in *The Christian Disciple* I, no. 4 (Boston, 1813), 17–22. Noah Worcester elaborates this hostility to human creeds and confessions in his book, *Causes and Evils of*

Contention Unveiled in Letters to Christians, a favorite of the reformer Lucretia Mott. See Otelia Cromwell, *Lucretia Mott* (Cambridge, Mass., 1958), pp. 39, 204.

14. Charles Beecher, *The Bible a Sufficient Creed* (Boston, 1850), pp. 24, 26.

15. For the importance of the idea of volitional allegiance in this period, see James H. Kettner, *The Development of American Citizenship, 1608–1870* (Chapel Hill, 1978), pp. 173–309. On these developments generally, see Gordon S. Wood, *The Creation of the American Republic, 1776–1787* (Chapel Hill, 1969), pp. 483–99; Alfred F. Young, *The Democratic Republicans of New York* (Chapel Hill, 1967); and Edmund S. Morgan, *The Challenge of the American Revolution* (New York, 1976), pp. 211–18.

16. Jackson Turner Main, *The Antifederalists: Critics of the Constitution, 1781–1788* (Chapel Hill, 1961); Eugene Perry Link, *Democratic Republican Societies, 1790–1800* (New York, 1942); Philip S. Foner, ed., *The Democratic-Republican Societies, 1790–1800* (Westport, Conn., 1976); Donald H. Stewart, *The Opposition Press of the Federalist Period* (Albany, 1969); and David Hackett Fischer, *The Revolution of American Conservatism: The Federalist Party in the Era of Jeffersonian Democracy* (New York, 1965).

17. Wood, *Creation of the American Republic,* pp. 483–99.

18. For extensive treatment of the role of Austin, see Richard E. Ellis, *The Jeffersonian Crisis: Courts and Politics in the Young Republic* (New York, 1971), pp. 184–229.

19. Benjamin Austin, Jr., *Constitutional Republicanism in Opposition to Fallacious Federalism* (Boston, 1803), p. 173.

20. Beyond William G. McLoughlin's five-page sketch in *New England Dissent, 1630–1833: The Baptists and the Separation of Church and State* (Cambridge, Mass., 1971), 2:745–49, no one has undertaken a serious study of Elias Smith, despite his prominence as a religious and political radical in New England from 1800 to 1820, his scores of publications addressed to a popular audience, his newspaper that ran for a decade, and his fascinating 400-page memoir. In his own right, he stands as an absolutely intriguing character; the numerous attacks against him and the popularity of his writings, moreover, suggest that he may be a far more important historical figure than has been recognized by historians who, all too often, have rested content to find the story line of New England religion in this period in the careers of men like Timothy Dwight, Nathaniel William Taylor, and Lyman Beecher. See Elias Smith, *The Life, Conversion, Preaching, Travels and Sufferings of Elias Smith* (Boston, 1840).

21. Elias Smith, *The Lovingkindness of God Displayed in the Triumph of Republicanism in America: Being a Discourse Delivered at Taunton* (Mass.) *July Fourth, 1809; at the Celebration of American Independence* (n.p., 1809), p. 32.

22. Smith, *Life,* pp. 256–57. For the same point, see Elias Smith, *Sermons, Containing an Illustration of the Prophecies* (Exeter, N.H., 1808), p. vi.

23. Smith, *Lovingkindness of God Displayed,* pp. 26–27; *Life,* pp. 352–53. "The Scripture," said Smith elsewhere, "is such a book that our minds must be shaped to that, and to do this, we must all be servants, and no one can be chief, or above his brethren." *Herald of Gospel Liberty* (April 14, 1809).

24. William Bentley, *The Diary of William Bentley, D.D.* (Salem, Mass., 1911), 3: 67, 490, 179, 271, 180. In May 1805 Bentley commented about Elias Smith that "the press has lately vomited out many nauseaus things from this writer" (*ibid.,* pp. 157, 370, 291).

25. For a discussion of Winchester's career, see Joseph R. Sweeny, "Elhanan Win-

chester and the Universal Baptists" (Ph.D. dissertation, University of Pennsylvania, 1969).

26. Elhanan Winchester, *The Universal Restoration* (London, 1788), pp. xvii–xviii.

27. See William Smythe Babcock Papers, American Antiquarian Society, Worcester, Massachusetts.

28. Miscellaneous Papers, William Smythe Babcock Papers.

29. Journal of Preaching, December 1809, William Smythe Babcock Papers.

30. Lucy Smith, *Biographical Sketches of Joseph Smith, the Prophet* (Liverpool, 1853; reprint ed., New York, 1969), pp. 37, 46–49.

31. George Wallingford Noyes, ed., *The Religious Experience of John Humphrey Noyes* (New York, 1923), pp. 50–65.

32. *Ibid.,* pp. 69–70.

33. Edmund S. Morgan, ed., *Puritan Political Ideas* (Indianapolis, 1965), p. xiii.

34. John W. Nevin, "Early Christianity," in Charles Yrigoyen, Jr., and George H. Bricker, *Catholic and Reformed: Selected Theological Writings of John Williamson Nevin* (Pittsburgh, 1978), p. 255.

35. The best treatment of O'Kelly is Charles Franklin Kilgore, *The James O'Kelly Schism in the Methodist Episcopal Church* (Mexico City, 1963); for Stone, see John Rogers, *The Biography of Elder Barton Warren Stone* (Cincinnati, 1847; reprint ed., New York, 1969); for Campbell, Robert Richardson, *Memoirs of Alexander Campbell,* 2 vols. (Cincinnati, 1913). For an extended discussion of this movement, see Nathan O. Hatch, "The Christian Movement and the Demand for a Theology of The People," *Journal of American History,* 67 (1980), 545–66.

36. Elias Smith, *The Age of Enquiry: The Christian's Pocket Companion and Daily Assistant* (Portsmouth, N.H., 1810), p. 23.

37. Elias Smith, *Herald of Gospel Liberty,* II, no. 22 (June 23, 1809), 87; Alexander Campbell, *The Christian Baptist,* III, p. 229.

38. Elias Smith, *Life,* p. 292.

39. Abel Sargent, *The Halcyon Itinerary and True Millennium Messenger* (Marietta, Ohio, 1807), p. 209.

40. Robert Marshall and John Thompson, *A Brief Historical Account of Sundry Things in the Doctrines and State of the Christian or . . . the Newlight Church* (Cincinnati, 1811), pp. 4–5.

41. Joseph Smith, *The Pearl of Great Price: Being a Choice Selection from the Revelations, Translations, and Narrations of Joseph Smith* (Salt Lake City, 1891), pp. 56–70.

42. Richard McNemar, "The Mole's little pathways" (1807?), ms. copy, Shaker Papers, Library of Congress; quoted in Mario S. De Pillis, "The Quest for Religious Authority and the Rise of Mormonism," *Dialogue: A Journal of Mormon Thought,* I (1966), 75.

43. Nevin, "Antichrist and the Sect System," Nichols, ed., pp. 97–99.

44. *Ibid.,* p. 101.

45. John Rogers, *Biography of Stone,* p. 45.

46. Joshua V. Himes, *A View of the Prophecies and Prophetic Oracles* (Boston, 1841), pp. 9, 11. On the Millerites, generally, see David L. Rowe, "Thunder and Trumpets: The Millerite Movement and Apocalyptic Thought in Upstate New York, 1800–1845" (Ph.D. dissertation, University of Virginia, 1974).

47. Charles G. Finney, *Memoirs* (New York, 1876), pp. 42–46.

48. George F. Parker, *Recollections of Grover Cleveland* (New York, 1911), p. 382; quoted in Francis P. Weisenburger, *Ordeal of Faith: The Crisis of Church-Going America, 1865–1900* (New York, 1959), p. 85.

IV

Everyone One's Own Interpreter?
The Bible, Science, and Authority
in Mid-Nineteenth-Century America

GEORGE M. MARSDEN
Calvin College

"Blind unbelief is sure to err,
And scan His work in vain,
God is His own Interpreter,
And He will make it plain."

William Cowper, 1774

The prestige of the Bible in the United States reached its apex in the mid-decades of the nineteenth century. Leaders as diverse as Nat Turner, Stonewall Jackson, and Abraham Lincoln seemed almost to speak naturally in biblical cadences. A radical like Turner or Ralph Waldo Emerson might regard himself as "a newborn bard of the Holy Ghost."[1] Or others, such as Joseph Smith or Herman Melville, might produce their own versions of the biblical sagas. But more typical, even among many progressives, was an unquestioning reverence for the Bible, exemplified, for instance, in Sarah Moore Grimké's determination in *Letters on the Equality of the Sexes* to "depend solely on the Bible" for her authority.[2] In antebellum Protestant America there was no higher court of appeal.

Two judges, however, sat in this court and the one never spoke without the other. The authoritative pronouncements of the ancient Scriptures always needed to be understood by the modern interpreter. No church or creed could guarantee uniformity of interpretation. So while a reformer

like Grimké might appeal to "the immutable truths of the Bible," she insisted none the less on her right "to judge for myself what is the meaning."[3] Here was the rub.

Protestants had long wrestled with these issues. From the outset of the
Reformation, Roman Catholics had attacked them at this vulnerable point.
Without the church, warned the Catholic critics, everyone would become
his own interpreter and spiritual anarchy would ensue. Protestants had
responded by insisting on the perspicuity of Scripture—in those things
necessary to salvation, the biblical meanings were plain to any normally in-
telligent reader. Not taking any chances, however, most sixteenth- and seventeenth-century Protestant groups doubly fortified their positions by drawing up creeds that effectively precluded private interpretations.

Nineteenth-century America was a different story. While creedalism
remained among some traditionalists, the stronger tendency was to renounce dependence on any ancient tradition or creed. Proclaiming the
"new order for the ages," many Americans viewed themselves as free people unencumbered by bonds of the past or of inherited authority. Without
the restraints of creeds of traditions, sects sprang up in America in bewildering varieties. The Roman Catholic predictions of spiritual anarchy
seemed on the verge of realization.

The main body of evangelical Protestants, however, did not let the spiritual eccentricities of their day dissuade them from their conviction that the
Bible spoke clearly and without equivocation. Behind this belief was the
broader philosophical assumption of the perspicuity of truth generally.
This assumption was deeply rooted in Western thought and had been
strengthened by the rise of the scientific method of the preceding two centuries. Through careful observation, humanity—and hence properly informed individuals—had access to the laws of nature. To Protestants it
seemed evident that the principles for knowing truth in one area of God's
revelation should parallel those of another area. Nature and Scripture
were analogous, as Bishop Butler had argued so persuasively in his *The
Analogy of Religion, Natural and Revealed* (1736). Neither our view of
nature nor our view of Scripture is complete or perfect but in each we can
be assured that we can know clearly something of the truth. Nature and
Scripture were equally perspicuous.[4]

A second assumption which helped combat anarchy was just as basic—
truth was unchanging throughout the ages. This doctrine of the immutability of truth went hand in hand with truth's perspicuity. This belief in the
changelessness of truth likewise had roots deep in ancient and medieval

thought and seemed reinforced by Enlightenment confidence in the power of scientific reason to discover the fixed laws of nature. As was true of the laws of physics uncovered by Newton, the truths thus discovered should be universal and invariable. Truth, whether found in nature or Scripture, was not relative to time or culture.

Of these two related doctrines—perspicuity and immutability—the immutability of truth was in more immediate trouble in nineteenth-century America. Everyone, it seems, thought that he or she could see truth clearly, but the sense of a new age and the disdain for old authorities promoted popular beliefs that truth—or at least humans' perception of it—was changing. The new Christian sects encouraged such views. As Mark Twain, feigning a stolid Presbyterian perspective, said of the "blamed wildcat religions," their idea of heaven was "progress pro-gress, pro-gress."[5] If change and newness were what Americans valued most, if trust in self was to be preferred to trust in authority and tradition, how could the faith in the changelessness of the Bible's truths be maintained?

The assault on these doctrines was strengthened by formidable romantic and philosophical forces imported from Europe. Transcendentalists, learning of Kant and of German idealism through the works of the English romantic Samuel Taylor Coleridge, reveled in change, sheer intuition, and individual uniqueness. Among the more conventional believers, even the "liberals" were shocked at this attack on the traditional ground for certainty. Such was clear, for instance, in the outraged reply of Unitarian Andrews Norton to Ralph Waldo Emerson's suggestion (at the Unitarian Harvard Divinity School of all places) that each person should be "a newborn bard of the Holy Ghost." "True Christianity," insisted the liberal Norton, "is always the same." "The facts," he added, ". . . admit of no change and no adaptation to the progress of men; and human speculations upon them, however far they may be carried, can have no claim to be considered parts of Christianity."[6] Academicians such as Norton who faced the onslaughts of European philosophies, and practical defenders of Protestant tradition who confronted the force of popular democratic opinion, had essentially the same problem. How could a concept of truth at once perspicuous and immutable survive in the modern world?

The Prevailing Solution: Common Sense and Baconian Science

The traditional Western ideas of the perspicuity and immutability of truth—found alike in Greek, medieval, and Reformation thought—had more recently been reinforced by the scientific revolution and the Enlightenment. In America these more recent traditions, so thoroughly identified with good thinking during the Revolutionary era, survived with great prestige well into the nineteenth century. Specifically, the prevailing intellectual opinion in nineteenth-century America was enamored of the "Common Sense" ideals of the Scottish Enlightenment, which provided an intellectual base for an unshakable faith in the inductive scientific method associated with the seventeenth-century philosopher Francis Bacon.

The strength of these ideals is evidenced by the difficulties that romantic and transcendentalist thinkers had in trying to displace them. "It is taken for granted," lamented James Marsh in introducing his important edition of Coleridge's *Aids to Reflection* in 1829, "that our whole system of philosophy of mind, as derived from Lord Bacon especially, is the only one which has any claims to common sense." Moreover, he said, this Baconian Common Sense system was so completely identified with Protestantism "that by most persons they are considered as necessary parts of the same system."[7] Proponents of inductive scientific reasoning agreed. "Protestant christianity and the Baconian philosophy originate in the same foundation," said Presbyterian philosopher Samuel Tyler. "There never could have been a Bacon without the Bible," concurred the Southern theologian Benjamin Morgan Palmer. "Francis Bacon was the offspring of the Reformation."[8]

During the forty years after James Marsh wrote, idealist and romantic currents would make a few inroads in the terrain of Protestant thought, while transcendentalism whistled loudly in the trees.[9] For most Protestants, however, the rock of ages and the rock of common sense scientific reasoning seemed to support each other. From the liberal Unitarians at Harvard to the conservative Presbyterians at Princeton, among the moderate Calvinists of Yale, to their more radical perfectionist offspring at Oberlin, among Methodists and Baptists, and including the "gentlemen theologians" of the South, there prevailed a faith in immutable truth seen clearly by inductive scientific reasoning in Scripture and nature alike.

Philosophically, this system found its strongest Enlightenment supports in the Scottish Common Sense teachings, originated by Thomas Reid (1710–96). Common Sense had a special appeal in America because it purported to be an anti-philosophy. The skepticism of the modern age, said Reid and his cohorts, was due to too many high-flown speculations by philosophers. The antidote was to begin the only sensible place where philosophy could—with what every person of good sense was obliged to believe. Common Sense philosophy could thus combat one of the nineteenth-century threats to certainty—Germanic speculations—by appealing to the American faith in the common person. But since the common sense starting points for thought were indeed *common* to all times, cultures and stations, the appeal to the common person seemed to answer the threat of anarchical individualism as well.

Specifically the Common Sense approach said that all normal people were endowed by their Creator with various faculties that produced beliefs on which they must rely. Everyone was obliged to believe in such things as the existence of the external world, in the continuity of self from one day to the next, that other minds existed, and in the reliability (under proper circumstances) of sense perceptions, of reasoning, memory, and the testimony of others. Only philosophers and other fools would doubt that people can normally rely on these sources of knowledge, even in matters of life and death. Courts of law and civilization itself depend upon them. These common sense beliefs are as instinctive to humans as the breathing of air—and almost as necessary for life.

These fundamental beliefs, accordingly, are not in essence culturally derived. Various cultures may develop vastly different ways of talking about these beliefs or acting upon them, but beneath those obvious surface diversities there is a core of shared basic common sense beliefs found in all ages and cultures. In the everyday affairs of the ancient world people relied upon their firm sense perceptions, their recent memories or the testimony of veracious friends just as we do. Despite our cultural difference we can understand much that they experienced and said because we share the faculties of a common humanity. On this foundation of common sense found throughout the race, humanity then ought to be able to erect sure and permanent systems of knowledge about many aspects of their experience.[10]

Having such a firm foundation in common sense, said the eighteenth-century Scottish philosophers, we can attain certainty about many of the laws of reality.[11] One need only build very carefully on this common sense foundation. Here is where Baconianism came in. In nineteenth-century America, Baconianism meant simply looking carefully at the evidence, determining what were "the facts," and carefully classifying these facts. One might scrupulously generalize from the facts, but good Baconianism avoided speculative hypotheses. The interpretation of Scripture, accordingly, involved careful determination of what the facts were—what the words meant. Once this was settled the facts revealed in Scripture could be known as surely and as clearly as the facts discovered by the natural scientist.

"The theologian should proceed," said James W. Alexander of Princeton, ". . . precisely as the chemist or the botanist proceeds. . . . [This] is the method which bears the name of Bacon." J. S. Lamar of the Disciples of Christ, invoking "Lord Bacon," agreed that "the Scriptures admit of being studied and expounded upon the principles of the inductive method; and that, when thus interpreted, they speak to us in a voice as certain and unmistakable as the language of nature heard in the experiments and observations of science."[12]

Such statements reflect a major theme in nineteenth-century American evangelical thought that would subsequently be obscured by the popular post-Darwinian conception that science and religion were inherently in conflict. By and large, mid-nineteenth-century American theologians were champions of scientific reasoning and scientific advance. Their own work was modeled on that of the natural scientists, and they had full confidence in the capacities of the scientific method for discovering truth exactly and objectively.

Common Sense and the Religion of the Heart

This does not mean that nineteenth-century American biblical interpreters were unrelievedly scientific and analytical in their approach to Scripture. In fact their main interest in Scripture was as a practical book to challenge the heart in matters of life and death. The heart-changing work of the Holy Spirit, they emphasized, complemented the objective understanding of Scripture. The theologians of this era were working after all in the midst of an extended revival, which most of them enthusiastically supported. The Second Great Awakening dominated American religious life and shaped much of American culture in the era from 1800 to 1860. American Protestant theologians provided the artillery cover for this evangelical advance, and often themselves were preachers who could be found in the front lines. The Bible, they said, was a two-edged sword challenging both head and heart.[13]

Timothy Dwight, president of Yale and early leader of the Second Great Awakening, explained the Bible's appeal to heart as well as head. The Scriptures, he said, contained not only instruction.

> They are also filled every where with Persuasion. Instead of being a cold compilation of philosophical dogmas, they are filled with real life; with facts; with persons; with forcible appeals to the imagination; and with powerful applications to the heart.

Dwight's presentation of these qualities of Scripture already reflected the vogue of Common Sense philosophy. Common Sense presented itself as a simple and popular teaching in contrast to tortured, abstract, and arcane "metaphysical" systems of "the philosophers." Said Dwight in a revealing passage:

> Common Sense, the most valuable faculty (if I may call it such) of man, finds all its premises either in revelation, or in facts; adopts arguments, only of the *a posteriori* kind; extends its reasonings through a few steps only; derives its illustrations from familiar sources; discriminates, only where there is a real difference; and admits conclusions, only where it can see their connexion with the premises. At theoretical philosophy it laughs. Theoretical divinity it detests. To this faculty the Scriptures are almost universally addressed. . . . Our Savior treats every subject in the direct manner of Common Sense. . . .[14]

Common Sense philosophy accordingly allowed plenty of room for the practical uses of Scripture, which were most important to American theologians and evangelists. The Bible appealed to the deepest emotions and was a down-to-earth guide to holy living. Through Scripture the Holy Spirit worked. These emphases were especially apparent in the new holiness movement emerging in the mid-decades of the century in both the Methodist and Reformed traditions. Subjective personal experience of God, "the Baptism of the Holy Spirit," confirmed objective proofs of the Bible's authority. For many simple believers, of course, the subjective experience was sufficient. The hymnody of the era reflected these trends; in contrast with the strictly Biblical psalm singing of Puritan days and the Biblical paraphrases and theological themes of the eighteenth-century hymns, nineteenth-century hymns shifted emphasis to recounting the feelings and experiences of the believer.[15]

Such popular romanticism, despite its subjectivistic tendencies, was not necessarily at odds with the scientific objectivism that dominated the Protestant intellectual community. Nowhere is this more evident than in the work of Professor Asa Mahan of Oberlin College. Mahan was a close associate of evangelist Charles Finney and perhaps the leading theorist of the new American holiness movement. Nonetheless Mahan was a thoroughgoing proponent of Common Sense philosophy and scientific reasoning. The Bible, he said, in phrases characteristic of the day, is "a scientific treatise" on morality. From it one can discover a "universal system of moral duty."[16] The truths of the Holy Spirit known in the heart and the truths from scientific biblical study would not conflict.

Science and the Bible

Whatever the popular appeals to the heart, it was also critical for Protestant scholars to show that the Bible could pass with flying colors a scientific review. The future of the civilization seemed to them to depend upon continued acceptance of the Bible's authority. America, Protestants held, was founded on the Bible, on *Scriptura sola*. Without respect for the Bible at the highest levels, intellectually and socially, the health and destiny of the nation would be hopelessly damaged. The heart alone, in this nation born of the Enlightenment, was not a sufficient or firm enough ground for intellectual certainty. Science, too, had to be revered. The objective truths of science, moreover, provided the essential corrective with which to oppose the subjective notions of that potential third authority in America—the individual. It was essential, then, to demonstrate that faith in Scripture was fully scientific. No impiety was involved in this enterprise. The God of science was after all the God of Scripture. It should not be difficult to demonstrate, therefore, that what he revealed in one realm perfectly harmonized with what he revealed in the other.[17] The perspicuity of nature should confirm the perspicuity of Scripture.

Evangelical apologists accordingly supplied publishers with a steady stream of books on "evidences of Christianity." All focused on the authenticity of the Bible, and all insisted that biblical truth was susceptible to scientific demonstration. "The proof of the authenticity of the Holy Scriptures as a revelation from God," wrote Baptist moral philosopher Francis Wayland, is "only a particular exemplification of the general laws of evidence."[18] "The Christian religion admits of certain proof," affirmed Mark Hopkins, president of Williams College, in his defense of the Bible. The proper inductive approach, said Hopkins, following the familiar Baconian formula, "decides nothing on the grounds of previous hypothesis, but yields itself entirely to the guidance of facts properly authenticated."[19] "A book comes to us purporting to be a revelation from God," declared James W. Alexander. "Examine the proofs which it brings to substantiate this claim. If they are incontrovertible, believe the book. . . . If they are insufficient, burn the volume."[20]

Modern scientific discoveries seemed to support this confidence. God the creator revealed in Scripture was God the designer of the wonderful laws of nature. The more complex the laws discovered, the better the evidence of God's design. Such marvelous engineering was unthinkable without an engineer. William Paley's famous argument in his *Natural Theology*

(1802), that the universe was like a finely-made watch whose presence decisively evidenced a watchmaker, was widely regarded as a definitive argument for theism.

Some details of the harmonies between nature and Scripture had, of course, to be worked into the picture, but as long as (prior to Darwin) the scientific community supported rather than questioned the premise of purposeful design, the problems could readily be surmounted. The most difficult questions during the first half of the century came from geology. Recent discoveries suggested that the earth was much older than would be supposed from simply reading the first chapters of Genesis. While some conservatives resisted making concessions to the new science, many other scholarly defenders of the Bible were quick to make the adjustment. The "days" of Genesis might be vastly lengthened, since the Hebrew word could mean an indefinite period of time as well as twenty-four hours. Or, some said, all the time necessary for primordial geological catastrophes could be found in Genesis 1:2, where the earth is described as "without form and void." Once the proper adjustments had been made, the scientific apologists for Scripture marveled at how well Moses had anticipated recent science. "Indeed," announced Professor L. W. Green in lectures on "evidences of Christianity" at the University of Virginia in 1850–51, "the whole tone and tendency of our modern geology, *when rightly understood,* is intensely and profoundly Christian." In a similar line of thought, rebutting arguments that Genesis is wrong because it says light was created before the sun, Green concluded that "the philosophy of Moses is infinitely superior to that of his German assailant in regard to the true nature of light, and its relation to the sun."[21]

Is the Bible Historically Accurate?

Behind such remarks was a more fundamental question. American scholars were well aware that German theologians, even many of the more evangelical among them, were developing theories of inspiration that effectively separated the Bible from questions of either scientific or historical fact. The Bible, said these theories, *contains* the word of God in distinction from *being* the word of God. What it contains is the essence of moral and religious truth, but it is not inspired in matters of history and science. This approach, which employed the new romantic and idealistic philosophies to defend against the rise of destructive biblical criticism, was applied in a wide variety of ways in Germany and to some extent in England.[22] In New England it had made a few inroads by mid-century, appearing in a radical form in the Transcendental Unitarianism of Theodore Parker, and in moderate evangelical varieties in the work of Horace Bushnell and of Edwards A. Park of Andover Theological Seminary.

Park brought the beginnings of the debate on the nature of Scripture that in the next generation would divide American Protestantism into liberal and conservative. In May of 1850 Professor Park, not a liberal by later standards, delivered an address to the Congregational ministers of New England suggesting that New England theology had been too much preoccupied with the precise statements of the "theology of the intellect" and should be more open to the "theology of the feelings." "The theology of the heart," said Park, "letting the minor accuracies go for the sake of holding strongly upon the substance of doctrine, need not always accommodate itself to scientific changes, but may often use its old statements, even if, when literally understood, they be incorrect, and it thus abides permanent as are the main impressions of the truth."[23] Charles Hodge of Princeton Theological Seminary responded in a series of long reviews that the theology of feeling could not be separated from that of correct teaching. Such ploys, said Hodge, were part of the whole trend of modern thought to abandon common sense in favor of ill-defined truths of the heart and were just the intellectual dangers to be avoided in this era of romanticism. Ultimately, he insisted, such teachings would undermine the whole authority of the Bible, "so the facts and doctrines of the Bible are the mere forms of the spirit of Christianity; and if you have the spirit, it matters not what form it takes."[24]

Lines of differences on the exact nature of the inspiration of Scripture were not yet sharply drawn in nineteenth-century America. The question to be decided, of course, was that of the relation of human authorship to divine authorship of the Bible. Skeptics on the one extreme insisted that the Bible was purely human. On the other extreme, it was not unusual to speak of the Bible as though the authorship were wholly divine. So for instance the Baptist New Hampshire Confession of 1833 began:

> We believe that the Holy Bible was written by men divinely inspired, and is a perfect treasure of heavenly instruction; that it has God for its author, salvation for its end, and truth, without any mixture of error, for its matter. . . .[25]

In between were those views that wrestled with the questions of how fully human and genuinely divine authorship could be combined. This problem was not at all new, but the recent rise of sophisticated biblical criticism had forced some refinement of distinctions.[26] Most American Protestant writers appear to have held that the Bible was inspired in all its parts and that God's guidance was present in choosing even the words of Scripture. The Bible was not, however, *dictated* by God; the human authors distinctively expressed their own thought and personalities. God's guidance for this "plenary" inspiration of Scripture was seen as a kind of superintendence. What this inspiration and superintendence might involve, however, was a matter for a lively discussion. Some suggested that while the whole Bible was inspired, it nonetheless might be inspired in different degrees. The authors could be closely superintended on substantial matters that God was teaching, but left on their own in matters of memory, scientific theories, or questions of common detail.[27]

On the other hand, a prominent contingent of American theologians insisted that there were no *degrees* of inspiration. The errorlessness of Scripture extended to all details of matters of fact. "If it is once granted that they are in the least degree alloyed with error," pronounced Methodist theologian Samuel Wakefield, "an opening is made for every imaginable corruption." "The sacred writers," concurred Congregationalist Leonard Woods, "had such a direction of the Holy Spirit, that they were secured against all liability to error, and enabled to write just what God pleased; so that what they wrote is, in truth, the Word of God, and can never be subject to any charge of mistake, either as to matter or form."[28]

Despite such strong statements, room for discussion of such fine points existed among those who agreed on the sure authority of Scripture. So among the revivalist (New School) Presbyterians and Congregationalists (a central grouping in mid-century evangelicalism) we find differences of opinion within the same fellowship. Charles Finney, considered a radical on some issues, nonetheless flatly insisted that the Bible was equally without error in its historical statements as in its doctrinal teachings.[29] Henry B. Smith, the leading New School theologian of the era, carefully balanced the human and the divine elements in his doctrine of inspiration. He insisted that the biblical writers were kept from error but also argued that because of the real humanity of the eye-witnesses, differences and omissions in details should be expected.[30] Albert Barnes, the era's leading biblical commentator, simply disclaimed any firm answer to the question of whether the biblical authors were "kept from error on all subjects." This was just one among many questions concerning inspiration that he thought were "yet to be solved."[31] Prior to 1870, however, differences on the exact theories of inspiration were not dividing evangelical Protestants, nor were they being used as tests of fellowship. When in 1869 the Old School Presbyterians reunited with their New School counterparts, the conservative Old School representatives, including the Princeton theologians who opposed the reunion, did not question the views of Scripture held by New School spokesmen such as Barnes.[32]

Common Sense and the Bible as a Scientific Book

In discussing the rise to prominence of the doctrine of the "inerrancy" of Scripture with respect to scientific and historical detail—a doctrine that eventually came to prevail among many Protestant conservatives—interpreters often have attributed the peculiarly American emphasis on this doctrine to the widespread influence of Common Sense philosophy and Baconianism. This point has been made especially with regard to the Princeton theologians.[33] Although the Princeton influence in determining such emphases has been overestimated, such interpretations have some merit. While it is of course true that many other intellectual and religious traditions also affected the outlook of nineteenth-century American evangelicalism, Common Sense Baconianism conditioned these traditions in the sense of giving them their exact shape. The inductive scientific bent of this outlook gave many American evangelicals a strong intellectual disposition to look for hard facts that could readily be classified. Viewing theology as an exact science, they tended to assume that God would reveal himself in terms that could be given very definite and precise meanings.

Even "figurative language," said Charles Hodge, who indeed was one of the more articulate and uncompromising proponents of this scientific framework for interpreting Scripture, "is just as definite in its meaning and just as intelligible as the most literal." "Such language," he insisted in his attack on Park's theology of feeling, "when interpreted according to established usage, and made to mean what it was intended to express, is not only definite in its import, but it never expresses what is false to the intellect."[34] So Hodge, like many of his contemporaries, treated Scripture quite frankly as a compilation of hard "facts" that the theologian had only to arrange in systematic order.[35] Such a scientific model, combined with a high view of God's role in inspiring the biblical writers, fit extremely well with the conclusion that God would do nothing less than reveal the facts of Scripture with an accuracy that would satisfy the most scrupulous modern scientific standards. While Common Sense and Baconianism certainly did not create the idea that the Bible was without error in detail, there can be little doubt that their influence contributed to giving the doctrine of the "inerrancy" of Scripture a more prominent role in modern America than it has had at almost any other time or place in church history.[36]

Common Sense and the Humanity of Scripture

The relationship of the Common Sense and Baconian outlook to nineteenth-century American views of Scripture was, however, not quite as simple as portrayed in this usual account. For one thing, as we have seen, Common Sense did allow for ordinary experience including "truths of the heart," so that Hodge's subordination of these themes was not entirely typical. Furthermore, Common Sense philosophy had much in it that might support an emphasis on the humanity of Scripture. Essential to the Common Sense account of the perspicuity of Scripture was an appeal to our common humanity with the biblical writers. A Common Sense premise was that we can understand other people, including those from other times and cultures, because the race is simply constituted with faculties that make such communication possible. Critical to the nineteenth-century apologists' arguments for the authenticity of Scripture, for instance, was an appeal to the very down-to-earth and everyday question of the reliability of human testimony. A law of our nature simply obliges us to believe the testimony of witnesses of known veracity. Courts of law in all cultures and all our knowledge of the past depend on such sources. All but the most hardened skeptics must agree that veracious testimony often is a legitimate ground for certainty. So ran the common argument for the authority of Scripture. The biblical writers recommend themselves by the unsurpassed system of morality which they taught. So it is "incredible and contradictory, contrary to all the known laws of mind, to suppose that men whose moral discrimination and susceptibilities were so acute . . . would, without reason or motive that we can see, deliberately attempt to deceive mankind."[37]

Critical then to the rational apologetic of the day was that the Bible was a human book, as well as a divine one. Here, however, were the seeds of a dilemma and the source of the most fascinating controversies over the Bible in mid-nineteenth-century America. Common Sense philosophy underlined the necessity of taking the humanity of the Bible seriously. Virtually all scholars, including the Princeton theologians, stressed this point. Crucial for understanding the Bible was the process of determining the original meanings of what the Biblical authors wrote. This was essentially a scientific question—a job for the philologist who studied closely the history of language. Once the original meaning was determined, it seemed to follow on Common Sense principles that the meaning of a Scriptures should be settled once and for all. Scripture would be speaking plainly— the anarchy of relativism and private interpretations would be avoided.

Yet the coastlines of this land of plain truth were surrounded by dangerous shoals. Everything in the Common Sense Baconian system assumed the stability of truth which could be known objectively by careful observers in any age or culture. Almost all the other trends in nineteenth-century thought, however, pointed toward an opposite conclusion. Change and progress were the things that counted in the history of humanity. Human knowledge was progressive. But did not the progress of human knowledge— especially in history and science—affect our interpretations of Scripture?

Moses Stuart of Andover Theological Seminary, the leading American biblical scholar of the era, forced the American intellectual community to face these perplexing issues. Stuart was a conservative in his view of the Bible and also a thoroughgoing champion of Common Sense philosophy. The meanings of Scripture, he insisted, must be plain. Interpretation, he said is *"a native art."* "Has any part of the race," he asked rhetorically, "in full possession of the human faculties, ever failed to understand what others said to them and to understand it truly?" Moreover, if God wished to *reveal* himself, Stuart reasoned, then he must have done so in plain language that could be understood by the common people who were the original hearers or readers of that revelation.

So far Stuart was saying nothing out of the ordinary.[38] He added, however, some startling implications of these Common Sense principles. If the meanings of Scripture passages were known to the original writers and hearers—if they spoke in the plain speech of humanity—then Scripture had in it no double meanings, such as one temporal and one spiritual, or meanings hidden from those to whom originally it was revealed.[39]

In drawing this conclusion Stuart was carrying through on Common Sense principles farther than most other American Protestants were willing to follow. In fact they almost all held that the Bible contained dual meanings. Many of the biblical prophecies were regarded in this way. Hidden in the words of the original sayings might be a secondary meaning not apparent until much later when the prophecy was fulfilled. Moreover, American Christians often employed typological interpretations of Scripture—that Old Testament figures and events were real historical types of

Christ and that these types were recapitulated in modern history, which indeed was already outlined in prophecy, especially in Daniel and Revelation.[40] These views continued to have great force in nineteenth-century America, as the view that the United States was the New Israel and the central site of the spiritual preparations for the millennial age. The progress of history was thus casting new light on the meanings of God's revelation.

Similar suggestions of hidden meanings were regularly made to accommodate the findings of modern science. The "days" in Genesis could be interpreted as long periods of time to take into account the findings of modern geology, and evangelicals could then marvel at how well the language of Moses anticipated recent scientific discoveries. To the modern Moses of Andover, this was sheer nonsense. "I am unable to see," he declared in one of the many polemics that surrounded his work, "how the discoveries of modern science and of recent date, can determine the meaning of Moses' words."[41] Stuart, moreover, had the courage of his convictions. Convinced that Moses thought the days of Genesis were of twenty-four hours, he was willing to discount the whole science of geology and to insist that the earth was less than 6000 years old.

The great irony of Stuart's position was that he arrived at this rigid conclusion because he was so modern a scholar. Like the biblical critics in Germany, whom he knew well, he took the humanity of the scriptural authors seriously and studied them scientifically in their original cultural contexts. With the critics he could answer the question, "Are the same principles of interpretation to be applied to the Bible as to other books?" with a resounding "Yes."[42] Yet with Stuart's Common Sense, anti-romantic anti-spiritualizing principles of interpretation this position meant taking simply at face value the apparent claims of Scripture, no matter how much of a strain these might create for other aspects of modern scientific thought. By eliminating hidden meanings, Stuart had established a basis for determining once and for all, scientifically and objectively, the true meanings of Scripture passages. In reaching for this goal Stuart epitomized the aspirations of nineteenth-century American theologians to make the interpretation of Scripture an exact modern science. The price, however, was high. Faced with the choice between the perspicuity of Scripture and the perspicuity of nature, Stuart bit the bullet and chose Scripture.

Stuart's dilemma pointed to an ominous weakness in the Common Sense Baconian outlook of nineteenth-century American Protestant thought. Eager to achieve complete intellectual stability—clarity and certainty that would avoid the ravages of private interpretations—theologians leaned the weight of divine Biblical authority squarely against the wall of humanity's current scientific knowledge and assumed that the two would support each other. The balance, however, was extremely precarious. Stuart's hard choices showed that the pieces did not all fit together as neatly as was often supposed. As long as sciences like geology were regarded as having their own rules, starting with no reference to biblical data, there was no guarantee that the current scientific understandings of nature would fit reverent scientific interpretations of Scripture.

The key to the problem were the assumptions involved. Basic to the Common Sense Baconian outlook was the assumption that science and philosophy were autonomous, rational, and objective disciplines. In fact, however, science and philosophy operate on various premises—often hidden premises. From a Christian perspective the crucial question is whether these premises reflect a strictly naturalistic outlook or one that may be shaped and guided by data derived from biblical revelation. Christian apologists, accordingly, were placing themselves in a highly vulnerable position by endorsing the Baconian ideal that the sciences should be completely neutral and freed from religious review at their starting points. Faith in the Bible was not in principle antagonistic to scientific inquiry. If, however, it was made to rest so heavily on the latest scientific findings it was always liable to disruption by what might appear on tomorrow's front page or in next month's scientific journal. For nineteenth-century Americans this vulnerability became startlingly apparent with the coming of Darwinism—science consistently without the tacit Christian premises of design and purpose. Almost without warning one wall of their apologetic edifice was removed and within a generation the place of biblical authority in American intellectual life was in a complete shambles.[43]

The balance, however, had involved more than purely intellectual factors. The "common sense" claims to objective and scientific demonstrations of biblical truths had rested also on a cultural consensus. This consensus had included essentially biblical assumptions that the universe was created and run by a being concerned with the spiritual and moral welfare of humanity. By the late nineteenth century this consensus began to erode. Moreover, in the Common Sense outlook there was little adequate means to account for cultural diversity. So as America shifted from a more-or-less unified culture dominated by British Protestant ideals to a notably pluralistic culture by the end of the nineteenth century, "common sense" lost much of its social base. The dominant philosophies of the day were those that could explain progress and varieties of legitimate points of view.

In the face of the demise of the old Common Sense consensus, Protestants who tried to keep the faith usually moved in one of three directions—each of which was already anticipated at mid-century. Protestant liberals followed essentially the route suggested by the earlier romantics of separating transcendental truths entirely from dependence on the vicissitudes of scientific data. The Bible's authority accordingly did not need to rest on any scientific or historical claims. Christianity was authenticated by personal experience, not by objective revelation. A second route was that followed by the Holiness Movement and its pentecostal heirs. As in the popular romanticism of mid-century, the subjective and personal experience was also accentuated without at all denying the objective authority of Scripture. Personal experience with the supernatural was all that was necessary to authenticate Christianity and such experience confirmed that the Bible was supernaturally inspired—no further argumentation was necessary. The third solution was that developed in American fundamentalism. Rather than conceding the issue, the old balance between scientific rationality and Scripture was shored up. The objective authority of Scripture and its inerrancy were affirmed and accentuated. Science and reason continued to be regarded as confirming Scripture, but Darwinian theories were declared speculative hypotheses and not true science.[44] Among these three positions much of American Protestantism still remains divided.

NOTES

1. Ralph Waldo Emerson, "The Divinity School Address" (1838), *Selections from Ralph Waldo Emerson: An Organic Anthology,* Stephen E. Whicher, ed. (Boston, 1957), p. 113.

2. Sarah Moore Grimké, *Letters on the Equality of the Sexes and the Condition of Women. Addressed to Mary S. Parker* (Boston, 1838), p. 4.

3. *Ibid.,* pp. 126, 4.

4. This parallelism was initially suggested to me by John W. Stewart, "The Princeton Theologians: The Tethered Theology" (uncompleted Ph.D. dissertation, University of Michigan, *ca.* 1978).

5. Mark Twain, "Reflections on the Sabbath," *Territorial Enterprise,* early March 1866, reprinted in *The Wilson Quarterly,* IV: 4 (Autumn 1980), 180.

6. Andrews Norton, *A Discourse on the Latest Form of Infidelity, Delivered . . . 19th of July 1839; with notes* (Cambridge, Mass., 1839), p. 48.

7. Page 40, 1840 London edition.

8. Samuel Tyler, *Discourse of the Baconian Philosophy,* 2d ed. (New York, 1850), p. 15; Benjamin Morgan Palmer, "Baconianism and the Bible," *Southern Presbyterian Review,* VI (1850), 250, quoted in Theodore Dwight Bozeman, *Protestants*

in an Age of Science: The Baconian Ideal and Antebellum American Religious Thought (Chapel Hill, N.C., 1977), pp. 128, 130. The connection was that the Bible taught nature was created with orderly laws. Bozeman cites many other examples of this connection. See also Herbert Hovenkamp, *Science and Religion in America 1800–1860* (Philadelphia, 1978), and George H. Daniels, *American Science in the Age of Jackson* (New York, 1968), for examples of the widespread reverence for Baconianism and Common Sense philosophy.

9. For the irrelevance of Emerson's transcendentalism to the common people in the mid-nineteenth century, see Lewis O. Saum, *The Popular Mood of Pre-Civil War America* (Westport, Conn., 1980), pp. xxi–xxii, 27–30.

10. Thomas Reid, *Essays on the Intellectual Powers of Man,* Baruch A. Brody, ed. (Cambridge, Mass., 1969 [1785]), *passim.* Essay VI, "Of Judgement," contains the most concise summary of Reid's first principles. There are many summaries of Reid's views. Probably the best is S. A. Grave, *The Scottish Philosophy of Common Sense* (Oxford, 1960).

11. Reid, *Essays,* VI:4, pp. 600–604, proposes following Baconian principles, building from Common Sense first principles to establish "unanimity" in philosophical issues like that established by Newton in physics.

12. James W. Alexander, "On the Use and Abuse of Systematic Theology," *Biblical Repertory and Princeton Review,* IV (1832), 171–90; J. S. Lamar, *The Organon of Scripture, Or, the Inductive Method of Biblical Interpretation* (Philadelphia, 1860), p. 176, cited in Bozeman, *Protestants in an Age of Science,* pp. 151, 144–45. Bozeman cites numerous other expressions of these views from representatives of a variety of denominations. Cf. John Miley's expression of such views late in the century, *Systematic Theology,* I, xx (New York, 1892), p. 50.

13. Bozeman, *Protestants in the Age of Science,* p. 171, says: "One of the most common refrains in orthodox literature was the primacy of 'heart' over head." These were the sentiments even of Princeton theologians, such as Charles Hodge, who was second to none in stressing the intellectual content of the faith.

14. Timothy Dwight, *Theology; Explained and Defended, in a Series of Sermons,* Vol. IV (New Haven, 1825 [from about 1800]), pp. 55, 260–61.

15. Sandra S. Sizer, *Gospel Hymns and Social Religion: The Rhetoric of Nineteenth-Century Revivalism* (Philadelphia, 1978). The slave spirituals, by contrast, include more direct biblical themes, often recounting narratives of salvation history. They also include emphasis on personal experience, as praying to Jesus to be close in time of need.

16. Asa Mahan, *A Science of Moral Philosophy* (Oberlin, 1848), pp. 187, 183. On Mahan as a Common Sense thinker, see, James E. Hamilton, "Nineteenth Century Holiness Theology: A Study of the Thought of Asa Mahan," *Wesleyan Theological Journal,* XIII (Spring 1978), 51–64.

17. Good examples of evangelical statements of this theme are found in *Lectures on the Evidences of Christianity delivered at the University of Virginia . . . 1850–1851* (New York, 1854), especially, for example, L. W. Green, "The Harmony of Revelation and Natural Science; with Especial Reference to Geology," pp. 459–520.

18. Francis Wayland, *The Elements of Moral Science,* Joseph L. Blau, ed. (Cambridge, Mass., 1963), p. 126.

19. Mark Hopkins, *Evidences of Christianity* (Boston, 1876 [1846]), p. 39. The evangelical arguments were accumulations of "probable" evidences that formed

strands of a rope of virtual certainty. Working from Common Sense premises, they argued that the authenticity of Scripture was as well established as many other of our beliefs that we rely on even in matters of life and death.

20. John Hall, ed., *Forty Years' Familiar Letters of James W. Alexander,* Vol. I (New York, 1860), p. 55, quoted in Bozeman, *Protestants in an Age of Science,* p. 141. Bozeman suggests this is a sarcastic allusion to a famous passage from skeptic David Hume, the favorite target of Protestant apologists.

21. Green, "The Harmony of Revelation," *Lectures on the Evidences,* pp. 462, and 507. See also Bozeman, *Protestants in an Age of Science,* and Hovenkamp, *Science and Religion,* for many other examples of this theme.

22. This account closely follows that provided by Henry B. Smith, *Introduction to Christian Theology* (New York, 1882), pp. 208–9. Smith had studied in Germany and is a reliable observer. His lectures were developed at Union Theological Seminary in the later 1850s. The tact of limiting biblical truths to essences had historical precedents, but never was as fully developed as it became in the nine-teenth century.

23. Edwards A. Park, "The Theology of the Intellect and That of the Feelings," *Bibliotheca Sacra,* VII (July 1850), 539.

24. Charles Hodge, "The Theology of the Intellect and That of the Feelings" (a Review), *Essays and Reviews* (New York, 1857); originally published in the *Princeton Review,* October 1850.

25. Quoted in T. Russ Bush and Tom J. Nettles, *Baptists and the Bible: The Baptist Doctrines of Biblical Importance and Religious Authority in Historical Perspective* (Chicago, 1980).

26. Smith, *Introduction,* p. 213. For a selective sampling of expressions emphasizing the human elements in Scripture, see Jack B. Rogers and Donald K. McKim, *The Authority and Interpretation of the Bible: An Historical Approach* (San Francisco, 1979). Among the reviewers who have pointed out a high degree of selectivity and bias in this work, the most thorough is John D. Woodbridge, "Biblical Authority: Towards an Evaluation of the Rogers and McKim Proposal," *Trinity Journal,* I (Fall 1980), 165–236. Woodbridge is selective in looking for counter examples to show that throughout church history people held that divine authorship entailed historical accuracy in detail. Despite overstating his case, Woodbridge certainly shows that Rogers and McKim overstate theirs.

Ian Rennie, "Mixed Metaphors, Misunderstood Models, and Puzzling Para-digms: A Contemporary Effort to Correct Some Current Misunderstandings Re-garding the Authority and Interpretation of the Bible, An Historical Response," paper presented at "Interpreting an Authoritative Scripture," a conference at the Institute for Christian Studies, Toronto, June 1981, argues that there were already two clearly defined positions reflecting a "battle for the Bible" in Great Britain. The plenary view was being attack by advocates of the "verbal inspiration" view, cf. note 27 below.

27. These distinctions are summarized in Smith's *Introduction,* pp. 209–12, and are assumed or discussed throughout the literature. The suggestions of degrees of inspiration seem to have come mainly from Scottish writers, whose works were very well known in America.

28. Samuel Wakefield, *A Complete System of Christian Theology* (Pittsburgh, 1869), p. 77. *Works of Leonard Woods,* I (Boston, 1851), p. 171. John Woodbridge and Randall Balmer, "The Princetonians and Biblical Authority: An Assessment of

the Ernest Sandeen Proposal," *Scripture and Truth* (Grand Rapids, Mich.: forth-coming), cite the Wakefield passage, comparable ones from Lutheran C.F.W. Walther, and that by Charles Finney, quoted below.

Woodbridge and Balmer demonstrate that the contention of Ernest Sandeen, followed to a large extent by Rogers and McKim, *The Authority and Interpretation,* is basically a misconception. Sandeen, *The Roots of Fundamentalism: British and American Millenarianism, 1800–1930* (Chicago, 1970), contends that a sys-tematic theology of biblical authority, stressing inerrancy of the original manu-scripts, was essentially a creation of the Princeton theologians after 1850 (for example, p. 106, "no such theology existed before 1850"). In fact such a theology (though far from universal) was commonplace by then and hardly the invention of Princeton theologians. Sandeen argues further that the appeal to the auto-graphs was a late invention in the Princeton defense, pp. 127–30 (Rogers and McKim refer to the "Retreat to the Original Autographs," p. 298). In fact, as Woodbridge and Balmer show, discussion of the autographs was commonplace in earlier nineteenth-century Protestant literature and was (like inerrancy) by no means a Princeton invention. In addition to the evidence that Balmer and Wood-bridge present, I can add the statement of Leonard Woods: "For what we assert is, the inspiration of the *original* scriptures, not of the translations, or the ancient copies." *Works,* I, p. 113. The appeal to the autographs was a strategy not solely of strict conservatives. Charles Elliott, professor at the Presbyterian Theological Seminary of the North-west, Chicago, *A Treatise on the Inspiration of the Holy Scriptures* (Edinburgh, 1877), said that "if any positive errors are found in the Scriptures, it must be proved that they existed in the original manuscripts. . . ." Elliott added, however, that "A document might contain an omission, or an in-accurate statement, and yet be of infallible authority on the point intended to be proved by it" (p. 249).

29. From quotation in G. F. Wright, *Charles G. Finney* (Boston, 1891), pp. 182–83, in Woodbridge, "Biblical Authority," p. 207.

30. H. B. Smith, *The Inspiration of the Holy Scriptures* (New York, 1855), pp. 3–31. Smith's views are summarized in George Marsden, *The Evangelical Mind and the New School Presbyterian Experience* (New Haven, 1970), pp. 169–72. Mark Hopkins, *Evidences of Christianity* (Boston, 1876 [1846]), p. 204, also uses the argument that discrepancies in the Gospels are evidence for their authenticity, since a fraud would have tried to make the details match previous accounts.

31. Albert Barnes, *Lectures on the Evidence of Christianity in the Nineteenth Cen-tury* (New York, 1872 [1867]), pp. 238–39. George Fisher, of Yale, *Essays on the Supernatural Origins of Christianity* (New York, 1890 [1866]), p. xxvii, dis-plays a similarly complete confidence in the Bible, but qualifications on the ques-tion of detail ("in the main") in the following remark: "That the narratives of miracles which are given in the Gospels are, in the main, a faithful record of facts which actually occurred, is the result of a sound unbiased historical criti-cism, and must, sooner or later, be generally acknowledged."

32. Cf. Marsden, *Evangelical Mind,* pp. 212–29. Norman H. Maring, "Baptists and Changing Views of the Bible, 1865–1918," *Foundations,* I (July 1958), 60, cf. pp. 52–60, suggests a similar stance among Baptists: "Thus, around 1870 Baptist theologians had a firm conviction that the Bible was inspired and a tendency to accept inspiration as implying inerrancy, but they were hesitant to accept any of the theories which tried to explain the nature and extent of that infallibility."

33. Among the helpful studies of this point are John C. Vander Stelt, *Philosophy and*

Scripture: A Study in Old Princeton and Westminster Theology (Marlton, N.J., 1978); Bozeman, *Protestants in an Age of Science;* John W. Stewart, "The Princeton Theologians: The Tethered Theology"; Rogers and McKim, *The Authority and Interpretation of the Bible.* These should be balanced by W. Andrew Hoffecker, *Piety and the Princeton Theologians* (Grand Rapids, Mich., 1981), who while pointing out strong elements of deep piety none the less acknowledges the dominance of objectivist and scientific tendencies, e.g., pp. 59–60, 70–71.

34. Hodge, "The Theology of Intellect," *Essays and Reviews,* p. 548.

35. "The Bible is to the theologian what nature is to the man of science. It is his store-house of facts. . . ." Charles Hodge, *Systematic Theology,* I (New York, 1874), p. 10.

36. The current debates over the precedents in church history for the doctrine of inerrancy can be clarified by observing that defenders of inerrancy are correct in showing that throughout church history the accuracy of the Bible in historical and scientific detail was often either assumed or stated. Opponents of inerrancy, however, are correct in showing that such statements were seldom emphasized in unambiguous ways prior to the nineteenth century and that there are precedents for seeing this issue as secondary or unimportant. Cf. the works discussed in note 28, above.

Whatever the other precedents, however, there is little doubt that the doctrine has had more prominence and more often been used as a test of the faith in America since about 1880 than it was previously. Since Christians in various countries have responded to modern biblical criticism in a variety of other ways, this peculiarly American phenomenon is worth trying to explain. Such explanations, of course, do not bear much on the merits of the cases for or against inerrancy. New emphases may or may not be correct.

One important factor not here discussed is the role of dispensational premillennialism in fostering the emphasis or inerrancy in America. Such influences and their relation to Common Sense Baconianism are discussed in Marsden, *Fundamentalism and American Culture,* and in the essay by Timothy Weber in this present book.

37. Mark Hopkins, *Evidences of Christianity,* p. 119. Charles Hodge uses this same argument, *Systematic Theology,* I, p. 634.

38. For instance, Charles Hodge had long employed this principle. "The only way in which the writer can be understood is to use words in the sense commonly attached to them by his readers. As this is perfectly obvious, it follows with equal clearness that if any other person wishes to understand such a writing, he must first ascertain how were the words and expressions understood by the persons to whom the writing was addressed." Hodge, "Biblical Criticism and Hermeneutics," *MSS,* 1823, Speer Library, Princeton Theological Seminary, Alumni Alcove. Quoted in Stewart, "The Tethered Theology," VI:32.

39. Moses Stuart, "Are the Same Principles To Be Applied to the Bible as to Other Books?", *Biblical Repository,* II (January 1832), 125, 129–37. Cf. "On the Alleged Obscurity of Prophecy," *Biblical Repository,* II (April 1832), 217–45. Stuart's work elicited many responses and counter-responses.

40. The most heated debate over this issue came from George Duffield, *Millenarianism Defended; A Reply to Prof. Stuart's "Strictures on the Rev. G. Duffield's Recent Work on the Second Coming of Jesus Christ"* (New York, 1843).

41. "Examination of Genesis I, in reference to Geology," *The Biblical Repository and Quarterly Observer,* VII (January 1836), 49. This was part of an extensive

debate with Edward Hitchcock, Professor of Chemistry and Natural Science, Amherst College. Cf. Hitchcock's reply, April 1836, pp. 448–87.

42. Article of this title, *American Biblical Repository,* II (January 1832), 124–37.

James R. Moore, *The Post-Darwinian Controversies: A Study of the Protestant struggle to come to terms with Darwin in Great Britain and America, 1870–1900* (Cambridge, 1979), shows that before 1900 some impressive attempts were made to hold the edifice together.

43. Cf. Marsden, "The Collapse of American Evangelical Academia" (a forthcoming paper from a Calvin Center for Christian Scholarship Project), for further discussion of this theme.

44. Cf. Marsden, *Fundamentalism and American Culture,* pp. 212–21.

V

The Two-Edged Sword:
The Fundamentalist Use of the Bible

TIMOTHY P. WEBER
Denver Conservative Baptist Theological Seminary

Since the 1920s fundamentalists have had an image problem. Many Americans equate fundamentalism with dogmatism, closed-mindedness, right-wing politics, and the "paranoid style." To some extent these popular views have been encouraged by the conclusions of historians. Until fairly recently most historians have seen fundamentalism as a movement of the socially backward, intellectually stunted, theologically naïve, and psychologically disturbed.

In the 1930s, for example, Stewart Cole and H. Richard Niebuhr set the fundamentalist-modernist controversy within a much larger urban-rural conflict. They believed that the religious battle was only one front in a bigger war between provincial people from the small towns and countryside and more progressive and sophisticated city dwellers.[1] In the 1950s Norman Furniss and Ray Ginger stressed fundamentalism's pervasive anti-intellectualism, especially in its opposition to evolution and other kinds of modern scholarship.[2] In the early 1960s Richard Hofstadter suggested that fundamentalism grew out of a certain class "status anxiety" over losing power, influence, and respect in society.[3] For the most part, then, these historians interpreted fundamentalism in terms of culture lag or social displacement.

That rather lopsided approach was ripe for revision. By the late 1960s historians began looking at fundamentalism as a *bona fide* religious, theological, and even intellectual movement. In an influential essay Paul Carter

challenged the old consensus by arguing that instead of being anti-intellectual, fundamentalists were actually intellectual in a way different from their
opponents.[4] Ernest Sandeen claimed that the roots of twentieth-century
fundamentalism were traceable to a nineteenth-century alliance between
advocates of the Calvinist orthodoxy of Princeton Seminary and millenar-
ians.[5] George Marsden has offered a more complicated thesis. Though the
movement eventually developed a distinct life and identity of its own, fundamentalism was closely allied with a number of older religious traditions,
including evangelicalism, revivalism, pietism, the Holiness Movement, premillennialism, Reformed confessionalism, Baptist traditionalism, and other
denominational orthodoxies. By interacting with their culture in complex
and sometimes ambivalent ways, fundamentalists put together "a loose,
diverse, and changing federation of co-belligerents united by their fierce
opposition to modernist attempts to bring Christianity into line with modern
thought."[6]

As a result of these more recent studies, we now know that fundamentalism is a much more complex phenomenon than previously imagined. It
is urban and rural, sophisticated and simplistic, intellectual and anti-intellectual, moderate and militant. In short, fundamentalism is much more
diverse—geographically, socially, politically, educationally, and theologically—than its negative public image portends.

Though they might disagree about the causes and clientele of fundamen-
talism, historians have recognized the importance of the Bible in shaping
the movement's identity. Fundamentalists were self-styled people of the
Book who defended against any attempt to undermine its power or prestige.
In contrast to more liberal Christians, fundamentalists called themselves
Bible-believers. When "modernisms" of one kind or another captured institutions of higher learning, they founded their own *Bible institutes* and
Bible colleges. They met often in *Bible conferences* to hear the old verities
expounded and extolled. They maintained their *Bible doctrine* when theologians in the seminaries started redefining the evangelical tradition. When
apostasy in the churches became unbearable, they withdrew and established their own *Bible Churches*. From one angle, then, fundamentalism
may be seen as an organized and often militant movement to protect the
Bible from all its enemies.

In the late nineteenth and early twentieth century, there were more than
enough enemies to go around. As far as conservative evangelicals were
concerned, most of them went by the name "higher critic." While some

biblical scholars used the new critical approach within the boundaries of theological orthodoxy, most did not. By the turn of the century, the more radical critics were convinced that Moses did not write the Pentateuch, Isaiah penned only half the book that bears his name, many so-called prophecies were actually written *after* the events they predicted, and large parts of both Testaments contained myths, legends, and gross historical and even theological errors.[7] Needless to say, such sentiments did not qualify as the old-time religion. As a result many evangelicals were genuinely mystified as to how scholars with such impeccable academic and religious credentials could come to such outrageous conclusions.

By 1900, then, just about everybody sensed that there had been a radical change in the way some evangelicals viewed and valued the Scriptures. To borrow a phrase from Thomas Kuhn,[8] a "paradigm shift" of enormous proportions had taken place. In his *Fundamentalism and American Culture,* Marsden noted the applicability of Kuhn's theory of "scientific revolutions" to the study of fundamentalism.[9] According to Kuhn, scientific thought does not progress by an orderly acquisition of new and more persuasive "facts." Rather it proceeds through "paradigm conflicts" between rival scientific world-views. With each revolution old presuppositions, perceptions, models (paradigms), and even language give way to new ones. One such paradigm shift occurred in the Copernican revolution. "Pre-Copernicans" viewed the earth as fixed in the universe, with the sun and the other planets in motion around it. Copernicans, on the other hand, reversed the model so that the sun was fixed, and the earth and the other planets were in motion. From Kuhn's perspective, the observable phenomena ("facts") had not changed, only the paradigm that explained them. Because the two sides used different models with radically different presuppositions, they found it difficult to communicate or even understand each other.

Another paradigm shift took place in the nineteenth-century conflict over evolutionary theory. In this case an older "mechanical" model gave way to a newer "organic" view of things. A static and empirical paradigm eventually lost ground to a developmental and more speculative model.[10] The shift from "Baconianism" to "Darwinism" was a revolution every bit as painful and difficult as the earlier shift from an earth-centered to a sun-centered perception of the heavens. From Kuhn's perspective, the transference of one's allegiance from one paradigm to another is a kind of conversion experience with profound personal consequences.

When paradigms change, the world itself changes with them. Led by a new paradigm, scientists adopt new instruments and look in new places. Even more important, during revolutions scientists see new and different things when looking with familiar instruments in places they have looked before. It is rather as if the professional community had been suddenly transported to another planet where familiar objects are seen in a different light and are joined by unfamiliar ones as well. Of course, nothing of quite that sort does occur: there is no geographical transplantation; outside the laboratory everyday affairs usually continue as before. Nevertheless, paradigm changes do cause scientists to see the world of their research-engagement differently. In so far as their only recourse to that world is through what they see and do, we may want to say that after a revolution scientists are responding to a different world.[11]

Without pressing Kuhn's theory to extremes, it does, however, seem that something like a "paradigm shift" occurred in the world of evangelical biblical scholarship during the last half of the nineteenth century. Worldviews changed; old ways of reading and understanding the Bible were laid aside for radically new ones. Many evangelical scholars, pastors, and even lay people suddenly found themselves living in a new world where nothing looked quite the same.

The experience of William Newton Clarke (1840–1912) can illustrate the shift from one biblical perspective to another. The son of a Baptist minister, Clarke grew up loving and respecting the Bible. After years of family and private devotions and hundreds of his father's sermons, Clarke trusted the Bible's truthfulness and accepted its authority in all matters of faith and practice. Studies at Hamilton Theological Seminary confirmed those convictions. When he graduated in 1863 and entered the pastorate, Clarke considered himself a "firm biblicist" and believed that the Bible was "so inspired by God that its writers were not capable of error."[12]

Despite this obviously high view of Scripture, Clarke had no carefully thought-out doctrine of biblical inspiration. He saw no real need for one. The verdict of the church and the quiet but convincing inner testimony of the Holy Spirit in the believer's heart were the only proofs he needed. Most Baptists of the mid-nineteenth century shared Clarke's devout but non-doctrinaire respect for the Bible.[13] In fact, loyalty to the Scriptures was so widespread that many theologians could get by without articulating any particular approach to the issue. As Norman Maring has noted, in 1870 "Baptist theologians had a firm conviction that the Bible was inspired and a tendency to accept inspiration as implying inerrancy, but they were hesitant to accept any of the theories which tried to explain the nature and extent of that infallibility."[14] Believing that the Bible is the inspired Word of God was one thing; being able or willing to say how God inspired it was quite another.

Clarke spent twenty-seven years in the pastoral ministry. From the start he dedicated himself to expository preaching and the regular and rigorous study of the Greek New Testament. During his first pastorate in New Hampshire, his beliefs about the Bible held firm; but after moving to Newton Center, Massachusetts, in 1869, he began having second thoughts. Contacts with liberal faculty members of Newton Theological Seminary led him to a personally painful conclusion: careful and open-minded exegesis of the Bible was "quite incompatible with permanent confidence in verbal inspiration."[15] In 1880 Clarke transfered to Toronto, where he began reading biblical criticism.[16] It was a shattering and unnerving experience for him. He had a difficult decision to make: should he ignore the conclusions of biblical criticism and stick to his earlier convictions or should he continue his critical studies and be forced to alter substantially his views of the Bible? After considerable struggle, Clarke concluded that there was no turning back. "There was no room for doubt. The inquiry that was undertaken by the higher criticism was perfectly legitimate, and I had no right to resist it or wish it away."[17]

The rest of Clarke's career is well known. In 1890 he left the pastorate and became professor of theology at Colgate Theological Seminary. There he had the time to rework evangelical theology from his new perspective. In 1898 he published *An Outline of Christian Theology,* the first systematic theology in America to be written from a liberal point of view.[18]

Clarke knew that a new approach to theology required a new approach to the Bible. Consequently, when asked to deliver the Taylor Lectures at Yale in 1905, he chose as his topic "The Use of the Scriptures in Theology."[19] Clarke called for a revolution in the way the church thought about the Bible and used it for doctrine. For Clarke the biggest obstacle to radical change was the older theory of biblical inspiration.

Though most evangelicals accepted the Bible's inspiration without exactly knowing why, a few theologians worked hard to clarify the issue once and for all. This was especially true of the men at Princeton Seminary, the citadel of Calvinist orthodoxy in nineteenth-century America. Drawing heavily on the then popular Scottish Common Sense philosophy and a Baconian approach to science,[20] the Princetonians reasserted a doctrine of inerrancy that they believed could stand up to the most skeptical scrutiny. Through a careful, inductive, and open-minded examination of the evidence, they concluded that the Bible had been uniquely inspired by God. God had so supernaturally superintended the biblical writers that everything recorded—including history, geography, geology, biology, and theology—was absolutely errorless. The Bible made such claims for itself; and an unbiased investigation of the internal evidence proved it. So-called "problem texts" were due to errors in the transmission of manuscripts over time, modern misunderstanding of what the texts really mean, or temporary confusion that would clear up with more time and scholarship. Under no circumstances, however, are good scholars ever forced to admit that errors occurred in the original texts which, unfortunately, were not available for examination.[21]

This doctrine of Scripture—which made the general assumptions of many earlier Christians considerably more concrete—caught on in conservative evangelical circles by the end of the century. It provided solid, scholarly reasons for popular evangelical sentiments. It was even "scientific" in that it followed the methods of induction that were still widely used by American scientists. Charles Hodge, an architect of the Princeton theology, believed that the "Bible is to the theologian what nature is to the man of science. It is his store-house of facts; and his method of ascertaining what the Bible teaches is the same as that which the natural philosopher adopts to ascertain what nature teaches."[22] Since the Bible could be "proved" to be inspired through careful induction, the theologian was free to use it as the scientist did the data in his laboratory. Because the Bible was inerrantly inspired in its entirety, each passage was the stuff out of which theology was made. Every proposition had to be sifted, analyzed, compared, and examined until larger connections emerged. Theologians with this view of the Bible believed that they were merely thinking God's thoughts after Him when they did their jobs correctly.

This was the biblical paradigm that Clarke rejected. In fact, he called it nonsense. Though he still maintained his belief in biblical inspiration, Clarke argued that modern criticism had uncovered numerous errors in the Bible. Ironically, Clarke too appealed to the inductive method to prove his point.

> But when we open our Bible to-day we open a book that is undergoing examination on the inductive method. Our generation is learning to read the Bible in the historical light, and let the book itself show what it is. We seek to discover how these utterances came to be made, and what they meant to the men who made them. The result is that the better we know the Bible in this manner, the less does it match the theory of an inspiration that im-

parts infallibility to all its statements, or even to all its utterances in the field of religion. There is no claim of such inspiration, and there is no proof of it. The high doctrine proves untenable, and consequently it is passing out of sight.[23]

Traditional views of inspiration tied Christians too closely to the text. "We are compelled to grasp at words. Precision is indispensable: uncertainty checks us, and inaccuracy admitted to our work would vitiate the whole. . . . Textual criticism confirms our general confidence, but slays our hope of absolute perfection."[24] Furthermore, if even half the conclusions of historical criticism were true, traditionalists might be "sorely tempted to lie in the interest of truth by denying or ignoring plain facts because they undermine [their] method or endanger [their] theology."[25]

For Clarke inspiration was not verbal, nor revelation propositional. God had inspired ideas, principles, and concepts, not words. He had allowed them to be somewhat entangled with primitive or even unChristian elements. One must recognize different levels of inspiration in Scripture, Clarke went on, and be willing to separate the good from the bad. Clarke was sure of one thing: theologians could no longer use the Bible in the way they had in the past. For practitioners of the modern perspective, "proof-texting" was passé.

Clarke believed that the proof–text approach to theology was inextricably tied to the doctrine of inerrancy. "If all is solidly divine, of course a citation is a proof."[26] Since inerrantists accepted the Bible as equally inspired throughout, they felt free to use all of it to construct their theology. In standard theology texts, Clarke observed, it is customary to find lists of Scripture references as doctrinal proofs. While he admitted that sometimes such selections were carefully done and theologically appropriate, Clarke asserted that very often they were not. Furthermore, if trained theologians could easily abuse the proof–text method, then only God knows how the Bible suffers at the hands of lay people. They cite a passage here, call on a passage there, assuming that they then have the mind of God on the matter. Clarke wanted to do away with proof–texting once and for all.

> Even if a proof–text method were a good method in itself, it could not be successfully employed now, since the texts of the Bible have suffered such serious though unintended distortion. One thing is certain. Theology must seize upon the help of criticism and history and exegesis and all else that can show what the Bible really means. But no one of these has a word to say in favor of continuing in the old, easy, superficial proof–text method which has come from taking the Scriptures as authoritative throughout. Theology has a deeper and harder work to do.[27]

In other words, the Bible had become too complicated to put into the hands of anybody but the experts. Common Christians needed theologians, historians, critics, and exegetes "to show what the Bible really means."

Naturally, until the experts completed their "deeper and harder work," most Christians were left high and dry. Clarke acknowledged that the average pastor was beginning to feel a bit unsure of himself. Thanks to the higher criticism, the Bible had become "more or less an unsolved problem." The ordinary minister remained loyal to the Scriptures and would not think of undermining his people's confidence in them. He longed to preach and teach authoritatively from the Bible but was now uncertain if he could. "Criticism has altered the book for his use, but just how far he does not know."[28]

Clarke knew that changing from one paradigm to another would be difficult and unsettling for many people. But he was confident that the church would be better for it. What should pastors and lay people do until theologians and biblical scholars finished their reconstructive work? They should follow their best Christian instincts.

> Frankly and fearlessly differentiate the Bible into its elements, Christian, Jewish, historical, traditional, and whatever they may be. Let the mountains rise, let the valleys sink, to the place that God had ordained for them. Set by itself that body of truth which our Savior taught concerning God and religion, and then give glory where glory is due. Put the Bible to its true use, as servant of Jesus Christ.[29]

Clarke believed that Christians would be able to adapt themselves to this new approach to the Bible. He had come to accept the new conviction that the Scripture was a very human book, complete with errors of every kind, through which God none the less still spoke. Though believers could no longer approach the Bible in the old way and with the old confidence, they would soon learn to make the necessary distinctions and to trust their own religious experience.

Needless to say, not everyone was willing to go along. Conservative Protestants found Clarke's eagerness to live with an errant Bible hard to understand. If the Bible has *any* mistakes, how can it be from God? If the critics are right about the multiple authorship of the Pentateuch, what about Jesus' apparent endorsement of Mosaic authorship?[30] If the apostles are wrong about some of the details of Jesus' life, why should anyone believe their statements about his atoning death or resurrection? For many evangelicals the integrity of God and the deity of Jesus Christ were riding

on the answers to those questions. Without an inerrant Bible, there could
be no religious certainty at all.

As a result, fundamentalists worked hard to maintain the old paradigm.
In no way should their defense be termed anti-intellectual, especially in the
years before World War I. Their views had been considered respectable
and even "scientific" throughout the nineteenth century. In fact before
1920 fundamentalists had no trouble finding reputable scholars to back up
their positions.[31] When conservatives published *The Fundamentals* in an
attempt to stem the liberal tide, they included articles from some of the
world's best known biblical specialists who were still dubious about the
"assured results" of higher criticism.[32] Such scholars had nothing against
higher criticism per se; they simply objected to the lack of hard evidence
to substantiate many of the higher critics' conclusions. W. H. Griffith
Thomas spoke for many conservatives:

> We do not question for an instant the right of Biblical criticism considered
> in itself. On the contrary, it is a necessity for all who use the Bible to be
> "critics" in the sense of constantly using their "judgment" on what is be-
> fore them. What is called "higher" criticism is not only a legitimate but a
> necessary method for all Christians, for by its use we are able to discover
> the facts and the form of the Old Testament Scriptures. Our hesitation,
> consequently, is not intended to apply to the method, but to what is be-
> lieved to be an illegitimate, unscientific, and unhistorical use of it. In fact,
> we base our objections to much modern criticism of the Old Testament on
> what we regard as a proper use of a true higher criticism.[33]

This is no anti-intellectual dodge. Conservative scholars sincerely believed that they could beat the higher critics at their own game. Higher
criticism was not critical enough. It based its conclusions on the slimmest
of evidence and twisted what evidence it had to fit its foregone conclusions,
which were usually predisposed against the Bible as a supernatural revelation. Destructive criticism was always *deductive,* then, not inductive. Nothing pleased conservatives more than the way higher critics kept changing
their minds. Their "assured results" were evidently not as certain as they
had supposed.[34]

From the fundamentalists' point of view, then, the old convictions were
intellectually superior to the new one. Accordingly, there was no reason to
repudiate traditional views of biblical inspiration and authority. Likewise
there was no need to reject the older use of the Scriptures in theology.
When carefully and properly done, there was nothing wrong with proof–

texting. Writing in *The Fundamentals,* Canon Dyson Hague of Toronto complained that the higher criticism threatened "the Christian system of doctrine and the whole fabric of systematic theology." Until criticism cast doubt on the approach, "any text from any part of the Bible was accepted as a proof–text for the establishment of any truth of Christian teaching, and a statement from the Bible was considered an end of controversy." Now if the critics get their way,

> The Christian system . . . will have to be re-adjusted if not revolution-ized, every text and chapter and book will have to be inspected and an-alyzed in the light of its date, and origin, and circumstances, and author-ship, and so on, and only after it has passed the examining board of the modern Franco-Dutch-German criticism will it be allowed to stand as a proof–text for the establishment of any Christian doctrine.[35]

Fundamentalists preferred to proof–text. They continued citing chapter and verse with, as Clarke had observed, mixed results. Probably the most blatant example of proof–texting among fundamentalists was the "Bible Reading." Coming out of the Holiness and Bible Conference movements, this approach consisted of stringing together a series of scriptural passages on a given topic. According to an expert, to do a Bible Reading one must "select some word . . . and with the aid of a good Concordance, mark down . . . the references to the subject under discussion . . . thus pre-senting all the Holy Ghost has been pleased to reveal on the topic."[36] No Bible conference was complete without Bible Readings; and many pastors and their congregations preferred public Bible Readings to regular ser-mons. But basically, this method was geared to lay people. Anyone with a concordance could pile passage upon passage and learn a lot in the pro-cess.[37]

A more sophisticated kind of proof–texting can be seen in Reuben A. Torrey's *What the Bible Teaches,* which came out in a number of editions between 1898 and 1933. In over five hundred pages, the popular teacher from Moody Bible Institute and the Bible Institute of Los Angeles put to-gether various theological propositions with their scriptural proofs. "This work is simply an attempt at a careful, unbiased, systematic, thoroughgo-ing, inductive study and statement of Bible truth. . . . The material con-tained in the Bible is brought together, carefully scrutinized, and then what is seen to be contained in it stated in the most exact terms possible." To liberal scholars Torrey's approach was the height of theological naïveté. From Torrey's perspective, "the methods of modern science are applied to Bible study–thorough analysis followed by careful synthesis."[38]

In addition to maintaining traditional views of biblical inspiration and the proof–text approach to theology, fundamentalists did their best to keep the Bible in the hands of common believers. Liberals were taking the Bible away from the church, causing a decline in personal Bible reading and family worship.[39] The Scriptures were slipping from the hands of ordinary Christians. As early as 1893 one pastor complained that the critics had forgotten that the Bible was dear to common folk and warned them not to "take it away until they have something better to give them than 'a series of tentative suggestions.' "[40] A few years later A. T. Pierson remarked that "like Romanism, [higher criticism] practically removes the Word of God from the common people by assuming that only scholars can interpret it; while Rome puts a priest between a man and the Word, criticism puts an educated expositor between the believer and his Bible."[41]

The higher criticism notwithstanding, fundamentalists believed that lay people could still read the Bible for themselves. According to William Evans, who taught the Bible at Moody Bible Institute and the Bible Institute of Los Angeles after the turn of the century,

> an English Bible; a devout and earnest spirit; a reverential and teachable mind; a willingness to do the will of God as it is revealed in the increasing knowledge of the Scriptures; the pursuance of a right, though simple method of reading and study—these are the essentials for profit and pleasure in Bible study.[42]

Certainly one did not have to be a scholar to study the Scriptures. Greek and Hebrew were unnecessary. James M. Gray, the president of Moody Bible Institute, could use both languages himself, but he downplayed their importance. While scholars may have an advantage in more technical areas, one must remember that the Bible was written for plain people.[43] Similarly, A. T. Pierson advised that "the humblest reader might, without any other guide than the Bible itself, by careful, prayerful searching, come to know the Word, exploring its contents till he became another Apollos, mighty in the Scriptures."[44]

Such statements are extraordinary in light of the warnings placed on popular Bible study methods by men like William Newton Clarke. But fundamentalist Bible teachers made them constantly. One pastor rather sarcastically inquired, "Have we to await a communication from Tübingen or a telegram from Oxford before we can read the Bible?"[45] Of course not. The simplest believer had something going for him that many of the best scholars did not: the guidance of the Holy Spirit. In fact, because of the Spirit's assistance, lay people frequently understood what trained scholars could not.[46] Thus the conclusions of the spiritually prepared but untutored Bible reader were preferrable to the learned but spiritually deficient professor. As R. A. Torrey observed, "In ninety-nine out of a hundred cases, the meaning that the plain man gets out of the Bible is the correct one."[47]

Despite the rhetoric, fundamentalist Bible teachers did not merely turn everyone loose to do his own thing. There was a right way and a wrong way to study the Bible. The Bible was understandable; but it was not always obvious. According to William Evans, "The Bible is a book that requires study. No superficial reading of its contents will reveal its hidden depths. We must dig deep if we would find its rich treasures. . . . The Bible requires not study merely, but methodical study. . . . We must have a system or we study in vain."[48]

Probably the most popular method of Bible study used by fundamentalists was James M. Gray's "synthetic method." As the name implies, "the synthetic study of the Bible . . . is an attempt to put it together rather than to take it apart."[49] Taking the Bible apart was higher criticism's greatest sin. Gray liked to tell A. J. Gordon's story about a disgruntled Baptist deacon who disliked his new preacher. "He's the best man I ever seen to take the Bible apart, but he don't know the first thing about putting it back together again."[50]

Gray developed his system in the 1890s, during his part-time teaching stints at Moody Bible Institute. D. L. Moody saw how the method helped his students and encouraged Gray to perfect it and make it available to more people. Gray took his mentor's advice and published a series of synthetic Bible studies in the *Union Gospel News* in 1900. In 1904 he published *How To Master the English Bible,* in which he explained the method in more detail.[51]

According to the synthetic method one must first see the Bible in its fullness before examining its parts. Gray was convinced that unless the student viewed the panorama of Scripture, he would get lost or be led astray by more detailed study. Therefore, Gray suggested reading the Bible through, from Genesis to Revelation, each book being read at a single sitting. After completing this enormous assignment, the student may begin a more careful reading of each book.

Gray advised a five-step approach to individual book study: 1) read the book entirely at one sitting; 2) read it continuously (i.e., without regard to chapter or verse divisions); 3) read it repeatedly until one has a feel for the flow of the book; 4) read it independently of any outside aid or authority; and 5) read it prayerfully. Once the whole was in hand, one could turn one's attention to a more detailed study of its component parts, the development of its themes, and even the meaning of individual words or phrases. After studying a number of books in this way, one would be able to consider common doctrines, overlapping ideas, and so on.[52]

Gray's synthetic method caught on. Though they rarely gave him a footnote, other fundamentalist Bible teachers used his techniques. William Evans taught what he called the "book-method of Bible study" and in language that sounds strangely familiar told his students to read each book through at one sitting, read it over and over again, read it prayerfully, and read it without any outside helps.[53] W. H. Griffith Thomas trained lay people to begin with the whole Bible, then work down to smaller units in a similar way.[54] So did I. M. Haldeman, A. C. Dixon, and A. T. Dixon.[55]

These teachers shared certain assumptions. They believed that the Bible was totally inspired, that it should be taken literally whenever possible, and that an inductive method of Bible study eliminated personal bias and provided a foundation on which to build interpretation. According to James Gray, "The facts must come first and interpretation afterwards. To a great extent, if we get the facts, the interpretation will take care of itself."[56]

By World War I these Bible study techniques had spread throughout the fundamentalist movement, thanks especially to the influence of the Bible institutes.[57] In 1899, for example, Moody Bible Institute helped to organize the Bible Institute Colportage Association, which distributed Bible study manuals by Gray, Evans, Griffith Thomas, and others.[58] The Institute's widely circulated magazines carried Bible studies as part of their regular format.[59] After 1912 the Moody Correspondence School required students to master Gray's synthetic method.[60] By 1928 Moody's extension department reached a reported quarter of a million people through its sponsored Bible conferences around the country.[61] Consequently, the fundamentalist Bible study methods that were developed before World War I continued through the ranks well into the twenties and beyond.[62]

It is safe to conclude that fundamentalists saw themselves as champions of the traditional approach to the Bible, heirs of the nineteenth-century evangelical tradition. They resisted the threats of the new approach to the Bible and believed that they had saved the Bible for the church. As we have seen, fundamentalists did maintain the old perspective even after the new one gained wide acceptance. But in some subtle and rather ironic ways, the fundamentalist use of the Bible was not what it seemed.

For one thing, despite the claims that lay people could study the Bible for themselves, their teachers rarely let them. When Gray, for instance, said that students must first see the Scriptures as a whole, he really meant that they should view them in *dispensational* terms. Originating in Great Britain in the 1830s and spreading to America through various means, including the *Scofield Reference Bible,*[63] dispensationalism is an intricate hermeneutic which "rightly divides the Word of truth" into different periods and divine programs and then rejoins them in a complicated way. In 1913 Gray told his students, "Get the whole Bible . . . in its dispensational relations, and then you can study it . . . to your heart's content."[64] When he finally published his own *Synthetic Bible Studies,* everything was arranged in a full-blown dispensational system.[65]

Needless to say, not every fundamentalist was a dispensationalist; but most of those who taught in the Bible institutes and conducted popular Bible teaching ministries were. They were convinced that dispensationalism provided a superior perspective from which to study the Bible and often claimed that non-dispensationalists were incapable of seeing the Scriptures in their fullness. According to I. M. Haldeman, "unless [the Bible student] understands dispensational truth, he will never fully lay hold of Bible doctrine."[66]

Few people would deny fundamentalists the privilege of reading the Bible in dispensational terms if they are so inclined. But many would deny that they are being inductive when they do. Whatever may be said for the virtues of a dispensational hermeneutic, the system is anything but inductive. How many students using purely inductive methods would conclude that the Lord's Prayer or the Sermon on the Mount were intended for Jews in the millennium and not for Christians in this age?[67] Most people would require extensive coaxing to arrive at such conclusions.

Ironically, by teaching an inductive method, then insisting that it would not work apart from an elaborate dispensational system, fundamentalist teachers made their students dependent on them for their biblical literacy. Since most lay people could not arrive at a dispensational understanding of the Bible on their own, they had to rely on their instructors to unravel the intricacies of the system. While assuring common Christians that they did not need scholarly help in Bible study, these teachers initiated them into a complicated system that most people could never maneuver without considerable assistance. In the final analysis, there is something incongruous about fundamentalists who say that they can read the Bible by themselves, then pore over Scofield's notes in order to discover what the text really means.

When fundamentalist leaders circumscribed the use of the Bible in this way, they demonstrated that the old paradigm was in more trouble than they were willing to admit. As numerous scholars have pointed out, much of nineteenth-century evangelical theology was buttressed—sometimes even unconsciously—by the Scottish Common Sense philosophy. According to this world-view, truth was pretty much the same for everybody everywhere. All people possessed a kind of pre-rational intuition for distinguishing right from wrong, truth from falsehood, and facts from illusion. Everyone could know facts directly, with a minimum of distortion and speculation, and could trust their observations of the world. Based on these assumptions, evangelicals wrote books on "Christian evidences," certain that people of good will and a minimum of intelligence could understand and accept them. Common Sense meant there was common ground between all kinds of people. And most of evangelical theology was done with the confidence that people—believers and unbelievers alike—knew a fact when they saw one and could recognize the truth if they wanted to.

It is not surprising, then, that believers in Common Sense were deeply troubled by the rise of new ideas in religion. As Marsden has pointed out, "The common sense tradition in America assumed a national consensus of rationality and morality wed to Protestant religion and the revival. This tradition provided a basis for holding on to the Christian faith at all costs—which of course was the principle issue. Yet it provided no fully adequate way to account for the collapse of the consensus."[68] If there was so much Common Sense around, why was there so much obvious error, especially among those who claimed to be open to the truth? Christians with this world-view did not have too many alternatives. Since they could not argue that people were basically irrational and incapable of knowing the truth, they had to resort to moral or spiritual explanations. Charles Blanchard, a leading fundamentalist educator, found it hard to believe that religious apostasy could ever come from common folks. The fault, then, must lie with morally defective teachers. "Ministers and teachers of theology seem to be the ones who lead the Church into error, and the more these are paid, the longer vacations they have, the higher positions they obtain, the more unfaithful to God and his Church they seem to become."[69] The only other possible explanation was that these teachers had "poisoned their nervous systems and injured their minds" by using alcohol and tobacco.

Fundamentalists of the Common Sense tradition were even less able to account for differences of opinion in their own ranks. None of the popular Bible study manuals dealt with the possibility that Christians who read the Bible openly, honestly, and prayerfully might disagree about what it meant.

How could they when the Bible was so clear and believers had the Holy Spirit as teacher and guide? In effect, Bible teachers oversold the perspicuity of the Bible and the role of the Spirit in interpretation to such an extent that many fundamentalists were unable to explain, let alone tolerate, other points of view.

This problem may be at the root of some of fundamentalism's intolerance. Since their use of the Bible did not really prepare them to arbitrate between rival positions, many fundamentalists chose to align themselves with a particular Bible teacher (or group of them who all agreed with each other), then eliminate or ignore all other perspectives. During times of theological subversion, any deviation from the "obvious" truth of God's Word was viewed with the deepest suspicion. Dissenters, even fundamentalist ones, must be deviates.

Naturally one should not put all the blame for fundamentalist combativeness on these Bible study techniques. Personal attitudes and the understandable fear that apostasy was on the rise played significant roles too. But fundamentalists' unwillingness to expect or provide for sincere differences of opinion among themselves seems to be at least partially responsible for the movement's militancy. As a result, fundamentalists have quarrelled with each other nearly as much as they have quarrelled with their enemies.[70]

To sum up, the fundamentalist use of the Bible was like a two-edged sword. It cut both ways. While fundamentalists claimed to be preserving the old paradigm, they were unintentionally undermining it. As dispensationalism became more dominant in militant fundamentalist circles in the 1920s, people actually had less control over their Bibles than before. Because of the intricacies of their "inductive" system, fundamentalist lay people were only slightly less reliant on their Bible teachers than liberal lay people were on the higher critics.

One should not look for anything sinister or underhanded here. Fundamentalist teachers did nothing more than their liberal counterparts. Modernists like Henry Ward Beecher, Washington Gladden, Phillips Brooks, William Newton Clarke, and Harry Emerson Fosdick helped their people adjust to changing times. So did fundamentalists like James Gray, William Evans, Reuben Torrey, and John Roach Straton. The church has always relied on its teachers to transmit the faith, interpret the creeds, and explain the difficult parts of the Bible. This is especially true during times of transition and uncertainty. Their rhetoric aside, fundamentalists needed help like everyone else. While it was relatively easy for the rank and file to believe in biblical inerrancy, it was nearly impossible for most of them to prove it. It was enough to know that there were trusted teachers who could.[71] In this way, at least, fundamentalist and liberal leaders acted pretty much the same: they helped their followers handle hard times and hang on to what they believed were the essentials of the faith.

The scandal in the fundamentalist use of the Bible, if there is one, is that most fundamentalists did not—and still do not—see the inconsistency between their ideology and their practice. Early fundamentalist leaders fought hard to keep the Bible accessible to ordinary believers but in the end made them nearly totally dependent on themselves. In order to save the old paradigm, they had to hedge it in. Though they still talked a lot about Common Sense, fundamentalists no longer could trust people to come to their own conclusions. Again according to Kuhn, this is only to be expected during a "scientific revolution." When people start "responding to a different world," leaders must be certain that their followers keep looking in the right places and finding what they are supposed to find.

The ultimate irony of the fundamentalist approach to the Scriptures is that it has produced so little really independent Bible study. While fundamentalist still claim that they are capable of doing it for themselves, most of them still derive their greatest "blessing" from hearing some notable Bible teacher tell them what the Bible really means.

NOTES

1. Stewart G. Cole, *The History of Fundamentalism* (New York: Richard R. Smith, 1931); H. Richard Niebuhr, "Fundamentalism," *Encyclopedia of Social Sciences* (New York, 1937), VI: 526–27.

2. Norman F. Furniss, *The Fundamentalist Controversy, 1918–1931* (New Haven: Yale University Press, 1954); Ray Ginger, *Six Days or Forever? Tennessee v. John Thomas Scopes* (Boston: Beacon Press, 1958).

3. Richard Hofstadter, *Anti-Intellectualism in American Life* (New York: Vintage Books, 1962); see also his *The Paranoid Style in American Politics* (Chicago: University of Chicago Press, 1979; orig. 1963).

4. Paul Carter, "The Fundamentalist Defense of the Faith," *Change and Continuity in Twentieth-Century America: The 1920s,* John Braeman, Robert Bremner, David Brody, eds. (Columbus: Ohio State University Press, 1968), pp. 179–214.

5. Ernest R. Sandeen, *The Roots of Fundamentalism* (Chicago: University of Chicago Press, 1970).

6. George M. Marsden, *Fundamentalism and American Culture: The Shaping of Twentieth-Century Evangelicalism, 1870–1925* (New York: Oxford University Press, 1980), p. 4.

7. See, for example, Stephen Neill, *The Interpretation of the New Testament, 1861–1961* (London: Oxford University Press, 1964); Robert M. Grant, *A Short History of the Interpretation of the Bible* (New York: Macmillan, 1963).

118   THE BIBLE IN AMERICA

8. Thomas Kuhn, *The Structure of Scientific Revolutions,* 2d ed. (Chicago: University of Chicago Press, 1970). For what other scholars say about Kuhn's thesis, see Gary Gutting, ed., *Paradigms and Revolutions* (South Bend: University of Notre Dame Press, 1980).

9. Marsden, *Fundamentalism and American Culture,* p. 215.

10. See James R. Moore, *The Post-Darwinian Controversies: A Study of the Protestant Struggle To Come to Terms with Darwin in Great Britain and America, 1870–1900* (London: Cambridge University Press, 1979); Paul E. Boller, Jr., *American Thought in Transition: The Impact of Evolutionary Naturalism, 1865–1900* (Chicago: Rand McNally, 1969).

11. Kuhn, *The Structure of Scientific Revolutions,* p. 111.

12. William Newton Clarke, *Sixty Years with the Bible* (New York: Scribner's, 1909), p. 42.

13. Norman Maring, "Baptists and Changing Views of the Bible, 1865–1918 (Part I)," *Foundations,* I (July 1958), 52–75.

14. *Ibid.,* p. 60.

15. Clarke, *Sixty Years with the Bible,* p. 47.

16. For helpful overviews of the history of higher criticism in America, see Ira V. Brown, "The Higher Criticism Comes to America, 1800–1900," *Journal of the Presbyterian Historical Society,* 38 (December 1960), 193–211; Jerry W. Brown, *The Rise of Biblical Criticism in America, 1800–1870* (Middletown, Conn.: Wesleyan University Press, 1969).

17. Clarke, *Sixty Years with the Bible,* pp. 176–77.

18. William Newton Clarke, *An Outline of Christian Theology* (New York: Scribner's, 1898).

19. These lectures were eventually published. William Newton Clarke, *The Use of the Scriptures in Theology* (Edinburgh: T. & T. Clark, 1907).

20. Theodore Dwight Bozeman, *Protestants in an Age of Science: The Baconian Ideal and Antebellum American Religious Thought* (Chapel Hill: University of North Carolina Press, 1977); S. A. Grave, *The Scottish Philosophy of Common Sense* (Westport, Conn.: Greenwood Press, 1973); John C. Vander Stelt, *Philosophy and Scripture: A Study in Old Princeton and Westminster Theology* (Marlton, N.J.: Mack Publishing Company, 1978), pp. 1–200; Jack B. Rogers and Donald K. McKim, *The Authority and Interpretation of the Bible: An Historical Approach* (New York: Harper and Row, 1979), pp. 200–369. But see also the careful qualifications to these authors in Marsden's essay in this volume, fns. 25, 27, 35.

21. The classic expression of the Princeton doctrine of inerrancy is A. A. Hodge and B. B. Warfield, "Inspiration," *Presbyterian Review,* 2 (1881), 225–38.

22. Charles Hodge, *Systematic Theology* (New York: Scribner, Armstrong and Company, 1873), 1:10.

23. Clarke, *The Use of the Scriptures in Theology,* pp. 25–26.

24. *Ibid.,* p. 146.

25. *Ibid.,* p. 147.

26. *Ibid.,* p. 31.

27. *Ibid.,* pp. 35–36.

28. *Ibid.,* p. 161.

29. *Ibid.,* pp. 163–64.

30. Leander Munhall, *The Highest Critics vs. the Higher Critics* (Philadelphia: E. & R. Munhall, 1896), p. 205; Franklin Johnson, "Fallacies of the Higher

Criticism," *Higher Criticism and the New Theology,* R. A. Torrey, ed. (New York: Gospel Publishing House, 1911), p. 110. A. T. Pierson, "Inspiration, Prophecy, and Higher Criticism," *Our Hope,* 5 (June 1899), 427.

31. For example, William H. Green, *The Higher Criticism of the Pentateuch* (New York: Scribner's, 1902); James Orr, *The Problem of the Old Testament* (New York: Scribner's, 1907); Sir Robert Anderson, *The Bible and Modern Criticism* (London: Hodder and Stoughton, 1903).

32. R. A. Torrey, A. C. Dixon, *et al.,* eds., *The Fundamentals* (Los Angeles: Bible Institute of Los Angeles, 1917), vol. I.

33. W. H. Griffith Thomas, "Old Testament Criticism and New Testament Christianity," *ibid.,* I:128.

34. Torrey, *The Fundamentals,* I:55–333.

35. Canon Dyson Hague, "The History of the Higher Criticism," *The Fundamentals,* I:33.

36. James H. Brookes, *The Truth,* 5 (1879), 314; *ibid.,* 23 (1897), 80–82.

37. The method was advocated and demonstrated in I. M. Haldeman, *How To Study the Bible* (New York: Charles C. Cook, 1904), pp. 481–84; see also Nancy Hardesty, Lucille Sider Dayton, and Donald W. Dayton, "Women in the Holiness Movement: Feminism in the Evangelical Tradition," *Women of Spirit,* Rosemary Ruether and Eleanor McLaughlin, eds. (New York: Simon and Schuster, 1979), p. 247; Sandeen, *The Roots of Fundamentalism,* pp. 72, 136–39; Timothy P. Weber, *Living in the Shadow of the Second Coming: American Premillennialism, 1875–1925* (New York: Oxford University Press, 1979), pp. 37–38.

38. Reuben A. Torrey, *What the Bible Teaches* (New York: Revell, 1898–1933), p. 1.

39. Johnson, "Fallacies of the Higher Criticism," p. 111; Munhall, *The Highest Critics . . . ,* pp. 204–6, 220; F. Bettex, "The Bible and Modern Criticism," *The Fundamentals,* I:89–92. Harold Lindsell, a current champion of inerrancy, makes the same charge in Harold Lindsell, *The Bible in the Balance* (Grand Rapids, Mich.: Zondervan, 1979), p. 301.

40. Joseph Parker, *None Like It* (New York: Revell, 1893), pp. 72–73, 244.

41. A. T. Pierson, "Antagonism to the Bible," *Our Hope,* 15 (January 1909), 475.

42. William Evans, *Outline Study of the Bible* (Chicago: Bible Institute Colportage Association, 1913), pp. 15–16.

43. James M. Gray, "Blasting at the Rock of Ages," *The Institute Tie,* 10 (October 1909), 116–17.

44. A. T. Pierson, *Knowing the Scriptures* (New York: Gospel Publishing House, 1910), pp. 2–3.

45. Parker, *None Like It,* p. 73.

46. James M. Gray, *How To Master the English Bible* (Chicago: Bible Institute Colportage Association, 1904), pp. 49–50; W. H. Griffith Thomas, *Methods of Bible Study* (Chicago: Bible Institute Colportage Association, 1926), pp. 101–20; R. A. Torrey, *The Bible and Its Christ* (New York: Revell, 1906), pp. 39–40.

47. Reuben Torrey quoted in William McLoughlin, *Modern Revivalism* (New York: Ronald Press, 1959), p. 372.

48. Evans, *Outline Study of the Bible,* pp. 14–15. See also Griffith Thomas, *Methods of Bible Study,* p. 2.

51. *Ibid., passim.*

50. *Ibid.,* pp. 31–32.

49. Gray, *How To Master the English Bible,* p. 32.

52. For another example of the synthetic method, see James M. Gray, "How To Master the English Bible," *The Institute Tie,* 1 (January 1901), 138. William M. Runyan, *Dr. Gray at Moody Bible Institute* (New York: Oxford University, 1935), pp. 64–79.

53. William Evans, *The Book-Method of Bible Study* (Chicago: Bible Institute Colportage Association, 1915). See also his *Outline Study of the Bible* for an example of the method used on a larger scale.

54. Griffith Thomas, *Methods of Bible Study*.

55. Haldeman, *How To Study the Bible;* A. C. Dixon, "The Scriptures," *The Fundamentals,* IV:264–72; Pierson, *Knowing the Scriptures;* see also A. T. Pierson, *Gods' Living Oracles* (London: James Nisbet, 1908).

56. James M. Gray, *Synthetic Bible Studies,* rev. ed. (New York: Revell, 1923), p. 11.

57. Gray, *How To Master the English Bible,* pp. 25–27.

58. Gene Getz, *MBI: The Story of Moody Bible Institute* (Chicago: Moody Press, 1969), pp. 229–36.

59. MBI's magazines have included the following: *The Institute Tie* (1900–1909); *The Christian Worker's Magazine* (1909–20); *The Moody Bible Institute Monthly* (1920–38); *The Moody Monthly* (1938–   ). Getz, *MBI,* pp. 254–64.

60. *Ibid.,* pp. 121–26.

61. *Ibid.,* p. 276.

62. Joel A. Carpenter, "A Shelter in the Time of Storm: Fundamentalist Institutions and the Rise of Evangelical Protestantism, 1929–1942," *Church History,* 49 (March 1980), 62–75.

63. C. I. Scofield, ed., *Scofield Reference Bible* (New York: Oxford University Press, 1909); see also Sandeen and Weber for overviews of the spread of dispensationalism in America.

64. James M. Gray, *Bible Problems Explained* (Chicago: Moody Press, [1913], 1941), pp. 18–19.

65. Gray, *Synthetic Bible Studies*.

66. Haldeman, *How To Study the Bible,* p. 7; see also Evans, *Outline Study of the Bible,* pp. 30–31; Pierson, *Knowing the Scriptures,* p. 431.

67. Gray, *Synthetic Bible Studies,* p. 193; *Scofield Bible* on Matthew 5–7.

68. Marsden, *Fundamentalism and American Culture,* pp. 220–21.

69. Charles Blanchard, quoted in *ibid.,* p. 220.

70. For instance, fundamentalists have fought over details of prophetic interpretation, the definition and extent of biblical "separation from the world," and the best tactics in the war against liberalism. See Sandeen, *The Roots of Fundamentalism,* pp. 208–32; Weber, *Living in the Shadow of the Second Coming,* pp. 162–66; Cole, *History of Fundamentalism,* pp. 65–97; George Dollar, *A History of Fundamentalism in America* (Greenville, S.C.: Bob Jones University, 1973), pp. 145–58.

71. Gray, *Bible Problems Explained;* R. A. Torrey, *Difficulties in the Bible* (New York: Revell, 1907).

VI

The Demise of Biblical Civilization

GRANT WACKER
University of North Carolina

> The fundamental principle of the higher criticism lies in the conception of the organic unity of all history.
>
> —W. Robertson Smith (1870)

> [Hodge] has no conception of the modern form of the problem.
>
> —W. Robertson Smith (1871)

I am uneasy with the title of this essay. The shadows that crossed the biblical civilization of the late nineteenth century were not, as many contemporaries believed, signs of impending winter. A long and genial Indian summer of biblical authority has persisted into the 1980s, and it may turn out that it is not an Indian summer at all, but the beginnings of a new spring.[1]

Nonetheless, no student of modern American culture could seriously say, as did English traveler James Bryce in 1888, that Americans are basically a religious people. "There are churches everywhere," he wrote, "and everywhere equally. . . . Possibly half of the native population go to church at least once every Sunday." Bryce even noted that the reading of the average family had a "religious tinge," for it largely consisted of religious books and magazines. The observations of Francis Grund, a Czech visitor in 1890, further highlight the contrast between our civilization and the civilization of the Gilded Age. "The religious habits of Americans form not only the basis of their private and public morals," said Grund, "but have become . . . thoroughly interwoven with . . . the very essence of their government." Indeed, religion "presides over their councils, aids in the execution of the laws, and adds to the dignity of the judges."[2]

We know of course that the United States has always been more culturally pluaristic than these comments suggest. Yet visitors like Bryce and Grund were not far wrong. A broadly evangelical Protestant consensus powerfully gripped mainstream culture—and there are good reasons to believe that this homogeneity was very much a product of common assumptions about what the Bible is and teaches.[3] We thus have to ask, when did the change come about? When and why did the biblical foundation begin to crumble?

For ordinary people the 1920s and 1930s seem to have been the decisive years of transition. In 1924, when Robert and Helen Lynd were doing their initial fieldwork in "Middletown," they found that the revival tradition was still strong. Most people claimed to believe in the exclusiveness of Christianity, the certainty of heaven and hell, the sacredness of the Bible, and the divinity of Jesus. When the Lynds returned a decade later, however, they found that the old beliefs had deteriorated to what they called an "unalert acceptance" of traditional verities. What the Lynds discovered, Richard H. Pells has said, is that during the inter-war years religion in America was transformed "from a set of beliefs to a social occasion." *Middletown* was, of course, only a laboratory study. Yet other scholars such as Winthrop S. Hudson, Robert T. Handy, and Edwin S. Gaustad—historians who have made it their business to see American religion in the long perspective—have similarly concluded that the 1920s and 1930s were a watershed. The average person did not disavow the Bible so much as simply abandon it. By the end of the 1930s, to borrow a phrase from Conrad Wright, Americans had grown accustomed to using "a secular rather than a theological vocabulary when issues really seem[ed] worth arguing about."[4]

Among the well-educated, on the other hand, erosion of confidence in the Bible had started at least a generation earlier. A sprinkling of biblical scholars such as Theodore Parker had been influenced by German criticism before the Civil War, but because of the war and other distractions, this initial interest had largely ebbed by 1870.[5] The real change seems to have begun, almost imperceptibly, in the late 1870s and 1880s. Washington Gladden described the beginnings of a new attitude toward many theological issues as "a going in the tops of the trees." The velocity of this wind rapidly accelerated: by the 1890s the gentle rustling in the trees had become a gale of critical innovation. Gaius Glenn Atkins, who lived through the entire period, said of the forty years following 1890 that "no other four decades, or forty decades either, in the history of Christian thought had seen so many and such momentous changes in fundamental religious attitudes." Although it is risky to isolate biblical from other forms of religious and theological scholarship, it seems safe to say that the biblical question, the problem of the source and the authority of Scripture, was the center of the storm. Atkins later remembered that other issues always seemed to be side issues: "the authority of the Bible was central."[6]

Professional biblical scholars did not constitute the whole army, but one could argue that they were the field marshals who led the revolution. Charles Augustus Briggs at Union Seminary in New York and William Rainey Harper at Yale and (later) the University of Chicago were probably the most illustrious. In the 1880s both went to the mat with formidable defenders of the old notions of verbal inspiration, infallibility, and inerrancy. In 1881 Briggs disputed the theory of verbal inspiration with Princeton's Archibald A. Hodge and Benjamin B. Warfield in a series of widely read articles in the *Presbyterian Review*. Seven years later Harper argued the documentary question with another Princeton dinosaur, William Henry Green, in the pages of *Hebraica,* a journal founded by Harper in 1884 as a forum for modern biblical scholarship. Crawford H. Toy at Harvard, George Foote Moore at Andover Seminary, Nathaniel Schmidt at Colgate Seminary, and in ancillary fields, James Henry Breasted at Chicago and Paul Haupt at Johns Hopkins were less theatrical than Briggs or Harper, but they too contributed mightily to the growth of a critical understanding of the Old Testament. There were fewer New Testament scholars of international stature in the United States, but early leaders included Benjamin Bacon at Yale, Ezra P. Gould at Colgate, and Ernest DeWitt Burton at Chicago.[7]

A mere listing of those theologians, church historians, and ministers of this period who argued that the Bible must be understood in a new way would run many pages. The most eminent of the academic theologians undoubtedly was Colgate's William Newton Clarke, whose *Outline of Systematic Theology* was one of the most widely read theology textbooks in the country. Other stars included Newman Smyth at Andover, Henry Churchill King at Oberlin, and George Burman Foster at Chicago. The modern conception of the Bible informed the work of church historians such as A. V. G. Allen at the Episcopal Theological School in Cambridge, A. C. McGiffert at Union, and Walter Rauschenbusch at Rochester. Scholarly ministers like George A. Gordon at Old South Church in Boston, Theodore T. Munger at United Church in New Haven, and David Swing at Central Music Hall in Chicago, as well as immensely popular preachers like Henry Ward Beecher at Brooklyn's Plymouth Church and Russell H. Conwell at Baptist Temple in Philadelphia, shared the same assumptions. The new attitude touched the thousands who each week read national religious newspapers such as Lyman Abbott's *Outlook* and Beecher's *Independent*.[8] William Rainey Harper, more than anyone, carried the message to ordinary folk through his semi-popular journal *The Hebrew Student,* as well as the Chautauqua Institution and the American Institute of Sacred Literature. The latter enrolled 10,000 students in its correspondence courses and prompted the formation of countless local study groups.[9] Then there was the publicity generated by the heresy trials and expulsions involving, among those already mentioned, Briggs, Toy, Schmidt, Gould, McGiffert, and Swing, as well as Henry Preserved Smith at Lane Seminary, Hinckley Mitchell at Boston University, Alexander Winchell at Vanderbilt, and Algernon Crapsey in the city of Rochester.[10] And finally we must remember the extraordinary influence of European scholars like Germany's Isaac Dorner and Scotland's William Robertson Smith, whose critical views gained a wide American audience because they seemed to be cushioned in warmly evangelical theology.[11]

To this point I have written in general terms about the new understanding of the Bible in the various fields of religious and theological scholarship. It is necessary now to think more precisely about the exact nature of the ideational revolution that took place in the late nineteenth century. Succinctly stated, for many—perhaps the majority of—persons well educated in the human or in the behavioral sciences, the Bible gradually ceased to be regarded as Scripture and came instead to be regarded as a mixture of Scripture and literature. Or, put another way, the Bible came to be seen as a human as well as a divine document.[12] Many changes followed. The new understanding meant, at the very least, that the Bible is not free from error, for it necessarily reflects the fallibilities of its human authors. And once it became clear that the Bible contains errors, it also became clear that other cherished notions about the nature of the Bible's authority would also have to be reworked—and in many cases defined and redefined until they bore little resemblance to the meanings traditionally ascribed to these terms.[13]

The embattled retreat of the closely related arguments for the inerrancy, infallibility, and verbal inspiration of the Bible is an important and still largely untold story.[14] Even that story, however, does not take us to the heart of the matter, for none of these concepts was at the center of the revolution. Rather, the real revolution appeared in a changed understanding of the nature of historical process. More precisely, it was a change in the way educated men and women understood the relationship between divinely sanctioned knowledge, on the one hand, and the flow of human history on the other.

Historians have ably charted the transformation of historical consciousness that so profoundly altered the intellectual landscape of the late nineteenth century. Morton White's *Social Thought in America* is probably the classic description, but Henry F. May's *The End of American Innocence* is more vivid. It was a process, says May, which saw "many different kinds of people cheerfully laying dynamite in the hidden cracks . . . [of] the massive walls of nineteenth-century America."[15]

That dynamite was, quite simply, the belief that culture is the product of its own history, that ideas, values, and institutions of every sort are wholly conditioned by the historical setting in which they exist. Among advanced social thinkers on both sides of the Atlantic belief quickly became first conviction, then assumption, then simply presupposition. It was classically illustrated in Justice Oliver Wendell Holmes's dictum that law—for centuries considered to be a coherent system of timeless juridical principles—is only a shrewd prediction of what a judge will do next. The same unflinching relativism was applied to sociology by Max Weber, to philosophy by John Dewey, to historical studies by J. B. Bury, and to political science by Charles Beard. There were exceptions, to be sure. A few eminent thinkers, of whom William James was one, refused to press the notion to such rigorous conclusions, and some of those who did, such as Ernst Troeltsch, left the back gate ajar for the re-entry of ideal values. But by and large the trend was unmistakable and irreversible. By 1931, when Kark Mannheim published his stunning article "The Sociology of Knowledge," most serious scholars in the human and behavioral sciences (except perhaps jursiprudence) were prepared to accept the radical relativism underlying the concept articulated by Mannheim. The assumption that historical process is the bed of human perception, that knowledge is the product of a fluid social process, had come to be the hallmark of the modern mind.[16]

The high noon of historical consciousness should not be dated too early. Georg Iggers, a leading authority on the subject, believes that historicism, as it was often called, was not carried to its logical conclusion until Max

Weber published his main work and, in any case, pure historicism did not saturate social thought in the West until after World War I.[17] Still, we can best see the total process by focusing upon the sunburst of the 1920s, before the spectre of Hitler drove many of the most hardheaded social thinkers back to the drawing boards.[18]

No one articulated the historical view of the world more compellingly than Cornell historian Carl L. Becker. In *The Heavenly City of the Eighteenth-Century Philosophers,* delivered as a series of lectures at Yale in 1931, Becker observed that to regard "all things in their historical setting appears, indeed, to be . . . [the] procedure of the modern mind. We do it without thinking," he noted, "because we can scarcely think at all without doing it." Becker was not simply talking about the way historians do their work, although that was part of it. He was really talking about the presuppositions of the modern mind. "What is peculiar to the modern mind," he said, "is the disposition and the determination to regard ideas and concepts, the truth of things as well as the things themselves, as changing entities . . . as points in an endless process." Here, then, was the fruit of radical historical consciousness: an insistence that every notion of truth and value and meaning is forged entirely within the process of history—a process, as Becker put it, not of linear development, but of "concurrence, renewed from moment to moment, of forces parting sooner or later on their way."[19]

Several historians have recently argued that scholars like Becker were not as consistent as they supposed.[20] But this was a failure of execution rather than intention. It does not force us significantly to qualify the judgment that between the 1880s and the 1920s the social disciplines were largely conquered by radically historical—or historicist—assumptions. Only thus, perhaps, are we able to understand the poignancy of Henry Adams's reflection that when he entered Harvard College in 1854 his conception of the world "stood nearer to the year 1 than to the year 1900."[21]

It is almost impossible to overestimate the impact of historical consciousness upon religious thought in the West. It could be argued that Protestant and Catholic liberalism was virtually defined by its sympathetic response to the historical understanding of culture. Liberals made their peace with modernity in various ways, but in the end they all insisted that God's self-revelation is mediated through the flow of history.[22] When we look at the foundation of biblical civilization in the 1880s and 1890s, it is apparent, I think, that the dynamite in the crevices was not the reconstruction of this or that particular doctrine. It was not the denial of the virgin birth of Jesus, nor the assertion of future probation for the heathen. Nor indeed was it the development of historical-critical method itself. Rather the dynamite that ultimately exploded the entire edifice was the assumption that knowledge of divine things, like knowledge of ordinary things, must be found squarely within the historical process or not at all.

The contrast to the assumptions undergirding conservative Protestantism could not have been sharper. Conservatives typically claimed that some parts of God's self-revelation escaped the grip of history. For them, knowledge of divine things was imposed upon history, mediated by human authors to be sure, but uncontaminated by the context in which it was received. This meant that revelation is subject to clarification, but not development. It also meant that the biblical writers were partly ahistorical persons, in significant respects transcending the setting of their lives in the ancient world.[23] Indeed, it could be argued that this insistence that the method and content of revelation were not a function merely of historical processes stood at the core of what came to be known, especially in the United States, as fundamentalism.[24]

It is important to stress the fact that conservatives did not necessarily lack a sense of history, defined as a keen interest in the events of the past, especially the events recorded in Scripture. Nor did they necessarily lack historical sensitivity, defined as willingness or even eagerness to conform to the traditions of the Church. What they lacked, rather, was historical consciousness: the recognition that the meaning of events is given not from outside history, not anterior to and independent of the process, but forged wholly from within the process. The conservative world was filled with people and issues drawn from the past, but it was, in the last analysis, a world without a modern sense of history.

The way in which these contrasts found expression in popular religious culture is illustrated by two of the most influential and eloquent preachers of the Gilded Age. The first was Adoniram Judson Gordon, pastor of Boston's Clarendon Street (Baptist) Church and the founder of what are now Gordon College and Gordon-Conwell Theological Seminary. The other, already mentioned, was George A. Gordon, pastor of Boston's Old South (Congregational) Church and, after Phillips Brooks, the prince of the American pulpit.[25]

For A. J. Gordon, who represented the conservative understanding of the origin and nature of the Bible, God's self-revelation was thrust into history from outside history. It was an intrusion into the process. "We are to find in the *words* of Scripture," he argued, "the exact substance of what [the Holy Ghost] saith. Hence verbal inspiration seems absolutely essential for conveying to us the exact thought of God . . . Vary the language by the slightest modification, and you by so much vary the thought." Unlike many conservatives, especially later on, who would squirm when verbal inspiration was construed by its opponents to mean mechanical dictation, Gordon stood firm. "And what if one objects that this theory makes inspiration purely mechanical, and turns the writers of Scripture into stenographers? . . . It must be confessed that there is much in Scripture to support this view of the case."[26] For George Gordon, on the other hand, God's self-revelation does not cut across the sphere of ordinary experience but is mediated in and through the flow of experience. Thus he explained that revelation must be considered as "something presented to the human mind," but also, and equally importantly, as an "achievement by the [human mind]." He waved aside the orthodox conception of a "wholly non-human" and "bloodless revelation" as an abuse of the "mechanism of miracle."[27]

So much for the method by which divine knowledge is revealed. The question remained, where is divine knowledge to be found? Here the contrast between ahistorical and historical ways of seeing the world was even sharper. For A. J. Gordon, God's message is uniquely held in the Bible. There is, he judged, "abundant evidence" that the "inspiration of the apostles and scribes of the New Testament was not transmitted to successors" and not embodied anywhere except in the Bible. God has inspired only one book, "thereby separating it and setting it apart from all other books."[28] For George Gordon, on the other hand, the locus of revelation was not just the Bible, but the whole human historical process. "Events, facts, circumstances, persons, national movements, are the forms through which the Divine world affirms its reality." The self-disclosure of the Spirit of God operates, in short, through the "entire term of history."[29]

These Boston ministers are interesting because they illustrate the way in which slowly diverging presuppositions, like drifting continents, eventually broke apart the biblical foundation of the late nineteenth century. But if we leave it there the story is not complete. The Gordons are too tidy. Early in life each staked out a clearly defined theological turf and set up camp. More interesting—and, I suspect, more representative of the period—were the men and women who gradually moved from one camp to the other, sometimes willingly, sometimes not.

I have already indicated that William Newton Clarke's *Outline of Sys-*

tematic Theology was one of the most widely used theology textbooks of the late nineteenth century.[30] But Clarke's autobiographical reflections, brought together in 1910 in a charming little book called *Sixty Years with the Bible,* give a better sense of the flow of thought and feeling in the half-century between the Civil War and the First World War. When he entered college in the 1850s, Clarke recalled, "it was assumed, and to me was real, that in dealing with the Bible I had to do with God." He could not remember that as a student at Colgate he had ever explicitly subscribed to the theory of verbal inspiration, but in practice, he said, he had inherited its effects.

> I looked upon the Bible as so inspired by God that its writers were not capable of error. I did not feel myself at liberty to dissent from its teachings, to doubt the accuracy of its statements, or to question the validity of its reasonings . . . God's written requirements were presumably universal.[31]

Clarke soon jettisoned these ideas, adopting the view—so characteristic of the golden age of Protestant liberalism—that the Bible consists of the "precious memorials" of the faith of the early church. Thus, "instead of being dictated by the Bible, a man's theology should be inspired in him by the Bible." Even the words of Jesus, Clarke believed, should not be regarded as final deliverances but as general principles that disclose the divine nature. The "utterances of Jesus himself," he insisted, "enter into theology with their sure and glorious testimony, but they must enter through the medium of religion and experience . . . These testimonies to divine reality must enter into theology through life."[32]

What is particularly interesting about Clarke's pilgrimage is that it seems not to have been principally impelled by the encroachments of science, nor by the exposure of errors and contradictions within the Bible, although both factors were undoubtedly present. Rather, the autobiography reveals that the transformation was chiefly a response to, or a manifestation of, his deepening awareness of the historicity of all things human. As he saw it, "God could not possibly require the assent of all . . . to provisional statements of some past time, the nearest true that the times were ripe for, but certainly to be superseded, containing truth partly wrapped up in temporary forms." Yet for Clarke even this, the conditioning power of history, was not the heart of the problem. The real issue, using Giles Gunn's phrase, was the "interpretation of otherness." Is it possible to leap over twenty centuries of cultural process, and somehow repossess the intentionality of the biblical authors? To Clarke, it is absurd to suppose that one can.

> The fact is that absolutely perfect understanding of what a writer meant
> . . . can never be obtained. . . . The historical setting can never be per-
> fectly reproduced in the reader's mind. But even farther beyond reach is
> the inner work of interpretation. One man cannot . . . think [another's]
> thoughts after him: least of all can this be done when the other speaks out
> of another age and training. . . . It is one of the delusions of theologians
> to think that they have done it.[33]

It is important to note the progression of Clarke's logic. It was because
he was persuaded that it is impossible to interpret infallibly the thoughts of
another age that he came to the conclusion that the book itself could not
be infallible—and not the other way around. If God had intended to give
us an infallible standard, Clarke judged, God "should, and would, have
inspired to us the power of understanding it perfectly."[34]

William Newton Clarke's theological journey was not unusual, but it
was too linear, too self-assured, to be typical. A more characteristic route
was a brave though often confused determination to have it both ways. The
individuals who fitted this pattern took the problems raised by historical
consciousness with utmost seriousness because they knew that they had no
choice. At the same time, they clung to the conviction that the faith once
delivered to the saints somehow stands above the vicissitudes of historical
process. The twists and turns in the spiritual odyssey of Augustus H.
Strong illustrate the dilemma of an honest man trapped in a vast process of
cultural realignment.

Strong reigned over the Rochester Theological Seminary for the forty
years from 1872 to 1912, and at one time or another led every major
Baptist organization in the North. He fathered a ponderous *Systematic
Theology* which, after eight editions (and now in its thirtieth printing) may
have been even more widely read than Clarke's. At the turn of the century
Strong was, in short, one of the most influential figures in American Protestantism, though he is now largely forgotten.[35]

Historians of American religion have never known quite what to do
with Strong. Some have called him an irenic fundamentalist, some have
suggested he was a closet liberal, and at least one has intimated that he
was simply befuddled.[36] The difficulty in classifying Strong stems from the
fact that as he grew older he also grew more determined to have things
both ways. Increasingly, he longed to appropriate the modern understanding of religious knowledge as a historical product, but at the same time he
resolved always to be, as he phrased it, a "great believer" in the cardinal
doctrines of Reformed Protestant orthodoxy.[37]

Through the 1870s and 1880s, Strong, like most evangelicals, was almost untouched by the going in the treetops. He rebuked biblical critics like Crawford H. Toy, who were motivated, he thought, not by strictly "literary considerations," nor by the "conclusion of science," but by a desire "to get rid of the supernatural." He strongly suspected that it was their assumptions, rather than their empirical findings, that led them to discover in Scripture a "concoction of fables."[38]

But early in the 1890s something started to stir in the immense and immovable edifice entombed in the first six editions of the *Systematic Theology*. In retrospect it seems clear that Strong had somehow caught a glimpse of process and movement that was at once profoundly religious and profoundly historical. The vision bathed every aspects of his thinking in a new light. He boasted that he had "outgrown the old scholastic terminology of substance and qualities" and had "gone back to the far simpler and more scriptural category of life and its powers." Again and again Strong declared that Christ is immanent in historical process, and to fail to see Christ in the "whole continuous process of history" is "to substitute a sort of half-atheism for real theism." "Our modern theology has immensely gained in candor and insight," he readily admitted, "by acknowledging that the same method of human growth which was adopted by the incarnate Word was also adopted in the production of this written word." Strong warned the Rochester trustees that "modern scholarship has modified our ideas with regard to the method of inspiration," and he confided to his children that he was "prepared now to acknowledge all that the higher criticism can prove as to the composition of the sacred documents."[39]

But it was so much easier said than done. Readers of Strong's later works, and especially the mammoth eighth edition of the *Systematic Theology*, published in 1907, found them strewn with signs of intellectual turmoil, if not fundamental confusion. One of many problems was the jungle of contradictions regarding the Bible's inerrancy.

> Do I say that there are errors in matters of historical details, errors in New Testament translation from the Hebrew, errors in exegesis, errors in Logic? I say nothing of the kind.

> Science has not yet shown any fairly interpreted passage of Scripture to be untrue.

Yet repeatedly Strong referred to "imperfections of detail"; "slight imperfections . . . of merely secular knowledge"; freedom from "essential error." He even allowed that Scripture's authority is "entirely consistent with its gradual evolution and with great imperfection in its essential parts."[40]

Strong's observations on the Bible's mode of composition are equally bewildering. He admitted the composite origin of the Pentateuch—but also claimed without flinching that the "sixty-six books . . . [and] forty writers" of the Bible "constitute a consistent system." He conceded that some or most of the books of the Bible may have been written at different times and by different authors than traditionally thought—but scored William Rainey Harper for esteeming "modern inspiration as better than that which is three thousand . . . years old."[41]

After a time Strong begins to remind us of the paunchy, middle-aged veteran who refuses to admit that the old uniform is too tight. With a lot of tugging we probably could squeeze all these opinions into a single suit. But it would not be worth the effort, for the simple truth is that Strong had come to intellectual maturity in the 1850s and 1860s, when critical biblical scholarship scarcely existed, not to mention real historical consciousness. In 1907 he was seventy-one years old, and obviously twisting in the wind. Yet he lived on to a great age, and as the years passed and he was swept into the thickening haze of the fundamentalist controversy, he was forced to rethink as never before the relation between history and Scripture.

By 1917 Woodrow Wilson was committed to making the world safe for democracy, and Augustus H. Strong was committed to making it safe for biblical civilization. He had no taste for polemics, but a world tour of missions had persuaded him that theological liberalism in general, and liberal biblical scholarship in particular, had gone too far. The critics had gone astray, he warned, not because they had used historical methods, but because they had used nothing else. They had been tyrannized by a technique that "proceeds wholly by induction." Yet in Strong's estimation the real problem was deeper. The root of the disease was not the method, but the radically historical presupposition that the Bible is "only a promiscuous collection of disjointed documents, with . . . no significance beyond that of the time in which they were written." Having butchered the Bible into "congeries of separate bits," the higher critics had failed to see the "divine intelligence and life throbbing through the whole." Even so, the aging patriarch thought the emergent fundamentalist faction not much better. Strong growled that the problem with the fundamentalists, who had become entangled in pointless arguments over inerrancy, evolution, and premillennialism, was that they were not "fundamental enough." They did not "get down to the rock-foundation, the omnipresent and eternal Christ, who has supervised in past ages the evolution of Scripture, so that it represents himself in all the forms of human composition."[42]

Strong's tortured attempt to come to terms with the great work of the nineteenth century without giving up the faith of his fathers was not unusual. George Frederick Wright at Oberlin, William Henry Green at Princeton, E. Y. Mullins at Southern Baptist, as well as thoughtful evangelicals in Britain like P. T. Forsyth and A. S. Peake, all seem to have followed the same path in pretty much the same way. And we now can see that "pietistic critics" like Briggs and Harper were much closer to Strong than they were to such real historicists as Shirley Jackson Case or Morris Jastrow.[43]

Still, there were many who knew that once the foundation of biblical civilization had cracked, it could never be restored in the way that Strong—or Clarke—imagined. One thinks of the great geologist John Wesley Powell, a minister's son, for whom the encounter with history proved an exhilarating liberation from all forms of supernatural religion. One also thinks of another minister's son, Charles Augustus Strong, a distinguished professional philosopher of the 1930s, whose painful loss of faith had been prompted by the "unnaturalness of the suppositions" in his father's *Systematic Theology*. On the other side were those who forthrightly challenged the governing principles of modern consciousness. One thinks of Princeton's Benjamin B. Warfield, or his younger colleague J. Gresham Machen, who hauled out the heavy guns of a superior classical education to blast the myth that there is a "truth for this race and a truth for that race, but no truth for all races." Or one thinks of another minister's son, John Henry Strong, whose intense personal piety and stalwart orthodoxy simply smothered the dilemmas that had troubled his father and tormented his brother.[44]

In the end they all had to find a way to choose between—or patch together—the historical processes revealed by the modern world and the timeless certitudes of an earlier era.[45] For some, both then and now, it might be possible, as Paul Riceour has urged, to achieve a "second naïveté" through the devices of mythic and imaginative reconstruction. But biblical civilizations are made of sterner stuff.

NOTES

1. Donald G. Bloesch, *The Evangelical Renaissance* (Grand Rapids: Eerdmans, 1973), esp. pp. 33–34, 55–59. Winthrop S. Hudson, *Religion in America* (New York: Scribner's, 1981, 3rd rev. ed. [1965]), pp. 442–50.

The first of the two epigraphs is taken from John Sutherland Black and George Chrystal, *Lectures and Essays of William Robertson Smith* (1912), quoted in T. O. Beidelman, *W. Robertson Smith and the Sociological Study of Religion* (Chicago: University of Chicago, 1974), p. 33. The second is taken from a letter to J. S. Black, 14 September 1871, Smith Papers, quoted in Warner M. Bailey, "William Robertson Smith and American Biblical Studies," *Journal of Presbyterian History,* 51(1973):287.

2. James Bryce, *The American Commonwealth,* 2 vols. (1910), II:781–82, and Francis Grund, in *America in Perspective,* ed. H. S. Commager (1947), pp. 85, 87, quoted, respectively, in Winthrop S. Hudson, *The Great Tradition of the American Churches* (Gloucester, MA: Peter Smith, 1970 [1953]), pp. 28, 39. For fundamental changes of attitude about the Bible's authority, especially in Britain and the United States, see James Barr, *The Bible in the Modern World* (New York: Harper & Row, 1973), esp. pp. 8–10.

3. Gaius Glenn Atkins, *Religion in Our Times* (New York: Round Table, 1932), p. 40. Paul Carter, *The Spiritual Crisis of the Gilded Age* (DeKalb, IL: Northern Illinois University Press, 1971), pp. viii, chap. 4. George M. Marsden, *Fundamentalism and American Culture: The Shaping of Twentieth-Century Evangelicalism, 1870–1925* (New York: Oxford University Press, 1980), pp. 11–17. For a comparable situation in Britain see Thomas A. Langford, *In Search of Foundations: English Theology, 1900–1920* (Nashville: Abingdon, 1969), pp. 13–14, 88.

4. Robert S. and Helen Merrell Lynd, *Middletown: A Study in Contemporary American Culture* (New York: Harcourt, Brace, 1929), pp. 315–31, 378–79. Lynd and Lynd, *Middletown in Transition: A Study in Cultural Conflicts* (New York: Harcourt, Brace, 1937), p. 295. Richard H. Pells, *Radical Visions and American Dreams: Culture and Social Thought in the Depression Years* (New York: Harper & Row, 1973), p. 27. Winthrop S. Hudson, *American Protestantism* (Chicago: University of Chicago, 1961), pp. 149–53. Robert T. Handy, *A History of the Churches in the United States and Canada* (New York: Oxford University Press, 1977), p. 377. Edwin S. Gaustad, *A Religious History of America* (New York: Harper & Row, 1966), p. 262. Conrad Wright, Introduction, in Wright, ed., *Three Prophets of Religious Liberalism: Channing-Emerson-Parker* (Boston: Beacon, 1961), p. 5. Wright's phrase is set in a different context than mine.

5. Jerry Wayne Brown, *The Rise of Biblical Criticism in America, 1800–1870: The New England Scholars* (Middletown, CT: Wesleyan University, 1969), pp. 180–82.

6. Washington Gladden, *Recollections* (1909), pp. 262–66, quoted in William R. Hutchison, *The Modernist Impulse in American Protestantism* (Cambridge, MA: Harvard University Press, 1976), p. 77. Atkins, *Religion in Our Times,* pp. 86, 39.

7. Ira V. Brown, "The Higher Criticism Comes to America, 1880–1900," *Journal of the Presbyterian Historical Society,* 38(1960):192–212. See also George Ernest Wright, "The Study of the Old Testament: The Changing Mood in the Household of Wellhausen," and Floyd V. Filson, "The Study of the New Testament: Through Historical Study to Biblical Theology," in Arnold S. Nash, ed., *Protestant Thought in the 20th Century: Whence and Whither* (New York: Macmillan, 1951), pp. 17–44, 47–69. See also J. M. Powis Smith, "Old Testament Interpretation," Shirley Jackson Case, "The Life of Jesus," and Harold R. Willoughby, "The Study of Early Christianity," in Gerald Birney Smith, ed., *Religious Thought*

in the Last Quarter-Century (Chicago: University of Chicago Press, 1927), pp. 1–25, 26–41, 42–69. See also the entries, s.v., in Henry Warner Bowden, *Dictionary of American Religious History* (Westport, CT: Greenwood, 1977).

8. Hutchison, *Modernist Impulse,* esp. chaps. 3 & 4. Sydney E. Ahlstrom, *A Religious History of the American People* (New Haven: Yale University, 1972), chap. 46, "The Golden Age of Liberal Theology." For a brief but exceptionally lucid account see Hudson, *Religion in America,* pp. 268–79.

9. Hudson, *Great Tradition,* p. 153.

10. George H. Shriver, ed., *American Religious Heretics: Formal and Informal Trials* (Nashville: Abingdon, 1966). William R. Hutchison, "Disapproval of Chicago: The Symbolic Trial of David Swing," *Journal of American History,* 59(1972): 30–47.

11. For Dorner's influence see Hutchison, *Modernist Impulse,* pp. 84–88. For Smith's see Bailey, "William Robertson Smith," and Beidelman, *W. Robertson Smith,* pp. 29–31.

12. See for example popular tracts like Washington Gladden's *Who Wrote the Bible? A Book for the People* (Boston: Houghton Mifflin, 1891), and Harry Emerson Fosdick's *The Modern Use of the Bible* (New York: Macmillan, 1924).

13. It is important to distinguish an articulated doctrine of biblical inerrancy from an unarticulated assumption that the Bible is without error. It may be true, as Ernest R. Sandeen, Jack B. Rogers, and others have argued, that the former view was imported from Swiss scholasticism in the mid-nineteenth century and adapted to the American setting by theological craftsmen at Princeton Seminary. Sandeen, *The Roots of Fundamentalism: British and American Millenarianism, 1800–1930* (Chicago: University of Chicago, 1970), chap. 5. Rogers and Donald K. McKim, *The Authority and Interpretation of the Bible: An Historical Approach* (San Francisco: Harper & Row, 1979), chaps. 5 & 6. Nonetheless, the latter view was extremely common among Victorian era evangelicals on both sides of the Atlantic. Norman H. Maring, "Baptists and Changing Views of the Bible, 1865–1918," *Foundations,* 1(July 1958):52–78, and 1(October 1958):30–61. John D. Woodbridge, "Evangelicals and the Bible," in Woodbridge, Mark A. Noll, and Nathan O. Hatch, *The Gospel in America: Themes in the Story of America's Evangelicals* (Grand Rapids: Zondervan, 1979), pp. 110–12, 116, 117–18. Kirsopp Lake, *The Religion of Yesterday and Tomorrow* (1926), p. 61, quoted in Kenneth S. Kantzer, "Evangelicals and the Inerrancy Question," in Kantzer, ed., *Evangelical Roots: A Tribute to Wilbur Smith* (Nashville: Thomas Nelson, 1978), p. 93. For Britain see Willis B. Glover, *Evangelical Nonconformists and Higher Criticism in the 19th Century* (London: Independent Press, 1954), chap. 3, and Barbara Zink MacHaffie, " 'Monument Facts and Higher Critical Fancies': Archaeology and the Popularization of Old Testament Criticism in Nineteenth-Century Britain," *Church History,* 50(1981):319–28.

14. A small part of the story has been recounted in James Barr, *Fundamentalism* (Philadelphia: Westminster, 1977), pp. 260–79, and Lefferts A. Loetscher, *The Broadening Church: A Study of the Theological Issues in the Presbyterian Church Since 1865* (Philadelphia: University of Pennsylvania, 1954), esp. chaps. 4–8. After a century of struggle these notions have been refined to a razor's edge. See for example the essays in Norman L. Geisler, ed., *Inerrancy* (Grand Rapids: Zondervan, 1979), especially Paul D. Feinberg, "The Meaning of Inerrancy," pp. 267–304.

15. Morton White, *Social Thought in America: The Revolt Against Formalism* (Bos-

ton: Beacon, 1957 [1947]). Henry F. May, *The End of American Innocence: A Study of the First Years of Our Own Time, 1912–1917* (Chicago: Quadrangle Paperbacks, 1964 [1959]), p. ix.

16. The literature is extensive. In addition to White and May, cited above, the most important synoptic studies include the following. Franklin L. Baumer, *Modern European Thought: Continuity and Change in Ideas, 1600–1950* (New York: Macmillan, 1977), Part IV, Part V, esp. chaps. 1, 6. H. Stuart Hughes, *Consciousness and Society: The Reorientation of European Social Thought, 1890–1930* (New York: Random House, 1958). Georg Iggers, *The German Conception of History* (Middletown, CT: Wesleyan University, 1968). Maurice Mandelbaum, *History, Man, and Reason: A Study in Nineteenth-Century Thought* (Baltimore: Johns Hopkins University, 1971). Hayden White, *Tropics of Discourse: Essays in Cultural Criticism* (Baltimore: Johns Hopkins University, 1978), esp. chap. 4, "Historicism, History, and the Figurative Imagination."

17. Georg Iggers, "The Idea of Progress: A Critical Reassessment," *American Historical Review*, 71(1965):8–9. See also Baumer, *European Thought*, p. 495.

18. Edward A. Purcell, *The Crisis of Democratic Theory: Scientific Naturalism and the Problem of Value* (Lexington, KY: University of Kentucky Press, 1973), chaps. 8–10. This is the best study of the growth of historical consciousness in the behavioral sciences in the United States.

19. Carl L. Becker, *The Heavenly City of the Eighteenth-Century Philosophers* (New Haven: Yale University, 1965 [1932]), pp. 18–19.

20. Robert A. Nisbet, *Social Change and History: Aspects of the Western Theory of Development* (New York: Oxford University Press, 1969), pp. 223–39. Robert H. Wiebe, *The Search for Order: 1877–1920* (New York: Hill and Wang, 1967), p. 154. Morton White, *Science and Sentiment in America: Philosophical Thought from Jonathan Edwards to John Dewey*, chaps. 6–11. Others have minimized the extent or depth of historical consciousness outside the academy. Richard Hofstadter, *The Age of Reform: From Bryan to F. D. R.* (New York: Random House, Vintage Books, 1962), pp. 15–16.

21. Henry Adams, *The Education of Henry Adams* (1931), p. 53, quoted in Brown, "Higher Criticism," p. 193.

22. Hutchison, *Modernist Impulse*, esp. p. 2. Ahlstrom, *Religious History*, pp. 772–74. Claude Welch, *Protestant Thought in the Nineteenth Century, 1799–1870* (New Haven: Yale University, 1972), esp. chap. 7. See also Shailer Mathews, "The Historical Study of Religion," in Gerald Birney Smith, ed., *A Guide to the Study of the Christian Religion* (Chicago: University of Chicago, 1916), pp. 19–81.

23. Glover, *Evangelical Nonconformists*, pp. 80, 106. Marsden, *Fundamentalism and American Culture*, pp. 56, 113.

24. Barr, *Fundamentalism*, pp. 15, 78, 84, 97. George Marsden, "Fundamentalism as an American Phenomenon," *Church History*, 46(1977):226–32. Sandeen, *Roots of Fundamentalism*, p. 268. See also the preface to the reprint edition (Grand Rapids: Baker, 1978), p. ix, where Sandeen makes the point even more sharply.

25. Bowden, *Dictionary*, s.v., Adoniram Judson Gordon, George A. Gordon.

26. Adoniram Judson Gordon, *The Ministry of the Spirit* (New York: Fleming H. Revell, 1894), pp. 171–73.

27. George A. Gordon, *Ultimate Conceptions of Faith* (Boston: Houghton Mifflin, 1903), pp. 338–39.

28. Gordon, *Ministry of the Spirit*, pp. 168–69.

29. George A. Gordon, *The Christ of To-Day* (Boston: Houghton Mifflin, 1895), pp. 283, 66.

30. For assessments of the extraordinary influences of Clarke's *Outline of Systematic Theology* see Hudson, *Religion in America*, pp. 276 n15.

31. William Newton Clarke, *Sixty Years with the Bible: A Record of Experience* (New York: Scribner's, 1910), pp. 13, 42–44.

32. Ibid., pp. 239–40, 203, 206–7.

33. Ibid., pp. 167–68. Clarke was particularly contemptuous of Plymouth Brethren, whom he pilloried as "profoundly ignorant," not because they were biblically illiterate, but because they tended to regard "their own understanding of the Bible as unquestionably the interpretation of the Holy Ghost." Pp. 141, 145.

34. Ibid., pp. 157–60.

35. Bowden, *Dictionary*, s.v., Augustus H. Strong. For one of many estimates of Strong's influence see Carl F. H. Henry, *Personal Idealism and Strong's Theology* (Wheaton, IL: Van Kampen, 1951), pp. 11, 13, 228.

36. For respective examples see the following. Allan Nevins, *John D. Rockefeller: The Heroic Age of American Enterprise*, 2 vols. (New York: Scribner's, 1940), II:173–243 (passim), 457. Henry, *Personal Idealism*, p. 229. LeRoy Moore, Jr., "Another Look at Fundamentalism: A Response to Ernest R. Sandeen," *Church History*, 37(1968):200. (Moore assesses Strong more generously, however, in his Ph.D. diss., "The Rise of American Religious Liberalism at the Rochester Theological Seminary, 1872–1928," Claremont, 1966.)

37. Compare Augustus H. Strong, "My Views of the Universe in General," *Baptist* 29 May 1920, pp. 625–26, with "Confessions of Our Faith," *Watchman-Examiner*, 21 July 1921, p. 910.

38. Strong to William Rainey Harper, 8 January 1889. President's Papers, 1889–1925, University of Chicago.

39. Augustus H. Strong, *Christ in Creation and Ethical Monism* (Philadelphia: Roger Williams, 1899), p. 158. Strong, *One Hundred Chapel-Talks to Theological Students* (Philadelphia: Griffith & Rowland, 1913), pp. 152–53. Strong, *Christ in Creation*, p. 206. [Rochester Theological Seminary] *52nd Annual Report* (1902): 33–34. Strong, "Autobiography of Augustus Hopkins Strong, 1896–1917," typed, p. 550 [American Baptist Historical Society, Rochester, NY].

40. Strong, *Christ in Creation*, pp. 127–28. Strong, *Systematic Theology*, 8th ed. rev. & enl., 3 vols. (1907–1909), reprint ed., 3 vols. in 1 (Old Tappan, NJ: Fleming H. Revell, 1970), pp. 224, 207, 218, 215, 220.

41. Ibid., pp. 171–72, 217, 145–46. Strong, "Modifications of the Theological Curriculum," *American Journal of Theology*, 3(1899):329.

42. Strong, *A Tour of the Missions: Observations and Conclusions* (Philadelphia: Griffith & Rowland, 1918), pp. 170, 177, 174–75. Strong, *What Shall I Believe? A Primer of Christian Theology* (New York: Fleming H. Revell, 1922), pp. 62–63.

43. For Wright see James R. Moore, *The Post-Darwinian Controversies: A study of the Protestant struggle to come to terms with Darwin in Great Britain and America, 1870–1900* (Cambridge: Cambridge University, 1979), pp. 280–340. For Green see Bailey, "William Robertson Smith," pp. 303–7. For Mullins see William E. Ellis, "Edgar Young Mullins and the Crisis of Moderate Southern Baptist Leadership," *Foundations*, 19(1976):171–85. For Forsyth and Peake see Glover, *Evangelical Nonconformists*, chap. 11, and Langford, *English Theology*,

chap. 4. For the contrast between "pietistic critics" and rigorous historicists see Robert W. Funk, "The Watershed of American Biblical Tradition: The Chicago School, First Phase, 1892–1920," *Journal of Biblical Literature,* 95(1976):4–22, and compare Charles A. Briggs, *Whither? A Theological Question for the Times* (New York: Scribner's, 1889), against Morris Jastrow, Jr., *The Study of Religion* (Chico, CA: Scholars Press, 1981 [1901]).

44. For Powell see Carter, *Spiritual Crisis,* pp. 5, 32. For Charles A. Strong see his "Nature and Mind," in George P. Adams and William Pepperell Montague, eds., *Contemporary American Philosophy: Personal Statements,* 2 vols. (London: George Allen & Unwin, 1930), II: 314. For Warfield and Machen see Hutchison, *Modernist Impulse,* chap. 8. The Machen quotation is from *Christian Faith in the Modern World* (Grand Rapids: Eerdmans, 1965 [1936]), p. 90. See also George M. Marsden, "J. Gresham Machen, History, and Truth," *Westminster Theological Journal,* 42(1979):157–75. For John H. Strong see LeRoy Moore, Jr., "Religious Liberalism," pp. 161–67.

45. Brevard S. Childs argues that the biblical theology movement of the 1940s was the first serious attempt by American biblical scholars to transcend the dilemma posed by historical consciousness. *Biblical Theology in Crisis* (Philadelphia: Westminster, 1970), chap. 1. It is not evident, however, that the biblical theology movement, or any other movement for that matter, has yet enabled us to do more than grope for the edges of a reconstructed biblical civilization.

VII

The Bible in Twentieth-Century Protestantism: A Preliminary Taxonomy

RICHARD J. MOUW
Calvin College

How has the Bible been viewed by North American Protestants in the twentieth century? To be specific, how have they used the Bible? How have they appropriated its content? How has the Bible functioned for them as they have participated in, and attempted to interpret, the patterns of North American culture?

There are not easy questions to answer, and this present attempt to discuss the issues must be, of necessity, somewhat sketchy and superficial. Not much scholarly attention has been directed toward questions of this sort. For example, the standard historical studies of North American Protestantism—or of the church in the United States, or of religion in America—seldom address questions regarding basic attitudes toward the Bible. Even when they do touch on such questions, the discussion seldom refers to twentieth-century attitudes, save for a few paragraphs here and there on the issue of biblical authority as a matter of dispute in the "fundamentalist–modernist" controversies.[1]

Other kinds of scholarly treatises do treat the subject of attitudes toward the Bible. Polemical and systematic writings on this subject abound. Recently some helpful attempts have been made to gain a "second order" perspective on the ways in which appeals to biblical authority function in theological discussions. David Kelsey's analysis of different theological "uses" of the Bible[2] is a ground-breaking work in this area. Kelsey even discusses the views of a few North American theologians—one a nineteenth-century Princetonian, and another a German import. Bruce Birch and Larry Rasmussen have co-authored a study[3] of the ways in which the Bible functions in the thinking of selected American ethicists, as well as in various confessional and theological traditions. But none of these treatments focuses on the specifically cultural or historical or North American *contexts* of the uses of the Bible.

The body of literature dealing with "American civil religion"[4] has a somewhat more direct bearing on the present topic; indeed that literature might provide one very helpful route into a discussion of our questions. The "civil religion" analysts have devoted considerable attention to the ways in which North American Christians have employed biblical images and themes in attempting to understand the history and calling of the American nation.

Even so, the discussions of civil religion do not cover exactly the same territory as our present questions. We are concerned here with possible differences in Protestant uses of the Bible. The analysts of the phenomenon of civil religion, on the other hand, have been concerned primarily with a "consensus" theology of the American experience—a common set of beliefs about the United States which many Christians share above and beyond the peculiar religious beliefs of their own denominations; the emphasis has been on the resultant consensus, rather than on the diversity of religious traditions out of which that consensus had to be forged.

The search for an existing consensus is legitimate and fascinating, but it is also important to attend to the residual differences that exist among adherents to the alleged civil religion. Suppose it is true, for example, that large numbers of North American Christians from a variety of church backgrounds believe, or have believed in the past, that the United States is in some special sense a "chosen" nation with a unique and privileged destiny to pursue in the community of nations.[5] How then did people *arrive* at their substantive belief? More particularly, how have persons from diverse theological and denominational traditions come to hold that belief in common? How did a Methodist get there? Or an Episcopalian? Or a Presbyterian? Or a Southern Baptist? What was it about each of these traditions or groups—or the ways in which the traditions or groups are perceived by their members—which allowed people to come to a point where they accepted this or that item in a consensus civil theology? The fact is that the alleged consensus does not exist uniformly within American religious life. Some Protestant groups have simply refused to accede to many of the beliefs associated with American civil religion. Many black Christians, Mennonites, Quakers, and recent European immigrant groups have resisted the consensus theology to one degree or another.[6] An understanding of the views of adherents to an American civil religion, then, hardly constitutes an understanding of the cultural uses of the Bible in American Protestantism as such.

Our present investigation shares a common methodological problem with the civil religion discussion: Where do we go to find our evidence? Whether the goal is to discover a consensus or to expose residual differences, whose views are to be cited as data in support of our conclusions? Where, for example, do we find canonical expressions of the attitudes of Presbyterians or Lutherans or black Methodists?

Survey data offer only a little assistance. An extensive recent poll undertaken by the Gallup organization for *Christianity Today* provided interesting, but still limited, information on the use of the Bible in America. It showed, for example, that Catholics and Protestants shared some of the same general feelings about Scripture—48 percent of Protestants polled and 41 percent of Catholics believed "the Bible is the word of God and is not mistaken in its statements and teachings." Catholics were somewhat more likely than Protestants to know at least five of the Ten Commandments (49% to 40%), even though more Protestants professed to read the Bible at least once a week (42% to 14%). The same poll also revealed differences among major Protestant groups: 53 percent of Southern Baptists and 50 percent of Lutherans said that the Bible does not make mistakes, compared with 33 percent of the Methodists. Southern Baptists and Lutherans were also more likely to read the Bible at least once a week than were Methodists (48% of Southern Baptists, 42% of Lutherans, and 32% of Methodists). Yet Methodists (50%) were just as likely as Southern Baptists (52%) or Lutherans (47%) to test religious beliefs first by "what the Bible says."[7] Such numbers are intriguing, but without knowing the reasoning processes that led to the different responses or the relationship between professed attitudes toward the Bible and the actual use of Scripture, it is difficult to construct a general interpretation upon the polls. Nor is it possible to move directly from the public attitudes of ministers to the actual practices of parishioners.

Harry Emerson Fosdick reports in his autobiography that as a young preacher who was somewhat critical of his colleagues' homiletical practices, he once exclaimed: "Only the preacher proceeds still upon the idea that folk come to church desperately anxious to discover what happened to the Jebusites."[8] Whether Fosdick was giving a fair assessment of either

the practices of his fellow preachers or the expectations of their congregations is, perhaps, a moot question. But he is at least correct in pointing to
a possible gap between clerical and lay criteria of biblical relevance.[9] And
each of these may, in turn, differ greatly from the criteria associated with
either official "churchly" theologies or the deliverances of academic theologians. Furthermore, there is no reason to expect uniformity within any
one of these groups.

A proper and thorough discussion of the questions raised in this present
essay would have to be based on some clear delineations among these
groups. A focus would have to be chosen, data collected and sifted, and
conclusions formulated with proper care and caution. Such is the stuff of
historical scholarship. This essay is not an exercise in historical scholarship. A philosopher writing in the company of historians would be fool-
hardy not to offer a disclaimer of this sort. In the present case this disclaimer is not only politic but true. No decision has been made here
regarding focus, class orientation, proper sources of evidence, or the like.
Rather, what is offered is a scheme which might be helpful in setting out
upon that larger investigation. Philosophers are well known for their insistence on writing "prologomena" to the work of other scholars. This essay, for better or worse, perpetuates that tradition.

Our questions point to a terrain which can be carved up in a variety of
ways. One such scheme will be proposed here. It is proposed as a struc-
tured way of organizing different basic answers to the question, "What
kind of book is the Bible?" It employs a set of distinctions borrowed and
adapted from Nicholas Wolterstorff's attempt to categorize the diverse
"minds" at work in one specific ethnic-religious group.[10]

Certain twentieth-century Protestants have placed a strong emphasis on
the importance of *doctrine,* and on having the right kinds of doctrinal beliefs. The presence of such an emphasis is not unique to the twentieth century. A stress on doctrinal "purity" has emerged whenever parts of the
church perceive threats to traditional beliefs. In the nineteenth century a
number of groups separated themselves from major European churches,
insisting that major ecclesiastical bodies had departed from traditional patterns of doctrinal formulation.

We will call this pattern of thought *doctrinalism.* Doctrinalists stress the
importance of believing the right kinds of doctrines. They tend to engage
in battles on at least two fronts. First, they oppose religious movements

which do not consider "correct doctrine" to be a highly valued commodity. Against such forces the doctrinalists argue for the importance of doctrine as such. But doctrinalists also argue with other doctrinalists. There are Lutheran doctrinalists who stress the importance of "true Lutheranism," Reformed doctrinalists who insist on the value of being "truly Reformed," Wesleyan doctrinalists, Anglo-Catholic doctrinalists, Baptist doctrinalists, and so on. Doctrinalists argue among themselves about *which* system of doctrine is correct.

Similarly, arguments can take place among doctrinalists within a given theological tradition. Some doctrinalists defend newer formulations of doctrine against older formulations. Thus, an argument between Reformed Barthians versus Old Princeton Calvinists is an intra-Reformed argument between doctrinalists, just as a debate between charismatic and noncharismatic Wesleyans is an intra-Wesleyan debate between doctrinalists.

The doctrinalists may consider other elements of the Christian life—such as piety or morality or social action—to have some importance. But the doctrinalist will consider doctrine to be of fundamental importance, such that a piety or morality or social program which is not in some sense based upon "sound doctrine" is defective.

Consequently, the doctrinalist sees the Bible as being primarily a source for doctrine, or religious *teachings*. Charles Hodge expressed a doctrinalist perspective when he insisted that

> Revelation is the communication of truth by God to the understanding of man. It makes known doctrines. For example, it makes known that God is . . . that Christ is the Son of God; that he assumed our nature; that he died for our sins, etc. These are logical propositions.[11]

David Kelsey attributes a similar account to Hodge's successor at Princeton, Benjamin Warfield, according to whom, as Kelsey describes his position, "Biblical texts, construed as containing a system of doctrine, strike with numinous power so that one's initial responses, as Warfield reports it, are awe, trembling, and submission."[12] And a central feature of the "submission" here is intellectual assent. For the doctrinalist understanding of the Bible, the most important and fundamental way in which human beings are to respond to the Bible is with intellectual assent to the "teaching" propositions asserted therein.

Similarities to the "Old Princeton" doctrinalism of Hodge and Warfield can be found in twentieth-century fundamentalism, among other places.

Philip Mauro, a New York attorney who contributed several essays to *The Fundamentals* (1910–1915), used language which is primarily intellectual (or "cognitive") in describing the Bible's authority:

> The Bible . . . although it treats of the greatest and most serious of all subjects, such as God, Christ, eternity, life, death, sin, righteousness, judgment, redemption—is always the latest, best, and only authority on all these and other weighty matters whereof it treats. Centuries of "progress" and "advancement" have added absolutely nothing to the sum of knowledge on any of these subjects. The Bible is always fresh and thoroughly "up to date." Indeed it is far, far ahead of human science. Progress cannot overtake it, or get beyond it. Generation succeeds generation, but each finds the Bible waiting for it with its ever fresh and never failing stores of information touching matters of the highest concern, touching everything that affects the welfare of human beings.[13]

A second mind at work in twentieth-century Protestantism is *pietism*. The pietist views the cultivation of certain pious ("godly" or "spiritual") experiences and habits as fundamental to the Christian life. We noted that the doctrinalist argues that piety not based on correct doctrinal formulations is not properly formed. The pietist responds by contending against "dead orthodoxy," or a faith that is "purely intellectual." Howard Colson expresses this attitude well:

> The Bible is supremely the Book of the heart. That is why some of the most brilliant intellects get but little out of it, while people of humble spirit and childlike faith get a wealth of meaning from its pages. . . . The open Book and the open heart must meet.[14]

The pietist speaks much of the "heart," utilizing the language of subjective or personal experience, and stressing the importance of "peace," "joy," "comfort," and assurance of one's personal salvation.

Sometimes pietistic emphases have developed in reaction against a stress on doctrinal orthodoxy. But they have also come about as a critical response to what is perceived as moral legalism or to a kind of Christianity which stresses social or political involvement. Pietism is a "turning inward" from these other emphases. The "charismatic renewal" is an example of a major pietistic development in twentieth-century Christianity.[15]

If the doctrinalist views the Bible as a doctrinal sourcebook, the pietist views it as a handbook for pious living. The Bible is a stimulus to certain kinds of experiences. Reading the Bible is crucial to fostering a personal sense of divine presence. The primary use of the Bible for the pietist is a devotional one. The "submission" to the Bible, which Warfield describes, is not for the pietist an intellectual act primarily; it is subjective and experiential.

This pietistic use of the Bible is probably the most important one for most American Protestants. It fuels a vast publishing enterprise that turns out thousands of devotional titles each year, including some that sell in the millions of copies.[16] It is a main feature in the burgeoning world of religious broadcasting. And it plays a major role in the great amount of literature produced for America's Sunday Schools.

In addition, pietism cuts across theological and denominational lines— the charismatic movement is a case in point for the ecumenical nature of pietistic Christianity. But pietism need not be associated exclusively with a "conservative" mentality. Unitarians and liberal Protestants can also be pietists. "Feeling close to God when I walk in the woods" can be a pietistic expression, as can "experiencing God's presence by drinking beer with my friends." Pietistic emphases can be formulated in the language of the "human potential" movement—as Thomas Oden has argued[17]—as well as in the language of Puritanism or Wesleyanism.

While the doctrinalist tends to define the human predicament in terms of ignorance, the pietist sees human beings as plagued by troubled hearts, doubts and fears. On the pietist view, then, the Bible's primary use is in speaking to these subjective states, as described in this classic statement of Dwight L. Moody:

> Bear in mind there is no situation in life for which you cannot find some word of consolation in Scripture. If you are in affliction, if you are in adversity and trial, there is a promise for you. In joy and sorrow, in health and sickness, in poverty and riches, in every condition of life, God has a promise stored up in His Word for you. In one way or another every case is met, and the truth is commended to every man's conscience.[18]

A third mind at work in twentieth-century Protestantism is one which can be labeled *moralism*. The moralist views Christianity primarily in terms of moral or ethical categories. Christianity is a system which helps human beings live the good life; it enables them to engage in right action. Doctrine which has no moral payoff is useless; piety which fails to express itself in the doing of what is morally right is mere sentimentality or emotionalism.

There are many different ways of being a Christian moralist. This is closely related to the fact that there are many different ways of understanding the basic tones and patterns of the moral life. Some people view morality as acting in accordance with moral rules or principles or laws. When this is understood within a Christian framework, it results in the phenomenon often referred to as "legalism." Christian legalism can in turn take different forms: it can focus on the Ten Commandments or the Sermon on the Mount; it can be spelled out in terms of "law and order" or it can manifest itself in a commitment to Christian pacifism. This kind of thinking tends toward a "litmus test" approach to spirituality. Some groups may question the religious character of anyone who smokes cigarettes, others the religious character of those who do not protest the Bomb.

Christian legalism views the Bible as a sourcebook for moral principles or rules. Biblical morality, on this view, curbs our sinful tendencies. It speaks directly to human immorality and wickedness, providing moral guidance in lives which would otherwise be confused and perverse.

Another kind of biblical moralism stresses the development of good "character." For example, some Christians view the Bible as providing human beings with stories about persons of good character. Christians ought to read the Bible, then, for the purpose of becoming aware of such examples. And the proper implementation of this awareness is imitation. This emphasis on imitation has played a major role in a number of American traditions. It received classic expression in the Victorian novel of Charles M. Sheldon, *In His Steps* (1897), which has encouraged generations of American readers to face all situations with the question, "What would Jesus do?"[19] It plays an important part in Anabaptist ethics.[20] And it was a major element in the older liberalism of Harry Emerson Fosdick, who once wrote:

> We claim that the heart of the Bible is its reproducible experiences. . . . For as one goes back to the Bible now in search of its repeatable experiences, it is clear that whatever else loyalty to the Book may mean, one element must be put first: the spirit and quality of Jesus were meant to be reproduced in his followers. Nothing is Christian which leaves that out or makes that secondary. In the New Testament the Master's life, like music, was meant to be reproduced. As a score of Bach or Beethoven, into which the composer's love of harmony once was poured, is meant to be caught up by each new generation and played over again, interpreted by organs, orchestras, choirs, by old instruments that may abide and by new ones that may be invented, so the life of Jesus in the New Testament was meant to be reproduced in all sorts of circumstances, by all sorts of temperaments, until the whole earth should be full of it.[21]

Christian moralism can also take other forms. It can view the Bible as a repository of "wise sayings" which are to be put to practical moral use; or it can see the Bible as a mosaic of characters and events which, viewed as a whole, presents us with a grand and inspiring "moral vision." The "wise sayings" approach came to life in the public rhetoric of Senators Everett Dirksen or Sam Ervin, who peppered their remarks with bits of biblical "wisdom" interspersed among quotations from Shakespeare and the Declaration of Independence. The "moral vision" perspective was expressed in a rhapsodic vein by Professor Mary Ellen Chase, who taught courses at Smith College on the literary significance of the Bible:

> . . . the Bible in its slow, patient evolution is the noblest record in any language of the hearts and the minds of men. Those who wrote it and those of whom it was written thought and wondered over the eternal questions of life and death, of man's lot upon this earth, and of his ultimate destiny. Amos on the Tekoan hills, the Great Isaiah by the waters of Shiloah and the Second Isaiah by those of Babylon, Job in the dust with his sententious friends, "physicians of no value" to him, St. John on the island of Patmos, Daniel by the river Ulai—these were men of dreams and of visions who struggled with the questions that beset us all. Consumed like Dante "by the Love that moves the sun and the other stars," they were intent upon the possible reaches of man's spirit even in a dry and thirsty land. In the midst of desolation and suffering, of oppression and greed, they saw hope; in war, the ways of peace; in the perennial processes of nature, the treasure of the snow, the former and the latter rain, the waste places of the deep, the singing of the morning stars, they saw the mysterious ways of God with men. Because of their vision, deep calleth unto deep in their pages; and the unanalyzed perception of the meaning and value of threescore years and ten is woven into the very texture of their speech. In their two-fold recognition of wisdom, that moral and ethical code by which a just man lives his life and that intangible and spiritual Power, set up from everlasting and possessed by God in the beginning of His way, only by the understanding of which man achieves his triumph, they encompassed all the affairs, small and great, of one's sojourn on this earth.[22]

It is clear that moralism also is associated with a certain way of viewing the Bible. The Bible, for moralists, is understood primarily in terms of what it can contribute to moral understanding and decision-making—although the moral content of the Bible will be variously interpreted by moralists, in relation to different understandings of the fundamental tones of the moral life.

A fourth mind at work in twentieth-century Protestantism is what we might call *culturalism*. Here the Christian life is viewed in terms of the Christian's involvements in broad institutions of society. "Culture" here is meant to include politics, economics, education, art, science and technology, and so on.

For the culturalist the crucial test is how Christians relate to the broad, even institutionalized, patterns of this world. This test is justified, in turn, on biblical grounds: the Bible becomes a book addressing primarily questions of culture. Thus, in articulating his "theology for the social gospel" Walter Rauschenbusch insisted that the growth of the "social gospel" movement was linked to a rediscovery of the proper understanding of the Bible:

> The biblical studies have responded to the spiritual hunger aroused by the social gospel. The historical interpretation of the Bible has put the religious personalities, their spiritual struggles, their growth, and their utterances, into social connection with the community life of which they were part. This method of interpretation has given back the Bible to men of modernized intelligence and has made it the feeder of faith in the social gospel.[23]

And more recently, Jim Wallis has defended a "radical Christianity" which views the Bible as a charter for living in opposition to the cultural status quo:

> The biblical witness presents a sharp contrast between "this world," dominated by the principalities and powers, and the inbreaking of the kingdom of God into human history which breaks the uncontested rule and dominion of the powers. The kingdom of God, inaugurated by Christ, is both a coming reality, eagerly anticipated, and a reality already present and in the making here and now. Jesus ushered in this new order by conquering death and bringing new life. The presence of this new order among us and the promise of its coming consummation provide the basis of hope and value for the Christian. Although not yet complete, the kingdom is a present reality, and the Christian community is to be that "new creation" living in the light of the new reality that we have experienced. Christians, then, are people of a new order and are not to walk in darkness but to walk as children of light (Ephesians 5:11). They are not to conform to the powers of the old order but are to be transformed—a people living by different values and standards.[24]

A similar emphasis can be found among those Calvinists who insist that because sin touches all of human life, redeemed people are called to manifest their obedience to the Gospel in all areas of human life. This means, they argue, that there must be uniquely Christian ways of pursuing education, science, politics, economic activity, art, and so on. Furthermore, these attempts must include the establishment of proper institutional settings for these activities. Hence the attempts either to impose Christian patterns onto the activities of the larger human community, or to establish alternative "Christian" schools, labor unions, art guilds, political movements, and so on.[25]

These kinds of cultural-Christian programs fit nicely into the fifth of H. Richard Niebuhr's patterns for relating "Christ and culture," namely "Christ transforming culture."[26] But culturalism can also fit into the first Niebuhrian category, "Christ against culture." The Old Order Amish, for example, also insist on cultural tests for Christian discipleship.[27] Proper Christianity is for them a life lived in separation from the cultural patterns of the larger human community. Christians are called to establish alternative cultural patterns: alternative technologies, alternative styles of family organization, alternative modes of dress, alternative educational designs.

Once again, culturalist Christianity has its own critique of the other "minds" which we have mentioned. Doctrine, according to the culturalist, must be viewed as part of the cultural patterns of the believing community; the same pertains to piety and morality.

These examples of culturalist proclivities come from the "edges" of North American Protestantism. Neither culturalist Calvinism nor the position of the Old Order Amish and other contemporary proponents of radical Anabaptism has made significant inroads into mainstream twentieth-century Protestantism in the United States. Yet other manifestations of culturalism have gained at least a hearing within the mainstream. Rauschenbusch's understanding of "the social gospel" is one such manifestation.[28] More recently Liberation Theology, with its emphasis on the primacy of structural change, seems to be a straightforward culturalism.[29] The same holds for the variety of "radical Christian" communities and programs which have emerged in the last decade or so; their "countercultural" posture points toward an entire reconstruction of life, and thus belongs with the culturalism described here.

Culturalism too is associated with a unique way of viewing the Bible. The Bible, for the culturalist, is a handbook for cultural action; it gives Christians marching-orders for their attempts at cultural transformation or cultural criticism. It also provides the means for interpreting contemporary patterns of culture. The Bible, then, becomes a set of instructions to a community of Christians who are called to live out their communal life in obedience to the Lord of culture. It is to be read for the purpose of discerning the proper patterns of cultural obedience.

An adequate treatment of the uses of the Bible among twentieth-century Protestants in North America also must attend to the full range of racial and ethnic diversity in American Christianity. In recent years racial and ethnic labels have come to be viewed as highly relevant coinage in theological discussion—thus "Black Theology," "Red Theology," "Immigrant Theology," or "Feminist Theology."

The insistence that these labels point to theologically relevant variables springs from an awareness that a group's cultural experiences shape its religious and theological formulations in many ways: Christians who have been the targets of sustained racist oppression will have different religious sensitivities than those who have wielded significant economic and political power; Christians who have experienced the trauma of geographical displacement will have a different religious self-understanding than those whose cultural experience is undergirded by geographical continuity.

Our present topic is an interesting case in point for these "contextualization" theses. How do cultural experiences shape or influence the ways in which the Bible is used and understood? How do, say, Korean Presbyterians differ in their use of the Bible from German Lutherans? Or black Methodists from native American Pentecostals? Or black Methodists from white Methodists? Such questions point to fascinating areas of investigation.[30] For the present it will have to suffice merely to point to these areas as ones which deserve scholarly attention.

A few observations are in order, however, about the way in which the Bible functions in the largest non-white Protestant community, namely, among black, or Afro-American, Christians. In assessing, however briefly, black attitudes toward the Bible it is important to remember that for the black slave community the fact that the Bible was a *book* was a matter of considerable social significance. Historical studies of the slavery experience record numerous examples of slaves who were punished for attempting to learn to read the Bible.[31]

The slaves' interest in Bible-reading was partly due to a desire for literacy as such. But Albert Raboteau, author of a notable synthesis on slave religion, notes some other factors: Christian slaves "were distrustful of the white folks' interpretation of the Scriptures and wanted to be able to search them for themselves"; in addition, there was a deep reverence for—almost a "worship" of—the Bible on the part of many slaves.[32] Raboteau reports a particularly poignant case of a young woman slave who learned from the white children how to recognize the name "Jesus" in print; she would spend long hours with a Bible, opened at random, tracing her finger along each line until she came across that name. This was for her a significant devotional exercise.[33]

The slaves compensated for their own illiteracy by extensive memorization of biblical materials which they had received orally. Again Raboteau:

> Illiteracy proved less of an obstacle to knowledge of the Bible than might be thought, for biblical stories became part of the oral tradition of the slaves. Oral instructions and Sunday School lessons were committed to memory. As one missionary to the slaves reported: "To those who are ignorant of letters, their memory is their book. . . . In a recent examination of one of the schools, I was forcibly struck with their remembrance of passages of Scripture. Those questions which turned upon and called for passages of Scripture, the scholars answered more readily than any other."[34]

Slave illiteracy may also have contributed to the development of one of the most prominent features of black preaching: its narrative or story-telling form. In a recent analysis of black preaching, Henry H. Mitchell describes this pattern:

> The Black preacher is more likely to think of the Bible as an inexhaustible source of good preaching material than as an inert doctrinal and ethical authority. He sees it as full of insights—warm and wise and relevant to the everyday problems of a Black man. It provides the basis for unlimited creativity in the telling of rich and interesting stories, and these narrations command rapt attention while the eternal truth is brought to bear on the Black experience and the struggle for liberation. The Bible undergirds remembrance and gives permanent reference to whatever illuminating discernment the preacher has to offer.[35]

It is quite likely that narrative assumed a special importance in the black Christian community because of the long tradition of illiteracy. Someone who is preaching to a literate audience takes for granted that they will have their own access to the text being exposited. The black preacher had the additional task of familiarizing his or her audience with the content of the text.

Mitchell's description of black narrative preaching is also interesting for its reference to terms employed by our brief analysis of the four "minds" at work in Protestant attitudes toward the Bible. At first glance he seems to contrast the "narrative" approach with both doctrinalism and ethicalism: the black preacher, he insists, is interested in the Bible as a fund of insightful stories and not as a source for "inert doctrinal and ethical authority."

Does this mean that there are no doctrinalist or moralist interests in the religion of the black slaves, or their twentieth-century descendants? On the contrary, it is not difficult to find instances of doctrinal divisiveness among black Christians—at the 1980 convention of the National Black Evangelical Association, for example, an organizational rift occurred over the question of doctrinal flexibility versus strictness.[36]

But many analysts of black Christianity would insist that these doctrinalist patterns are atypical. William Bentley, a prominent leader in the Black Evangelical Association, suggests that some black Christian leaders have accepted the standards for "orthodoxy" set by middle-class white evangelicalism, standards which lead them to view "mainstream black Christianity . . . as virtually apostate."[37] Bentley insists that mainstream black Christians have

> an implicit rather than formalized approach to theology. It is not the theology of the Academy, it is the theology of the involved participant-actor on the stage of life. In this restricted sense it may be more American than the theology of most academies which are to a great extent based on a European model and reflect implicitly a European social experience.[38]

It is more difficult to argue, however, that there are no moralist tendencies in black Christianity. When Mitchell notes that black Christians do not look to the Bible for "inert . . . ethical authority," emphasis ought to be placed on the word "inert." What he seems to be suggesting is that black Christians do not view the Bible's moral authority in terms of rules or principles which function apart from the biblical narratives themselves. There can be no doubt, however, that there are strong "moral-example" themes in black spirituality: for example, the Christian is regularly encouraged to imitate the example of Daniel or of the three young men in the fiery furnace.[39]

Similarly there are clear elements of personal piety in black Christianity. The social unavailability of "the Book" led to an emphasis on personal communion with God, the leading of the Spirit, and even "direct revelation."[40]

But the central emphasis in accounts of black uses of the Bible seem to be culturalist in tone. This is Mitchell's understanding of the role of narrative in black preaching: "these narrations command rapt attention while the eternal truth is brought to bear on the Black experience and the struggle for liberation." Latta R. Thomas analyzes black uses of the Bible even more explicitly in culturalist terms:

> The greatest tragedy that could happen to Black people in a day when full liberation is the password is to have them pass up the greatest collective

document of human liberation that has ever come out of human experience and the effort of God. Black people must find out for themselves, especially in these days, what the Bible is really about. For it is a book in which it is recorded that the God and Sovereign of all history is always in the business of creating and freeing a people to clear the earth of injustice, bigotry, hatred, human slavery, political corruption, tyranny, sin, illness, and poverty. It is a book in which there is an invitation to all people who will hear and respond to put all else aside and join God in the job of renewing the earth, believing that it must and can be done.[41]

Culturalism, then, seems to be a dominant pattern in black Christianity, although the other patterns are not completely absent. At the very least it is apparent that the basic categories of our explanatory scheme apply also to the ways in which black Christians have understood and used the Bible.

A number of elements in the preceding discussion beg for clarification. A few observations are certainly in order concerning the applicability and implications of the explanatory scheme which we have sketched out.

First, it is probably most helpful to think of the four "minds"—doctrinalism, pietism, moralism, and culturalism—as representing Weberian "ideal types."[42] It could undoubtedly be demonstrated that there are both individual Christians and groups of Christians who conform very closely to one or another of these types; but such correspondence is not necessary for the scheme to be considered helpful or legitimate.

Indeed it is extremely difficult to go about proving that a given individual or group is "really," say, a doctrinalist. A person may describe his view of the Bible in decidedly doctrinalist terms, but then proceed to treat the Bible as something more than a doctrinal sourcebook.[43] On the other hand, a person may describe the Bible in very "rich" terms, but actually use the Bible in a narrowly doctrinalist or pietist manner.

Therefore none of the previous examples cited from actual writers should be taken as suggesting that the writer in question is in fact a "pure" example of type of position being illustrated. For example, a passage from Fosdick was cited to illustrate a certain variety of moralism. On other occasions, however, Fosdick uses doctrinalist and culturalist, even pietist, language to describe the Bible. And similar patterns hold for many of the other persons and groups cited.

If we think of the four "minds" as ideal types, then it is best to view individuals and groups as exhibiting different tendencies and emphases to which our labels can be applied. And very often when we look at actual statements and practices it will be necessary to treat specific viewpoints as "hybrids" of two or more tendencies. The evangelical apologist Francis Schaeffer provides a good example of such a hybrid statement. He contends that

> God has given us two kinds of propositional revelation in the Bible. First, didactic statements and commands. Second, a record of how he himself has worked in space-time history. With these two together we really have a very adequate knowledge, both as knowledge and as a basis for action.[44]

What is being proposed here is a doctrinalist-moralist perspective on the nature of biblical revelation.

Second, it should be noted that nothing much hangs on the actual labels which have been used in spelling out this scheme. In some quarters, for example, labels such as "pietistic" and "moralistic" are terms of reproach. That is not the intention here. "Pietism" seems to be a helpful way of describing an emphasis on piety, and "moralism" an emphasis on morality. The labels are not meant as evaluative terms.

Third, the labels used here are meant to point to actual emphases in American Protestantism. But the fourfold classification is not necessarily exhaustive. There may be twentieth-century attitudes toward the Bible which do not fit into this scheme. Some people view the Bible as primarily an historical record. Others see it as "great literature."[45] It is likely that these, and other, perspectives do not fit neatly within the proposed scheme. The four categories are meant, however, as a means of organizing the *dominant* Protestant Christian perspectives.

A final observation requires considerable elaboration. This scheme does seem to provide a helpful way of viewing many of the conflicts and tensions which have occurred within twentieth-century Protestantism. For example, the "fundamentalist-modernist" controversy of the early decades of this century can be viewed as a battle between doctrinalists and moralists.[46] Fundamentalism also had strong pietist tendencies, but the struggles against modernism combined a broad strand of non-Calvinistic pietism with the Calvinistic Theology of Old Princeton, which was doctrinalist. The fundamentalists, then, drew upon a doctrinalist arsenal for the battle, but when the battle was lost the pietistic tendencies seemed once again to predominate in some forms of the movement.[47]

The more recent "battle for the Bible" among evangelicals—which centers on the notion of "inerrancy"—includes a number of sub-conflicts.[48] One dispute is between inerrantist doctrinalists and non-inerrantist doctrinalists. But the voices of conservative pietists can also be heard, expressing public regret over the fact that some Christians would require agreement on a mere point of doctrine as a crucial basis for fellowship and cooperation. On the other hand, the "radical evangelicals" have been known to observe that they are more concerned about the "literal" interpretation of the Sermon on the Mount than they are about the "literal" interpretation of Genesis 1–3. This remark happens to come from a culturalist-evangelical orientation, but it could just as easily be expressed by a moralist.

So-called "liberal" twentieth-century Protestantism has been characterized for the most part by moralism and pietism, with occasional manifestations of culturalism. Indeed, it can be suggested as a rather cautious generalization that pure doctrinalism has been a very minor presence in liberal Protestantism—at least on a "popular" level—while pure moralism has been a very negligible presence in conservative Protestantism.

This last observation may seem puzzling, since we often associate "legalist" moralism with conservative Protestantism. And rightly so. But in those environs moralist tendencies seldom exist in pure form. For example, conservative "confessionalist" denominations with strong ethnic roots (e.g., the Missouri Synod Lutherans and the Christian Reformed Church) often manifest a hybrid form of doctrinalism-moralism. Similarly, "left-wing" charismatics might be pietist-culturalists (a pattern also found among Mennonites, Brethren, and Quakers), whereas "social Gospel" Methodists might be moralist-culturalists.

The fact that each of the types or perspectives, and their hybrid forms, is associated with a distinct way of viewing the Bible explains why Christians often seem to be talking at cross-purposes with each other when they argue about important matters. David Kelsey suggests that one of the important questions to ask about a theology which claims to be based on "scripture" is: "What aspect(s) of scripture is(are) taken to be authoritative?"[49] He insists on the importance of this question because different theologians construe "scripture" in different ways. For some, "scripture" is a set of doctrines; for others, it is a recital of saving events; for still others, it is a series of stories which point to, and can lead to, divine-human encounters, and so on.

The same concern emerges from our present discussion. What is at stake in arguments among doctrinalists, pietists, moralists, and culturalists are differing conceptions of what is meant by "scripture." Differing understandings also appear concerning which aspects of the biblical "content" are most authoritative or normative. This is not to suggest a relativism, according to which each person is right in his or her own eyes concerning what counts as the authoritative aspect of "scripture." But the fact that there *are* differing conceptions at work should at least convince us that arguments from the Bible often look confusing because they occur on a number of levels of discourse.

And now a very bold, and risky, generalization. The major thrust of twentieth-century white Protestantism can be explained in terms of moralism and pietism. Indeed, predominantly doctrinalist Christianity and predominantly culturalist Christianity do not seem to fare well in twentieth-century North American environs. There was, of course, a strong doctrinalist tone to early American Puritanism—along with a dose of culturalism. But Puritanism gradually moved away from doctrinalism in the direction of pietism.[50] Sydney Ahlstom has suggested, for example, that what began as a Puritan interest in the *doctrine* of election evolved into a pious, introspective focus on experiencing the *assurance* of one's elect status.[51]

Many have suggested that North Americans, by nature, consistently stress the pragmatic and experiential.[52] This may explain the attractiveness of moralism and pietism. Doctrinalist disputes take place, for the most part, among denominational and movemental elites—e.g., in theological schools and leadership caucuses. The same is true for culturalist discussions. Except for groups who are on the fringes of twentieth-century white Protestantism, predominantly culturalist themes also have attraction primarily among the elites. At the very least, it seems clear that the popular figures in twentieth-century American Protestantism come from either the moralist or pietist camps. On the contemporary scene, for example, Billy Graham and a host of lesser figures in evangelism are pietists, while Norman Vincent Peale and Robert Schuller are moralists or, perhaps, pietist-moralists.[53] Anita Bryant, Jerry Falwell, and other proponents of occasional "change America" themes use rhetoric which sounds culturalist, but their proposals are, it can be argued, essentially moralist in nature.

None of this is meant as a suggestion that Protestant America in the twentieth century has ignored the realm of culture. Rather, Protestants *have* interpreted cultural phenomena. But they have often done so from a moralist or pietist base, inherited from the nineteenth century. Winthrop Hudson has described this inheritance well:

> While Evangelicalism in general, with its stress upon feeling rather than doctrine, tended to undermine the theological foundation of a self-consciously formulated social and cultural ethic, the "romanticism" of popular Evangelicalism denied the necessity for such an ethic. It operated

on the assumption that converted individuals would automatically produce a Christian society and Christian culture.[54]

Subsequent perspectives on American corporate life, espoused by Henry Ward Beecher, Phillips Brooks and Russell Conwell, and the like, merely built on the assumption—as described by Hudson—that "good culture" would automatically flow from "good people."[55] This outlook is indeed an outlook *on* cultural phenomena, but it is a moralistic-pietistic outlook on those phenomena. Such an outlook denies that there are uniquely cultural norms or criteria which must be brought to bear on the understanding of cultural phenomena.

This essay has been primarily an exercise in taxonomy, and very primitive taxonomy at that. It might seem to some, however, that taxonomical pursuits, when the objects of classification are religious phenomena, are much too modest—asking, as it were, "little" questions about "big" issues. But in the study of attitudes toward the Bible these seemingly modest and small classificatory efforts can themselves be a way of getting clearer about the answers to the big, immodest questions. One of the benefits of the scheme outlined here is to provide new ways for looking at ongoing debates among Christians.

There have been groups of immigrant Christians, for example, who—in a picture painted with broad strokes—would have to be classified as "theological conservatives," but who have confessed great difficulties in choosing sides in the battles between "conservatives" and "liberals" in American Protestantism. Perhaps this sense of alienation from traditional North American patterns of theological debate is more than an immigrant quirk— and it is worth noting that a similar complaint is sometimes heard from black Christians. It may be that such groups perceive a harmony underlying many of the standard debates among North American Protestants. From their "outsider" vantage point they may see a pattern wherein Anglo-Americans, both conservative and liberal, presuppose a common pietist-moralist approach to the Bible, an approach which gives the traditional debaters a mutually agreed-upon framework for their arguments, but which puzzles those onlookers who operate out of predominantly doctrinalist or culturalist perspectives.

But none of this will, by itself, resolve the ultimate question: What is the *truth* of the matter? How *ought* the Bible to be viewed and used? Here, of course, some Christians at least will be tempted by a synthesis of sorts. And rightly so. Christians are committed to living by every word which proceeds from the mouth of the Lord. And it will not do to limit him, *a priori,* to speaking only certain kinds of words. Some of his words require our intellectual assent, others our pious submission, others our moral obedience, and others our cultural faithfulness. To know when the Lord is speaking one kind of word rather than another is not always an easy matter. But the difficulty is lessened somewhat by the recognition that he has refused to allow his words to be easily categorized.

NOTES

1. Sydney E. Ahlstrom's perceptive comments on the Bible in twentieth-century Protestantism are concentrated in his discussion of the fundamentalist-modernist struggle, *A Religious History of the American People* (New Haven: Yale University Press, 1972), pp. 772, 780–82, 810–14, 914. Winthrop S. Hudson's excellent but briefer survey also limits its discussion of the Bible's role to the same controversy, *Religion in America* (2nd ed., New York: Scribner's, 1973), pp. 208, 264–69, 282–83.

2. David H. Kelsey, *The Uses of Scripture in Recent Theology* (Philadelphia: Fortress, 1975). A similar sophistication informs Hans W. Frei, *The Eclipse of Biblical Narrative: A Study in Eighteenth and Nineteenth Century Hermeneutics* (New Haven: Yale University Press, 1974), whose treatment of European approaches to the Bible offers a potentially useful way of understanding American attitudes as well.

3. Bruce C. Birch and Larry L. Rasmussen, *Bible and Ethics in the Christian Life* (Minneapolis: Augsburg, 1976).

4. A good sampling of the "civil religion" discussion is collected in *American Civil Religion,* eds. Russell E. Richey and Donald G. Jones (New York: Harper & Row, 1974). See especially the key essay by Robert N. Bellah, "Civil Religion in America," *Daedalus* (Winter 1967), reprinted in Richey and Jones, pp. 21–44. Bellah updates his own thinking in *The Broken Covenant: American Civil Religion in Time of Trial* (New York: Seabury, 1976). Sidney E. Mead, *The Old Religion in the Brave New World* (Berkeley: University of California Press, 1977), sums up a lifetime of provocative reflection on "civil religion" by concluding that the principles of American constitutional government and of America's Christian traditions "stand in a relation of mutual antagonism and are perhaps logically mutually exclusive" (p. 2). The most perceptive recent treatment of the topic is John F. Wilson, *Public Religion in American Culture* (Philadelphia: Temple University Press, 1979), who finds a number of different kinds of American public piety and who asks searching questions about the methods used to discover, and to discuss, civil religion.

5. See above, essays by Harry Stout, Mark A. Noll, and Nathan O. Hatch.

6. For an Anabaptist critique of American "civil religion," see John A. Lapp, "The Evangelical Factor in American Politics," in *Evangelicalism and Anabaptism,* ed. C. Norman Kraus (Scottdale, Pa.: Herald, 1979), pp. 83–100.

7. "Evangelical Christianity in the United States: National Parallel Surveys of General Public and Clergy," conducted for *Christianity Today* by the Gallup Organization, Inc., and the Princeton Religion Research Center (Princeton: Gallup, n.d.), pp. 94, 120, 126, 132.

8. Harry Emerson Fosdick, *The Living of These Days: An Autobiography* (New York: Harper & Bros., 1956).

9. Charles B. Wheeler presents a cogent statement, from a novel vantage point, of the gap between pulpit and pew, in "But Where Did Cain Get His Wife?—Reflections on Teaching the Bible as Literature," *South Atlantic Quarterly,* 80 (Winter 1981), 56–57. This same theme is interwoven through the several essays addressing the topic, "The Bible in the Church Today," *Theology Today,* 37 (April 1980), 1–84.

10. Nicholas Wolterstorff, "The AACS in the CRC," *The Reformed Journal,* December 1974, pp. 9–16. Wolterstorff distinguishes between three "minds" in Dutch Calvinism: "doctrinalism," "pietism," and "Kuyperianism." This last label refers to the cultural perspective of the Dutch theologian and political leader, Abraham Kuyper (1837–1920). As a label, it obviously lacks ecumenical applicability, thus my use of the term "culturalism" in this essay. I introduce a fourth category, "moralism," which plays no significant role among Dutch Calvinists.

11. Charles Hodge, "The Theology of the Intellect and That of Feelings," *Essays and Reviews* (New York: Robert Carter & Bros., 1857), p. 610.

12. Kelsey, *Uses of Scripture,* p. 24.

13. Philip Mauro, "Life in the Word," in *The Fundamentals: A Testimony to the Truth,* Vol. V (Chicago: Testimony Publishing, n.d.), p. 16.

14. Howard P. Colson, *I Recommend the Bible* (Nashville: Broadman, 1976), p. 147.

15. On the way in which the charismatic movement approximates earlier pietist emphases, see James H. Smylie, "Testing the Spirits in the American Context: Great Awakenings, Pentecostalism and the Charismatic Movement," *Interpretation,* 33 (January 1979), 32–46.

16. This literature has been a staple in recent American history, as attested by the best-seller status of Hannah W. Smith's *Christian's Secret of a Happy Life* (1875), Henry Drummond's *Greatest Thing in the World* (1890), E. Stanley Jones's *Victorious Living* (1936), Fulton J. Sheen's *Peace of Soul* (1949), Billy Graham's *Peace with God* (1953), and the current works of popular authors like Catherine Marshall, Philip Keller, Watchman Nee, and Marjorie Holmes, to mention only a few of the many who practice this genre successfully. A helpful study of this literature is Louis Schneider and Sanford M. Dornbusch, *Popular Religion: Inspirational Books in America* (Chicago: University of Chicago Press, 1958). See also Willard Thorp, "The Religious Novel as Best Seller in America," in *Religious Perspectives in American Culture,* eds. James Ward Smith and A. Leland Jamison (Princeton: Princeton University Press, 1961).

17. Thomas Oden, *The Intensive Group Experience: The New Pietism* (Philadelphia: Westminster, 1972), pp. 57–59.

18. Dwight L. Moody, *Pleasure and Profit in Bible Study* (Chicago: Moody, n.d.), p. 11.

19. A 1968 edition of *In His Steps* announced that the book had sold over 8,000,000 copies (Old Tappan, N.J.: Revell). Sheldon's moral vision is the subject of several recent studies, including P. S. Boyer, *"In His Steps:* A Reappraisal," *American Quarterly,* 23 (May 1971), 60–78; and James H. Smylie, "Sheldon's *In His Steps:* Conscience and Discipleship," *Theology Today,* 32 (April 1975), 32–45.

20. See the discussion of *Nachfolge Christi* (Imitation of Christ) in Abraham P. Toews, *The Problem of Mennonite Ethics* (Grand Rapids, Mich.: Eerdmans, 1963), *passim,* especially p. 217.

21. Harry Emerson Fosdick, *The Modern Use of the Bible* (New York: Macmillan: 1958), p. 195.

22. Mary Ellen Chase, *The Bible and the Common Reader* (New York: Macmillan, 1944), pp. 10–11.
23. Walter Rauschenbusch, *A Theology for the Social Gospel* (Nashville: Abingdon, 1945), p. 6. On the importance of biblical themes for the early Social Gospel, see C. Howard Hopkins, *The Rise of the Social Gospel in American Protestantism 1865–1915* (New Haven: Yale University Press, 1940), pp. 43–48.
24. Jim Wallis, *Agenda for Biblical People* (New York: Harper & Row, 1976), pp. 69–70.
25. These themes are prominent in periodicals associated with the Christian Reformed Church, such as *The Banner* or *The Reformed Journal.*
26. H. Richard Niebuhr, *Christ and Culture* (New York: Harper & Row, 1951).
27. For Anabaptist culturalism, the best studies are by John A. Hostetler, *Hutterite Society* (Baltimore: Johns Hopkins University Press, 1974) and *Amish Society* (3rd ed., Baltimore: Johns Hopkins University Press, 1980). For the way in which Mennonite culturalism is adapting to more common patterns in American life, see Barbara B. Wiesel, "From Separatism to Evangelicalism: A Case Study of Social and Cultural Change Among the Franconia Conference Mennonites, 1945–1970," *Review of Religious Research,* 18 (Spring 1977), 254–63; and J. Howard Kaufmann, "Boundary Maintenance and Cultural Assimilation of Contemporary Mennonites," *Mennonite Quarterly Review,* 51 (July 1977), 227–40.
28. Rauschenbusch's early proposals for a Christian transformation of culture have recently been published as *The Righteousness of the Kingdom,* Max L. Stackhouse, ed. (Nashville: Abingdon, 1968). Something of the current interest in Rauschenbusch as both theologian and social theorist is suggested in Glenn C. Altschuler, "Walter Rauschenbusch: Theology, the Church, and the Social Gospel," *Foundations,* 22 (April–June 1979), 140–51; and Charles R. Strain, "Walter Rauschenbusch: A Resource for Public Theology," *Union Seminary Quarterly Review,* 34 (Fall 1978), 23–34.
29. The literature on liberation theology is mushrooming, but some hints as to its many dimensions can be glimpsed in the following essays: John Bennett, "Fitting the Liberation Theme into Our Theological Agenda," *Christianity and Crisis,* 37 (July 18, 1977), 164–69; James H. Cone, "Asian Theology Today: Searching for Definitions," *Christian Century,* 96 (May 23, 1979), 589–91; Roger L. Shinn, "Liberation, Reconciliation, and 'Just Revolution,'" *Ecumenical Review,* 30 (October 1978), 319–32; and Ronald J. Sider, "An Evangelical Theology of Liberation," *Christian Century,* 97 (March 19, 1980), 314–18.
30. See Timothy L. Smith, "Religion and Ethnicity in America," *American Historical Review,* 83 (December 1978), 1155–85; *Immigrants and Religion in Urban America,* eds. Randall M. Miller and Thomas D. Marzik (Philadelphia: Temple University Press, 1977); and the significant sections on religion in *Ethnic Leadership in America,* John Higham, ed. (Baltimore: Johns Hopkins University Press, 1978).
31. For a general picture, see Albert J. Raboteau, *Slave Religion: The "Invisible Institution" in the Antebellum South* (New York: Oxford University Press, 1978), pp. 234, 239; and Eugene D. Genovese, *Roll, Jordan, Roll: The World the Slaves Made* (New York: Vintage, 1976; orig. 1972), pp. 169, 186, 191, 561–66, 725n4.
32. Raboteau, *Slave Religion,* pp. 239–40.
33. *Ibid.,* p. 240.
34. *Ibid.,* p. 241.
35. Henry Mitchell, *Black Preaching* (New York: Harper & Row, 1979), p. 113.

36. See "Theology-Culture Rift Surfaces Among Evangelical Blacks," *Christianity Today*, May 23, 1980, p. 44. Another example is the participation of blacks in early doctrinal disputes within Pentecostalism, including divisive debate on the "Jesus Only" Movement (a Unitarian focus on Christ). See Vinson Synan, *The Holiness-Pentecostal Movement* (Grand Rapids, Mich.: Eerdmans, 1971), pp. 220–22.

37. William H. Bentley, "Bible Believers in the Black Community," in *The Evangelicals: What They Believe, Who They Are, Where They Are Changing*, eds. David F. Wells and John D. Woodbridge (Nashville: Abingdon, 1975), pp. 110, 118.

38. *Ibid.*, p. 112.

39. See Donald Mathews, *Religion in the Old South* (Chicago: University of Chicago Press, 1977), p. 218. For discussions of moral-imitation themes in "black spirituals" see Miles Mark Fisher, *Negro Slave Songs in the United States* (New York: Citadel, 1953); and James Cone, *The Spirituals and the Blues* (New York: Seabury, 1972).

40. Raboteau, *Slave Religion*, p. 242.

41. Latta R. Thomas, *Biblical Faith and the Black American* (Valley Forge, Pa.: Judson, 1976), p. 13. A somewhat broader consideration of the Bible and blacks appears in Charles B. Copher, "Perspectives and Questions: The Black Religious Experience and Biblical Studies," *Theological Education*, 6 (Spring 1970), 181–88.

42. Max Weber, *The Theory of Social and Economic Organization*, ed. Talcott Parsons (New York: Free Press, 1964; orig. 1947), pp. 13–14, 89–90.

43. See W. Andrew Hoffecker, *Piety and the Princeton Theologians: Archibald Alexander, Charles Hodge, and Benjamin Warfield* (Grand Rapids, Mich.: Baker, 1981), for examples of piety among the doctrinalists.

44. Francis Schaeffer, *The Church at the End of the Twentieth Century* (Downers Grove, Ill.: InterVarsity Press, 1970), p. 53.

45. An apologetic note is strong in the manuals for teaching the Bible as literature which followed the Supreme Court's 1963 ruling prohibiting the religious use of the Bible in public schools: e.g., James S. Ackerman, *On Teaching the Bible as Literature* (Bloomington: Indiana University Press, 1967); *The Bible as Literature*, ed. Alton J. Capps (New York: McGraw-Hill, 1971) James S. Ackerman *et al., Teaching the Old Testament in English Classes* (Bloomington: Indiana University Press, 1973). That note is largely absent in more mature studies which take for granted that a book read by millions of people for centuries deserves serious study: e.g., Kenneth R. R. Gros Louis *et al., Literary Interpretations of Biblical Narratives* (Nashville: Abingdon, 1974); and Leland Ryken, *The Literature of the Bible* (Grand Rapids, Mich.: Zondervan, 1974).

46. See George M. Marsden, *Fundamentalism and American Culture: The Shaping of Twentieth-Century Evangelicalism 1870–1925* (New York: Oxford University Press, 1980), "Holiness," pp. 72–101, and "The Defense of the Faith," pp. 102–23.

47. See Joel A. Carpenter, "A Shelter in the Time of Storm: Fundamentalist Institutions and the Rise of Evangelical Protestantism, 1929-1942," *Church History*, 49 (March 1980), 62–75.

48. See note 13 in the Introduction above.

49. Kelsey, *Uses of Scripture*, p. 2.

50. The classic study of this change which, however, uses key phrases differently than

I do, remains Joseph Haroutunian, *Piety Versus Moralism: The Passing of the New England Theology* (New York: Henry Holt, 1932).

51. Sydney E. Ahlstrom, "From Puritanism to Evangelicalism: A Critical Perspective," in Wells and Woodbridge, eds., *The Evangelicals*, p. 272. Richard Niebuhr described a similar process in the shift from "covenant" to "compact." "The Idea of Covenant and American Democracy," *Church History*, 23 (June 1954), 126–35.

52. The pragmatic orientation is a major theme in Daniel J. Boorstin, *The Americas*, 3 vols. (New York: Vintage, 1958–73), e.g., Vol. I: *The Colonial Experience*, "An American Frame of Mind," pp. 147–68.

53. See, for example, the sensitive articles on Billy Graham by Richard V. Pierard, "Billy Graham and the U.S. Presidency," *Journal of Church and State*, 22 (Winter 1980), 107–27; and "Billy Graham and Vietnam: From Cold Warrior to Peacemaker," *Christian Scholar's Review*, 10 (1980), 37–51.

54. Winthrop S. Hudson, *American Protestantism* (Chicago: University of Chicago Press, 1961), p. 135. Sidney E. Mead has noted how American denominationalism works against a doctrinal orientation in "Denominationalism: The Shape of Protestantism in America," *The Lively Experiment* (New York: Harper & Row, 1963), p. 114.

55. Brooks and Conwell have not received notable scholarly attention, but William G. McLoughlin provides ample documentation for looking at Beecher this way, *The Meaning of Henry Ward Beecher: An Essay on the Shifting Values of Mid-Victorian America* (New York: Knopf, 1970).

VIII

The Quest for a Catholic Vernacular Bible in America

GERALD P. FOGARTY, S.J.
University of Virginia

Roman Catholicism in the United States is part of the universal Catholic Church. Unlike other American denominations, therefore, it has neither an approach to nor an appropriation of the sacred Scriptures different from the Catholic Church elsewhere. It is not only biblically based but sacramentally oriented. It accepts as its own the decree of the fourth session of the Council of Trent in 1546 pertaining to Revelation, the canon of Scripture, and the pre-eminence of the Latin Vulgate. Trent had taught that Revelation is "contained in the written books and unwritten traditions which have come down to us, having been received by the apostles from the mouth of Christ himself, or from the apostles themselves, by the dictation of the Holy Spirit, having been transmitted, as it were, from hand to hand." The Council also listed as canonical those books of the Old Testament found in the Septaugint but not found in the Hebrew Bible. Normative for all "public readings, disputations, sermons and expositions" was to be the Latin Vulgate. Finally, the Council decreed that

> in order to restrain irresponsible minds, that no one shall presume in matters of faith or morals pertaining to the edification of Christian doctrine to rely on his own conceptions to turn Scripture to his own meaning, contrary to the meaning that Holy Mother Church has held and holds—for it belongs to her to judge the true sense and interpretation of Holy Scripture—or to interpret the Scripture in a way contrary to the unanimous consensus of the Fathers, even though such interpretations not be intended for publication . . .[1]

Trent had responded to the challenge of the Reformers by prohibiting private interpretation of Scripture and also by holding up as normative the Latin Vulgate and the books contained in it.

Catholicism in the United States was loyal to Trent's teaching, but it faced a unique situation which placed a particular emphasis on that teaching. The American Church was primarily composed of immigrants, whom Church leaders sought to preserve from the proselytizing overtures of evangelical Protestants. The Catholic Church's prohibition of private interpretation of Scripture varied from American society's quest for liberty and admittedly was too often construed by Catholics as a prohibition of private reading of Scripture. Lyman Beecher was a representative Protestant opponent to Catholicism and its stance on Scripture. A Boston sermon of his had led to the burning of the Ursuline Convent in Charlestown, Massachusetts, in the summer of 1834.[2] In his *Plea for the West,* he placed his own construction on the Catholic Church's prohibition of private interpretation as meaning "that none may read the Bible but by permission of the priesthood, and no one be permitted to understand it and worship God according to the dictates of his own conscience."[3] The Catholic teaching on Scripture, he thought, prohibited the private reading of the Bible and subjected Catholics to a condition of servitude to priests and a foreign pope. For him, the solution to this anti-American attitude was simple:

> If they could read the Bible, and might and did, their darkened intellect would brighten, and their bowed down mind would rise. If they dared to think for themselves, the contrast of protestant independence with their thraldom, would awaken the desire of equal privileges, and put an end to an arbitrary clerical dominion over trembling superstitious minds. If the pope and potentates of Europe held no dominion over ecclesiastics here, we might trust to time and circumstances to mitigate their ascendence and produce assimilation. But for conscience sake and patronage, they are dependent on the powers that be across the deep, by whom they are sustained and nurtured; and receive and organize all who come, and retain all who are born, while by argument, and a Catholic education, they beguile the children of credulous unsuspecting protestants into their own communion.[4]

Beecher had, of course, created a stereotype of Catholic teaching. His complaints against Catholics included their loyalty to the Roman pontiff and the insidious nature of their schools, to the destruction of which he had contributed. But his chief irritation was their failure to read the Bible. The Bible for American Protestants, however, meant the Authorized Version, more familiarly known as the King James Bible. This, indeed, Catholics were forbidden to read since it was not a translation of the Vulgate. In the 1840s, one priest in New York State was overly zealous in enforcing Trent's regulation. He collected the Bibles given to his immigrant parishioners by one of the Protestant Bible societies and publicly burned them.[5]

The incident obtained national notoriety and seemed to provide clear evidence that the Catholic Church prohibited the reading of the Bible. The New York *Freeman's Journal,* perhaps with the overt support of the fiery Bishop John Hughes, declared that:

> To burn or otherwise destroy a spurious or corrupt copy of the Bible, whose circulation would tend to disseminate erroneous principles of faith or morals, we hold to be an act not only justifiable but praiseworthy.[6]

Not only were Catholic leaders opposed to their people's reading the Protestant version of the Bible, they were also adamant that their children not be compelled to read it in the public schools. In New York, Bishop Hughes waged an unsuccessful campaign from the fall of 1840 to the spring of 1842 either to gain a share of the funds administered by the Public School Society for Catholic schools or to provide for neighborhood school boards to determine the content of any religious instruction given. As a last resort he would even urge the removal of religion from the public schools altogether. His failure resulted in the entrenchment of the King James Version of the Bible in the New York public schools and also in an increase in parochial schools.[7]

In Philadelphia, Bishop Francis P. Kenrick, inspired by Hughes's activity in New York, complained to the Board of Controllers of the public schools that Catholic children were being read the King James Version exclusively and were compelled to attend religious exercises. He requested that his children be allowed to use a Catholic version of the Bible and be excused from religious instruction. In January 1843 the school board complied with his request by allowing children to read from any version of the Bible selected by their parents. The decision of the school board, however, appeared to the nativists as a surrender to papist designs to remove the Bible from the public schools. In vain did Kenrick attempt to explain that he only wished to preserve the right of Catholic children to read their own Bible. During the following year, the feeling of the nativists was fired to fever pitch and resulted in rioting. In May, two Catholic churches were burned and several people killed in three days of clashes between Irish Catholics and native Americans. In July, the militia was called out to defend a Catholic church, where a cache of arms had been found. In the ensuing foray thirteen men were killed and over fifty wounded in three days of rioting. The Grand Jury appointed to conduct an official investigation of the causes of the rioting and destruction concluded that it was due to "the efforts of a portion of the community to exclude the Bible from our Public Schools." The entire trouble was ascribed exclusively to the Irish.[8]

It was impossible for the native Americans of the 1840s to distinguish between the Catholic prohibition of private interpretation of the Bible and private reading. They were likewise blinded to the distinction between allowing the Catholic version of the Bible to be read and the exclusion of the Bible altogether. "Native Americans" meant Protestants, and they were watching their hegemony over American culture begin to collapse. By the census of 1840, Catholics were the single largest denomination, and the hordes of Irish and Germans who fled the potato famine and the failed revolts of 1848 had not yet arrived.[9] Yet the long-term result of the religious clashes in the 1830s and 1840s was to remove the Bible and religious instruction from the public schools. In 1890, Archbishop John Ireland of St. Paul asserted that his only reservation about public schools was that they excluded from their curriculum the religion which civilized Western society and preserved the family and society.[10] The issue raised by Catholics in the 1840s about the Protestant values inculcated in public schools, however, remains in 1981, when the Anti-Defamation League of B'nai B'rith has sought to prevent public school boards from allowing the Gideon Society to distribute copies of the New Testament in the schools.[11]

The battle to allow Catholic children to read their own version of the Bible in the public schools is, of course, directly related to the issue of providing a Catholic translation of the Bible in the United States. The standard Catholic translation of the Bible into English was familiarly known as the "Douay Version." More properly this was the work done by English Catholic exiles on the Continent. The New Testament was published at Rheims in 1582 and the Old Testament at Douay in 1609. This translation was subsequently revised by Bishop Richard Challoner, coadjutor of the Vicar Apostolic of the London District between 1749 and 1763.[12] This revision of the Douay-Rheims translation with Challoner's notes was the standard English Bible in use among Catholics on the eve of the Revolution and during the nineteenth century.

Providing copies of the Douay Bible was one of the primary concerns for the American Church. Early in 1789, Mathew Carey, an Irish publisher who immigrated to Philadelphia, suggested to John Carroll, who had recently been named the first Bishop of Baltimore, that he publish the Douay Bible. Carroll was enthusiastic for the project, for he desired to see that version "in the hands of our people, instead of those translations, which they purchase in stores and from Booksellers in the Country." But he was not sanguine as to the support Carey could expect from the people for the project.[13] Subsequently he remarked that the people in Maryland, at least, were so accustomed to receiving books free-of-charge from the clergy that they were not generous in subscribing to the publication.[14] Despite a meager response to his endeavor, Carey published the complete Douay Bible in 1790.[15]

Carroll continued to be concerned with providing his people with copies of the Douay Bible. In 1810, two years after he was elevated to Archbishop of Baltimore, he met with his suffragans. Recognizing the danger to their flocks of the use of non-Catholic Bibles, they decreed that the Douay Bible was to be used for any section of Scripture quoted in Catholic prayer books. In 1829 the bishops of the Province of Baltimore, which then included the entire United States, assembled for their first council. They decreed that the Douay Bible was to be used throughout the country. At the request of the Congregation of Propaganda, to which the American Church was subject, they inserted in their decree the clause that all future editions of the Bible were to be accompanied with "explanations selected from the holy Fathers of the Church or from learned Catholic men." This clause was taken from the rules of the Congregation of the Index governing the publication of vernacular Bibles and was virtually that prescribed by the Council of Trent in 1564.[16]

In their pastoral letter to the laity, the bishops exhorted the faithful to recognize that "one of the most precious legacies bequeathed to us by the Apostles and Evangelists is the sacred volume of Holy Scriptures." These were "profitable to the pastor . . . to reprove, to correct, to instruct unto justice" and "when used with due care, and an humble and docile spirit, for the edification and instruction of the faithful." While warning against raising "vain questions and strifes of words" and private interpretation, the bishops urged that "when in the moments of leisure and reflection you take up the sacred book, be impressed with the conviction that you then converse with God Himself; commence therefore by prayer, to obtain that it may be to you a lamp to guide your feet in safety through the shades of this valley of death." Citing the Council of Trent's decree that the Scriptures were to be understood according to the sense and interpretation of the Church, the bishops warned against "new and arbitrary interpretations," which flowed from other religious movements or from "the improvement of science" and "the progress of the arts," for "the word of God, being unalterable truth, cannot vary its meaning with the fluctuating opinions of men."[17]

Relating the approval of translations of Scripture to the authority of bishops, they declared

> Equally anxious to fulfill our important trust, we too desire to guard you against mistake and error. We therefore earnestly caution you against the indiscriminate use of unauthorised versions, for unfortunately many of those which are placed within your reach are extremely erroneous and defective. The Douay translation from the Vulgate of the Old Testament, together with the Remish translation of the New Testament, are our best English versions; but as some printers have undertaken in these States, by their own authority, without our sanction, to print and publish editions which have not been submitted to our examination, we cannot hold ourselves responsible for the correctness of such copies.[18]

The bishops, therefore, were anxious to provide the Douay translation but unable to prevent the dissemination of other versions.

In a separate letter addressed to the clergy, the bishops exhorted them to "seek daily to extend your knowledge, that you may improve your people. . . . The sacred volume of the Scriptures should be to you as the rolled book was to Ezechiel; you should eat it before you go to speak to the children of Israel." On the other hand, "to those who are negligent or arrogant, on this hear, the same book is like to the flying volume of Zacharias; it is a curse that goeth forth over the face of the earth for judgment and destruction." The priests were especially to familiarize themselves with those passages of Scripture which were disputed.[19]

The Second Provincial Council in 1833 did not pass any new legislation on the Bible, but it did address the subject in its pastoral letter. For the clergy, especially, "the continual study of the Holy Bible is absolutely of obligation." "The people," continued the bishops, "seek the law from the lips of the priest, and how shall he communicate that with which he has not been intimately conversant?" But that Scripture was the word of God was known only "by the testimony of that cloud of holy witnesses which the Saviour vouchsafed to establish as our guide through this desert over which we journey towards our permanent abode." These same witnesses "together with the book . . . gave to us the testimony of its meaning; and this explanation no man has power to change." Both Scripture and tradition, therefore, were to be the guides for the priests' understanding and preaching of Scripture, but Bishop John England of Charleston, the author of the pastoral letters from 1829 to 1840, did not specifically mention "tradition." Rather he spoke of Scripture and its "interpretation." In expounding where this interpretation was to be found, he gave one of the first expressions of what was to be a strong American tradition—the collegiality of bishops:

> Thus the recorded testimony of those ancient and venerable witnesses, who in every nation and every age, proclaimed in the name of the Catholic Church, and with its approbation, the interpretation of the Holy Bible, whether they were assembled in their councils or dispersed over the surface of the Christian world, is an harmonious collection of pure light, which sheds upon the inspired page the mild lustre which renders it pleasing to the eye, grateful to the understanding, and consoling to the heart. By this learning the true sense and meaning of the divine writings, Reverend and learned brethren, you will "keep that committed to your truth, avoiding the profane novelties of words, and oppositions of knowledge falsely so called"; you will, "shun profane and vain speeches; for they grow much towards impiety"; you will be easily distinguished from those who are "always learning and never attaining the knowledge of truth"; you will "continue in the things you have learned, and which have been committed to you"; you will "hold the form of sound words," which you have heard from *us and from our predecessors* in the faith, and in the love of Christ Jesus.[20]

By interpretation, then, England and the other bishops meant the constant witness to the meaning of the Scripture as given by the fathers and the teaching authority of the Church, the bishops together with the Pope.

The American bishops, it should be noted, did not particularly emphasize the study of Scripture in their councils, for these had been summoned for other purposes. That they took time in the pastoral letters to exhort the faithful to read the Scriptures, however, does indicate their desire to disseminate the sacred books. But the only aspect of Scripture on which they legislated was to provide for the Douay Bible. This gave rise to one of the most ambitious undertakings in American Catholic scholarship in the mid-nineteenth century.

Francis P. Kenrick, the Bishop of Philadelphia, was widely regarded as the most learned theologian among the bishops. He had studied at the Urban College of Propaganda in Rome before coming to the United States, where he taught theology at St. Thomas Seminary and St. Joseph's College, Bardstown, Kentucky. In 1830 he was named coadjutor bishop of Philadelphia and succeeded to the see in 1842. In the midst of his debate with the public school board to allow Catholic children to read the Douay Bible, which led to the Philadelphia riots described above, he undertook to make a new edition of the Douay Bible, which was in essence a new translation of the Vulgate as compared with the original languages. Originally, he seems to have envisioned this as a joint venture with his brother, Peter R. Kenrick, then the coadjutor bishop of St. Louis and subsequently bishop and archbishop of that see.

Although Francis Kenrick's understanding of what would later be called higher criticism was defective, his openness to the concept of development within the sacred books was novel among American Catholics at the time. The "recent theory about the composition of the book of Genesis," he wrote his brother in September 1843,

> appeals to me as having merit—[namely] that the book of Genesis is the result of the labors of various [earlier] writers, who, divinely guided, described contemporary facts: Moses then recognized these [older documents] and gave them the [new] form of his narrative; so also the Pentateuch, the books of which he is the chief author, later bear the authority of his name. I am not sure how well this theory could be verified in the text of Scripture. I do not hold to it as absolutely certain. But there are reasons to be found in the diversity of style, and the minute and accurate description of facts, if I may form a judgment of this subject. For, while I admit that main facts could easily be accounted for by tradition, I can hardly believe that the genealogical tables and other points more minute could have been preserved [to the time of Moses] without some form of written monument. I will ask to have your judgment on this subject.[21]

From time to time, Francis would chide his brother for not giving him more advice on the translation.

Kenrick's translation appeared in separate volumes from 1849 to 1860. In 1849, he published the four Gospels and began work on the Acts of the Apostles with the help of Father Augustine Hewitt, a convert, at that time a Redemptorist and later one of the first Paulists.[22] As his work progressed his attitude toward the Vulgate began to shift. Early in 1850 he wrote Peter that he could see the advantage of having a Catholic exegete go over his translation, but he felt that any subsequent editions of his work would follow his method, "so that all may understand how admirable the [Greek] codices and their critics agree with the [text of the Latin] Vulgate." He did not think it "prudent to give points of controversy [differences of opinion] on various interpretations; as the true meaning will be clear enough to the reader by [simple] notes to clear up the meaning of obscure passages." For the present, he hoped only to receive corrections, so that if his version should gain general approval among the bishops, "I would like to make it smaller in bulk for the use of the faithful."[23]

In 1851 Kenrick was named the Archbishop of Baltimore but he continued work on his translation. Late in 1858 he reported to his brother about the plan for a common English Bible for England, Ireland, and the United States. The work was to be under the general direction of John Henry Newman, who waited only for the approval of the English bishops. Kenrick had heard that his own version was that most favored by Newman for the common translation. Unfortunately, this plan came to nought, when the English bishops failed to give their approval.[24] But Archbishop Kenrick was developing as a biblical scholar. In October of 1859 Kenrick told his brother of the advice of Orestes Brownson, apparently to make use of the King James Version in his translation. But the archbishop could not do this "since the Holy See holds the [Latin] Vulgate to be the norm for translations into the vernacular." While he found that the Vulgate and the King James Version differed on many points, he feared that he might be thought too "daring" if he followed the latter on such points. The translator of the Pentateuch of the King James Version, he thought, had "turned the text with much freedom," but "if I set forth all the peculiarities of the text as they are, and follow closely the way of the Protestant translations, it will appear that I am betraying the cause which I have undertaken to vindicate, that is, the integrity of the Vulgate." He closed his discussion of his translation with the report that "Brownson believes that Newman ought to do the work, with hardly any consideration of the Vulgate."[25]

Kenrick published his volume on the Pentateuch, the next to last volume in his translation, in 1860. In his introduction, he said that he had revised the Douay Version in the light of the Hebrew, "which, however, I did not always feel at liberty to render closely where it would imply a departure from the Vulgate."[26] Kenrick died in 1863, and in 1866 the bishops of all the provinces of the United States assembled for the Second Plenary Council. Archbishop John Baptist Purcell of Cincinnati, in the name of a subcommittee, proposed that Kenrick's translation with the notes of Bishop Challoner be adopted as the standard version for the United States. Archbishop Peter R. Kenrick strongly opposed this, for reasons unstated, and ultimately the proposal was dropped.[27] When the decrees of the Council went to Rome for approval, however, the Congregation of Propaganda instructed the American bishops to compare the Douay and other English versions of the Scripture and in the next plenary council propose the one version approved for common use.[28]

In 1884 the American bishops held the Third Plenary Council, the last national legislative assembly of the American hierarchy. They again discussed a common English version of the Bible, recalling that nothing definitive had been decided at the previous Council. Several of the bishops praised Kenrick's "version," but Peter Kenrick stated that this was not "a version properly speaking, but rather a new edition of the Douay version."[29] The Council passed no new legislation concerning the Bible in the vernacular, but it did call for seminarians to study the Vulgate and for the Gospel to be proclaimed in the vernacular language on Sundays and Holy Days. The sacramental orientation of the American Church was evident with the prescription that a long sermon was unnecessary, especially at Solemn Masses, but that a "sermon properly speaking should occur at the last mass [on Sunday] which is regarded among us as the mass of the community or parish."[30]

In their pastoral letter, however, the bishops did treat of the role of the Scripture in the spiritual lives of their faithful. They reminded their people "that the most highly valued treasure of every family library, and the most frequently and lovingly made use of, should be the Holy Scriptures." Thomas à Kempis, they said, had often thanked "our Lord for having bestowed on us not only the adorable treasure of His Body in the Holy Eucharist, but also that of the Holy Scriptures." Here was one of the few statements in which the bishops linked word and sacrament. But, as to the proper version of the Scripture, the bishops were ambivalent. "We hope that no family," they wrote,

> can be found amongst us without a correct version of the Holy Scriptures. Among other versions, we recommend the Douay, which is venerable as used by our forefathers for three centuries, which comes down to us sanctioned by innumerable authorizations, and which was suitably annotated by the learned Bishop Challoner, by Canon Haydock, and especially by the late Archbishop Kenrick.[31]

In retrospect, it is difficult to determine whether the failure to specify a particular English version of Scripture was intentional, but it may be interesting to note that the personal copy of the New Testament used by Denis J. O'Connell, one of the secretaries of the Council and later one of the principal leaders of the liberal party in the American Church, was the Revised Version, i.e., the revision of the King James Version.[32]

Of greater importance, however, was that the Council also legislated for the foundation of the Catholic University of America, which was the conscious expression of the American Church's desire to enter into the mainstream of scholarship. By and large, American Catholic scholarship in most areas reflected what was happening in Europe rather than original work. The Catholic University of America thus heavily depended upon professors brought over from Europe. Bishop John Keane, the university's first rector, procured the services of Henri Hyvernat as the professor of Assyriology and Egyptology. Hyvernat was to initiate a tradition of excellence at the university in the study of ancient and Near-Eastern languages, an area which would not be affected by the condemnation of Modernism in 1907. For the Old Testament, however, Keane chose an American, Father Charles P. Grannan, whose teaching reported on the progressive tendencies of European scholarship.

Grannan's openness to the historico-critical method in Scripture actually contributed to the forced resignation of Keane. In 1895 Monsignor Joseph Schroeder, professor of dogmatic theology at the university, complained to Cardinal Mariano Rampolla, the Vatican secretary of state, that Keane was tolerating heresy. As an example, he cited the list of theses recently defended by a student, Father William Russell, later the Bishop of Charleston, that the Council of Trent had not defined the canon of Scripture as that contained in St. Jerome's edition of the Vulgate. This, said Schroeder, was a thesis lifted from the writings of Alfred Loisy,[33] a liberal biblical scholar who had been dismissed from his professorship at the Institut Catholique in Paris. Schroeder's complaint was but one issue leading to Keane's resignation in 1896. Keane's resignation, in turn, was the first in a series of defeats, which ultimately led in 1899 to the condemnation of Americanism by Pope Leo XIII. Americanism was an attempt on the part of a group of liberal American churchmen, including Keane, Cardinal James Gibbons, Archbishop of Baltimore and chancellor of the Catholic University, Archbishop John Ireland of St. Paul, and Monsignor Denis O'Connell, who was dismissed as rector of the American College in Rome, to reconcile Catholicism to American culture and modern movements.

Grannan, however, was at this point untouched by the controversy. In 1895 he had drawn up a detailed program for scriptural studies, based on Leo XIII's encyclical of 1893, *Providentissimus Deus*. In 1902 he was the first American named to the newly formed Pontifical Biblical Commission. What caused his difficulty was a personality conflict with Denis O'Connell, who became the rector of the university in 1903. After the condemnation of Americanism, O'Connell seems to have wished to cleanse himself of any taint of heterodoxy. Though he originally had enjoyed Grannan's support in being named rector, he rapidly turned against him in the years immediately preceding Pius X's condemnation of Modernism. In 1906 O'Connell personally complained to the Pope about Grannan, without mentioning his name. Through a tragicomedy of errors, the Pope was led to conclude that O'Connell meant another professor of Old Testament, Henri Poels, a Dutchman, who was then forced to resign.[34] For the next generation, biblical scholarship at the university was to be restricted to language study and lower criticism.

Catholic biblical scholarship, however, was not limited to the Catholic University of America. From 1905 to 1908, the scholarly *New York Review* was published at St. Joseph's Seminary, Dunwoodie, New York. But on a more popular level, the *American Ecclesiastical Review,* intended for priests, showed a surprising openness to the new historico-critical method in the 1890s. Though the articles were admittedly non-controversial, Loisy published at least four.[35] Among the most interesting—and tragic—of the American contributors to the AER, however, was Joseph Bruneau, S.S., then the professor of Scripture at Dunwoodie. His columns on biblical studies and reviews of books during the 1890s praised the historical approach of Loisy and Marie-Joseph Lagrange, O.P. In 1897 he published his *Harmony of the Gospels,* which printed in parallel columns the various Synoptic accounts. In the preface he stated that he was not claiming to provide a solution to the Synoptic Problem but to give a popular guide to how the problem had arisen. For anything of value in his work, he said, he was indebted to his professors at the Institut Catholique, Loisy, Fulcran Grégoire Vigouroux, Louis Fillion, and Paulin Martin.[36] Vigouroux was a conservative scholar and later was the secretary of the Biblical Commission, but that Bruneau praised Loisy could be seen in retrospect as nothing short of daring.

Unfortunately, the condemnation of Modernism ended the openness represented by Bruneau. Already in the late 1890s his place as reporter on biblical scholarship was taken by Anthony J. Maas, S.J., rector of Woodstock College. He was succeeded in turn by Walter Drum, S.J., professor of Scripture at Woodstock. Neither of these Jesuits was capable of dealing with the new historical method, and both were to inculcate a narrow view of biblical studies in a whole generation of priests who read their columns.[37] The American Church, still reeling from the condemnation of Americanism, was all too eager to avoid any identification with anything associated with Modernism.

Until the 1940s there was virtually no scriptural scholarship and, consequently, very little attempt to revitalize the spiritual life of the faithful with the Bible. In 1901 Francis Aloysius Spencer, O.P., a convert to Catholicism and a former Paulist, had published his translation from the Greek of the four Gospels, but the remainder of the New Testament, completed in 1913, was published only in 1937 at the request of the American bishops. This was the first American Catholic translation of the New Testament from the Greek.[38] In general, however, the danger of the historical criticism of the Bible condemned by Pius X reinforced the danger of private interpretation of the Bible condemned by the Council of Trent. In the United States and Europe, biblical scholarship was largely a Protestant affair. Fear of scholarship may have reinforced the notion that the Bible was a Protestant book. Priests, of course, were required to read daily passages of the Bible in their breviaries, but the laity were probably conversant only with those portions of the sacred texts read at the Sunday Mass.

Though Catholic scholars continued to engage in lower criticism, i.e., establishing the texts of the Scripture, and engaged in archaeological research, renewed efforts to place a readable text of the Bible in the hands of the faithful occurred through two initially unrelated events. First, Bishop Edwin Vincent O'Hara of Great Falls, Montana, founder of the Catholic Rural Life Conference and chairman of the episcopal committee of the Confraternity of Christian Doctrine, invited a group of Scripture scholars to a meeting in Washington in 1936 to discuss the revision of the Douay Version. This meeting ultimately led to the formation of the Catholic Biblical Association.[39]

In 1937 the Scripture scholars assembled in St. Louis further to discuss the project. They heard Romain Butin, S.M., a guiding influence on O'Hara and professor of ancient Near-Eastern languages at the Catholic University, speak on the "Revision of the Hebrew Text of the Pentateuch," in which he acknowledged that Moses was "substantially" the author of the Pentateuch, but then proceeded to show how the language of the books had developed since the time of Moses as the Israelite community altered and gave new meaning to his words.[40] Butin's was a far more advanced notion of the development within Scripture than that so naïvely represented by Kenrick's a century earlier.

Father William L. Newton, who headed the group of translators, then went to Rome in the summer of 1938 to consult members of the Biblical Commission about making a translation from the original languages. While some were in favor, all urged that any translation from the Vulgate take into consideration the original languages which underly the Latin. In England, Newton also spoke with C. Lattey, S.J., one of the editors of the

Westminster translation of the New Testament from the Greek, which had been published under the auspices of the hierarchy of England and Wales from 1913 to 1935. Lattey suggested that the Americans adopt this British endeavor. But O'Hara was adamant that the work was to be done by American scholars. After Newton's report on his trip, the translators decided to undertake a translation from the Vulgate.[41] The translation of the New Testament, the Confraternity Edition, was hastened into print in 1941 in time to provide copies for the millions of American Catholics entering the armed forces. The Catholic Biblical Association then began to translate the Old Testament.

The second event occurred in the midst of World War II and paved the way for full Catholic participation in biblical scholarship. In 1943 Pius XII issued his encyclical *Divino Afflante Spiritu* calling for new translations into the vernacular to be made from the original languages and for Catholic exegetes to use the historico-critical method, so suspect at the time of the condemnation of Modernism. Though the scholarly repercussions of the encyclical would not be felt until after the war, Catholic scholars could now join their Protestant counterparts in the methods they used to interpret the Bible. Of more immediate effect was the decision of the Catholic Biblical Association to abandon the translation of the Old Testament from the Vulgate and turn to the original languages. Though the translations of several books appeared from 1948 to 1951, the entire project awaited the impetus of the Second Vatican Council to bring it to completion. Work on the New Testament likewise proceeded slowly. In 1954, the translation from the Greek of James Kleist, S.J., and Joseph Lilly, C.M., was published, but was not generally accepted as the representative American revision needed.[42]

The Second Vatican Council threw open the doors of biblical scholarship still further. In its constitution on Divine Revelation, *Dei Verbum,* it stated that not only were new translations to be made from the original languages but, since the Bible was the common heritage of Catholics and Protestants, the translations should be a collaborative effort.[43] The American appropriation of this new approach ultimately led to the New American Bible, translated collaboratively by Catholic and Protestant scholars under the auspices of the American bishops.[44]

The new translations were first introduced into the liturgy late in 1964. For some Catholics, the new translation of the New Testament from the Greek was a source of consternation; for example, whereas the Confraternity Edition, following the Vulgate, had proclaimed that Christ rose from the dead, the new text read that Christ was raised from the dead.[45] Just as the adoption of the vernacular liturgy was the most obvious change of Vatican II which the people perceived, the translation of the Bible from the Greek and Hebrew, rather than from the Vulgate, was the most obvious effect which they saw of the new orientation in biblical scholarship.

The general effects of the Second Vatican Council on American Catholicism were both scholarly and pastoral. On the scholarly level, Catholic scholars began their ambitious undertaking to produce the *Jerome Biblical Commentary*, published in 1968. One purpose of the work, done exclusively by Catholics, was to show the maturity of American Catholic biblical scholarship. They had, moreover, moved into the mainstream of biblical scholarship. Although the Society of Biblical Literature, a predominantly Protestant organization, had already had a few Catholic members, including Walter Drum, Catholics now joined the Society in increasing numbers. Two have been elected president, Raymond E. Brown, S.S., in 1977 and Joseph A. Fitzmyer, S.J., in 1979.

The pastoral effect of the Council is more difficult to assess. Though the Council placed an increased emphasis on Scripture and established a three-year cycle of readings for the Sunday liturgies, which has been adopted by many mainline Protestant denominations, recent polls indicate that American Catholics still read the Scripture less frequently than Protestants.[46] The emphasis for American Catholicism seems still to be on sacrament rather than on both word and sacrament.

The role of the Bible among American Catholics, then, has to be seen in the context of the sacramental orientation of Catholicism in general, a context heightened in the United States by the Church's being composed of immigrants and by the attacks made on Catholicism by the Protestant majority. The charge that Catholics were forbidden to read the Bible was in reality unfounded, for, even as the charge was being made, the bishops of the nineteenth century were urging their people to read the Scripture and were attempting to provide an authentic version of the Douay Bible. Nevertheless, circumstances led to the popular conception that the Bible was a Protestant book. First, there was the nineteenth-century reaction to the bishops' demand that Catholic children be allowed to read the Douay Version in public schools; the alternative was to make the schools totally neutral. Second, there was the Catholic reaction to Modernism, which seemed to relegate Scripture scholarship exclusively to Protestants. Only as Catholic Scripture scholarship was again encouraged and as the ecumenical movement developed, could the Bible become recognized as a common heritage of both Catholics and Protestants. The liturgical renewal and the joint Protestant-Catholic translations of the Scripture have fostered this recognition. Yet it will still take time for what is basically a scholarly endeavor to work its way down to the people, who have yet to realize what the bishops called for in 1884, "that the most highly valued treasure of every family library, and the most frequently and lovingly made use of, should be the Holy Scriptures."

NOTES

1. Karl Rahner, S.J., ed., *The Teaching of the Catholic Church,* originally prepared by Josef Neuner, S.J., and Heinrich Roos, S.J. (Staten Island, N.Y.: Alba House, 1967), pp. 59–61.
2. Ray Allen Billington, *The Protestant Crusade: A Study of the Origins of American Nativism* (Chicago: Quadrangle Books, 1964), pp. 68–76.
3. Lyman Beecher, *Plea for the West* (Cincinnati: Truman and Smith, 1835), p. 67. For obtaining sections of this work, I am grateful to my student Leo Hirrel.
4. *Ibid.,* pp. 118–19.
5. Billington, *The Protestant Crusade,* p. 157.
6. Quoted, *ibid.,* p. 158.
7. *Ibid.,* pp. 144–55.
8. *Ibid.,* pp. 221–30.
9. Gerald Shaughnessy, *Has the Immigrant Kept the Faith?* (New York: Macmillan, 1925), pp. 119–26.
10. Gerald P. Fogarty, S.J., *The Vatican and the Americanist Crisis: Denis J. O'Connell, American Agent in Rome, 1885–1903* (Rome: Università Gregoriana Editrice, 1974), p. 188.
11. B'nai B'rith Anti-Defamation League *News 'n Notes,* May 1981.
12. Patrick W. Skehan, George W. MacRae, S.J., and Raymond E. Brown, S.S., "Texts and Versions," *Jerome Biblical Commentary* (Englewood Cliffs, N.J.: Prentice-Hall, 1968), p. 588.
13. John Carroll to Mathew Carey, Baltimore, Jan. 30, 1789, in *The John Carroll Papers* (3 vols.; Notre Dame: University of Notre Dame Press, 1976), 1:348.
14. Carroll to Carey, Baltimore, April 8, 1789, *ibid.,* 355.
15. Margaret T. Hills, *The English Bible in America: A Bibliography of Editions of the Bible & New Testament* (New York: The American Bible Society and the New York Public Library, 1961), p. 4. Eleven years later Carey published the King James Version with the Apocrypha in small print which may have been his attempt to provide a common Bible; see *ibid.,* p. 15.
16. *Collectio Lacensis,* III, 28. Thomas F. Casey, *The Sacred Congregation de Propaganda Fide and the Revision of the First Provincial Council of Baltimore (1829–1830),* vol. LXXXVIII of *Analecta Gregoriana* (Rome: Università Gregoriana Editrice, 1957), pp. 116–22.
17. Hugh J. Nolan, ed., *Pastoral Letters of the American Hierarchy, 1792–1970* (Huntington, Ind.: Our Sunday Visitor, 1971), pp. 27–28.
18. *Ibid.,* p. 28.
19. *Ibid.,* p. 38.
20. *Ibid.,* pp. 51–52.

21. Francis Kenrick to Peter Kenrick, Philadelphia, Sept. 25, 1943, *The Kenrick-Frenaye Correspondence: Letters Chiefly of Francis Patrick Kenrick and Marc Antony Frenaye: 1830–1862,* translated by Frederick E. Tourscher (Philadelphia: Philadelphia Archives, 1920), p. 174. The "recent theory" of which Kenrick wrote may have been that of J. G. Eichhorn or of A. Geddes, an English Catholic; see Alexa Suelzer, S.P., "Modern Old Testament Criticism," *Jerome Biblical Commentary,* pp. 592–93.

22. Francis Kenrick to Peter Kenrick, Philadelphia, Oct. 2, 1847, *Kenrick-Frenaye Correspondence,* p. 299.

23. Francis Kenrick to Peter Kenrick, Philadelphia, Feb. 10, 1850, *ibid.,* p. 305.

24. Francis Kenrick to Peter Kenrick, Baltimore, Nov. 30, 1858, *ibid.,* pp. 415–16. See also, letter of Jan. 19, 1959. On Newman, see p. 417n.

25. Francis Kenrick to Peter Kenrick, Baltimore, Oct. 25, 1859, *ibid.,* p. 430.

26. Quoted in Hills, *English Bible in America,* pp. 206–7.

27. *Collectio Lacensis,* III, 357.

28. *Ibid.,* 380.

29. *Acta et Decreta Concilii Plenarii Baltimorensis Tertii . . .* (Baltimore: John Murphy & Co., 1886), lxvi–lxvii.

30. *Ibid.,* no. 216, pp. 117–18; no. 167, p. 86.

31. Nolan, ed., *Pastoral Letters,* pp. 177–78.

32. This copy was given to the present writer by Ellen Caskie Witt of Richmond, Va.

33. Archivio Segreto Vaticano, Rub. 43 (1903), fasc, 2, 78r–80v, Schroeder to Rampolla, Washington, June 18, 1895.

34. Robert North, S.J., "The American Scripture Century," *American Ecclesiastical Review,* CL (May 1964), 320. Poels, himself a member of the Biblical Commission, had difficulty subscribing to the Commission's decree on the Mosaic authorship of the Pentateuch. On a visit to Rome, he saw the Pope and expressed his misgivings, but received the assurance that he could continue teaching. When O'Connell mentioned that one of his professors raised questions with students without giving answers, the Pope assumed he meant Poels, when O'Connell meant Grannan.

35. Loisy published "Scriptural Account of the Two Disciples of Emmaus," *American Ecclesiastical Review,* XIV (1896), 446–47; "Vobiscum Sum," *ibid.,* XVI (1897), 495–504; "The Transfiguration of Our Lord," *ibid.,* XVII (1897), 169–79; and "Gethsemane," *ibid.,* XVIII (1898), 234–42.

36. North, "American Scripture Century," p. 322.

37. *Ibid.,* pp. 322–23. This presentation is in no way intended to be an exhaustive treatment of American Catholic biblical scholarship. For the variety of approaches in American scholarship to historical criticism and inspiration, see Mary Ellen Trahan, "Theories of Inspiration in American Catholic Biblical Scholarship," unpublished seminar paper, University of Virginia.

38. S. J. Hartdegen, "Bible, IV," *New Catholic Encyclopedia* (14 vols.; New York, McGraw-Hill, 1967), 2:267.

39. North, "American Scripture Century," pp. 332–33.

40. Romain Butin, S.M., "Revision of the Hebrew Text of the Pentateuch," *Proceedings of the Catholic Biblical Association,* St. Louis, Mo., Oct. 9 & 10, 1937, pp. 16–28.

41. James Gerard Shaw, *Edwin Vincent O'Hara: American Prelate* (New York: Farrar, Straus and Cudahy, 1957), p. 185. For O'Hara's role in founding the CBA, see also pp. 173–91. Patrick W. Skehan, "The Old Testament Revision Project," *Catholic Biblical Quarterly,* V (1943), 214–19.

42. North, "American Scripture Century," p. 335.
43. Walter Abbott, ed., *Documents of Vatican II* (New York: Guild Press, 1966), p. 126.
44. The New American Bible appeared in 1970. The Protestant collaborators were David Noel Freedman, Frank M. Cross, and J. A. Sanders.
45. Raymond E. Brown, S.S., "Our New Translation of the Bible," *America,* CXI (Nov. 14, 1964), 601–4.
46. "Evangelical Christianity in the United States: National Parallel Surveys of General Public and Clergy," conducted for *Christianity Today* by the Gallup Organization, Inc., and the Princeton Religion Research Center (Princeton: Gallup, n.d.).

INDEX

Index

Abbot, Abiel, 55n39
Abbott, Lyman, 124
Adams, Henry, 4, 9n13, 126
Adams, John, 40, 62
Adams, Sam, 65
Adventists, 75
Ahlstrom, Sydney, 11, 14n18, 156
Aitken, Robert, 15n25
Alexander, Archibald, 52n5
Alexander, Caleb, 54n35
Alexander, James W., 84, 86
Allen, A. V. G., 123
America: as biblical nation, 10–
    11, 13n14, 18n52, 39–51; as
    Redeemer Nation, 27; as anti-
    type of biblical Israel, 43; as
    a biblical civilization, 121–
    23; as Chosen Nation, 140
American Revolution, 33–34, 41,
    43–44
Americanism, in Catholic church,
    174
Amish, 149
Anabaptists, 146, 149

Anderson, Robert, 119n31
Antinomianism controversy, 31–
    33
Atkins, Gaius Glenn, 123
Austin, Benjamin Jr., 65–66
authority—see democratic
    individualism

Babcock, William Smythe, 68–69,
    71
Backus, Isaac, 55n41, 61, 71
Bacon, Benjamin, 123
Bacon, Francis, 82–84
Baconianism, 83–84, 90–95, 103
Balmer, Randall, 97n28
Baptists, 33, 39, 88, 104–5; see
    Free-Will Baptists and
    Southern Baptist Convention
Barbour, Hugh, 27
Barker, Christopher, 36n20
Barnes, Albert, 89–90
Beard, Charles, 125
Becker, Carl L., 126

Beecher, Charles, 64
Beecher, Henry Ward, 116, 124, 157
Beecher, Lyman, 64, 77n20, 164
Belknap, Jeremy, 62
Bellamy, Joseph, 47
Benezet, Anthony, 56n54
Bentley, William (black evangelical), 152
Bentley, William (19th-cent. diarist), 67, 77n24
Bercovitch, Sacvan, 10, 19, 30
Berkowitz, David, 10
Beza, Theodore, 20
Bible: characters from: Abel, 44, 55n44; Abner, 41, 44, 55n44; Abraham, 55n44; Absalom, 4, 42; Adam, 49; Ahab, 4; Amos, 147; Apollos, 111; Belshazzar, 41; Cyrus, 44; Daniel, 44, 49–50, 147, 152; David, 41–42, 44, 49, 55n44; Elijah, 44; Eve, 49; Ezekiel, 168; Hezekiah, 43; Isaiah, 103, 147; Ishmael, 4; Jacob, 44, 49, 55n43; James, 73; Jehoiada, 44; Job, 147; John, 147; Jonah, 49; Joseph, 55n44; Joshua, 24, 39, 44, 49; Josiah, 44, 55n43; Judas, 44; Mordecai, 44; Moses, 4, 40, 43–44, 49–50, 55n44, 87, 93, 103, 175; Noah, 49; Othniel, 44; Pharoah, 44; Samuel, 44; Solomon, 42, 55n44; Stephen, 55n43; Zacharias, 168
Bible: doctrine of, 7, 15–16n27, 102–6, 123–25, 163–64
Bible: interpretation, 7, 11, 72, 79, 111
Bible: marginal notes, Geneva Bible, 21–25, 32; Scofield Bible, 114; Challoner, 166.
Bible: names, in United States, places, 3–4; people, 40.
Bible: Protestant approaches, 139–58; culturalist, 147–49; doctrinalist, 142–44; moralist, 145–47; pietist, 144–45
Bible: sermons, 41–42, 151
Bible: societies, 40, 165; American Bible Society, 6; Gideon Society, 166
Bible: texts cited: Genesis 1:2, 87; Genesis 13:10, 3; Exodus 1:8, 41; Exodus 20:15, 48; Exodus 21:16, 8; Leviticus 25:44–46, 9; Deuteronomy 26:19, 44; Joshua 7:13, 41; Joshua 12:24, 3; Joshua 18:28, 4; Judges 5:23, 44; II Samuel 3:38, 41; II Samuel 18:32, 42; II Kings 23:36, 3; I Chronicles 12:32, 43; II Chronicles 6:34–35, 42; Psalms 49:6, 24; Psalms 82:6–7, 43; Psalms 93:1, 43; Psalms 112:6, 43; Psalms 147:20, 44; Proverbs 31:9, 48; Isaiah 11:1, 24; Isaiah 27:6, 31; Jeremiah 7:6, 48; Daniel 5:27, 41; Daniel 11:13, 51; Micah 5:7, 31; Habakkuk 2:15, 48; Malachi 2:10, 50; Matthew 9:15, 32; Matthew 22:39, 48; John 21:22, 70; Acts 10:34, 50; Acts 17:26, 50; Romans 13:1–6, 34; Galatians 1:7, 32; Ephesians 5:11, 148; Ephesians 6:5–6, 48; Ephesians 6:9, 48; Colossians

2:21, 41; I Timothy 6:1, 48;
II Timothy 4:7, 56n55;
I Peter 2:18, 48; Revelation
10:5–6, 56n55
Bible: translating, 6–7; Geneva
Bible, 20–21; American
Catholic efforts, 169–77
Bible: typology, 43–48, 92–93
Bible: versions: Bishop's Bible,
21; Confraternity Edition,
176; Douay-Rheims-
Challoner, 9, 166–73, 175–
77; Geneva Bible, 20–33;
Good News Bible, 6; Holy
Scriptures (Jewish Publica-
tion Society), 15n21; King
James (Authorized Version),
9, 15n21, 20, 25–33, 164–66,
171–72; Living Bible, 6;
New American Bible, 15n21,
176; New American Standard
Bible, 15n21; New English
Bible, 14n21; New Interna-
tional Version, 6; Revised
Standard Version, 6; Revised
Version, 172; Scofield Refer-
ence Bible, 114; Vulgate,
163–65, 170–71, 175–77
Bible—*see also,* evidences; higher
criticism; historico-critical
method; inerrancy; inspira-
tion; *and other individual
subjects*
Birch, Bruce, 140
Blacks, and the Bible, 48–51,
150–53; spirituals, 49,
96n15; and sermons, 151
Blakeslee, Solomon, 54n34
Blanchard, Charles, 115
B'nai B'rith, Anti-Defamation
League, 166
Bodley, John, 35n6

Boucher, Jonathan, 56n54
Bozeman, Theodore Dwight, 95n8,
96n13, 97n20
Bradford, William, 4
Breasted, James Henry, 123
Brethren, Church of, 155
Briggs, Charles Augustus, 123–24,
133
Brookes, James H., 119n36
Brooks, Phillips, 116, 127, 157
Broughton, Hugh, 36n22
Brown, Raymond E., 177
Brownson, Orestes, 171
Bruce, F. F., 21, 36n22
Bruneau, Joseph, 174
Bryan, William Jennings, 9
Bryant, Anita, 156
Bryce, James, 121–22
Bulkeley, Peter, 37n35
Bunyan, John, 4
Burroughs, Peleg, 55n43
Burton, Ernest DeWitt, 123
Bury, J. B., 125
Bushnell, Horace, 88
Butin, Romain, 175
Butler, Bishop, 80
Butterfield, Herbert, 6
Byrd, William II, 9

Calvin, John, 20–22, 26, 61, 71
Campbell, Alexander, 10, 71–72
Carey, Matthew, 166–67
Carroll, John, 166–67
Carter, Jimmy, 4
Carter, Paul, 101
Cartwright, Thomas, 26
Case, Shirley Jackson, 133
Catholic Biblical Association,
175–76
Challoner, Richard, 166, 171
Charismatic movement, 145, 155

Chase, Mary Ellen, 147
Chauncy, Charles, 53n24, 63–64, 76n9
Chesnut, Mary Boykin, 39
Chesterton, G. K., 10
Christian Movement, 71, 75
Christian Reformed Church, 155, 159n10
civil religion, 140
Civil War, U.S., 40–44, 51
Clarke, John, 33
Clarke, Samuel, 63, 76n9
Clarke, William Newton, 104–8, 111, 116, 123, 128–30, 133, 137n33
Clay, Henry, 40
Cleveland, Grover, 4, 75–76
Cobb, Howell, 8, 16n38
Cole, Stewart, 101
Cole, William, 35n6
Coleridge, Samuel Taylor, 81–82
Colson, Howard, 144
Common Sense—see Scottish Common Sense Philosophy
Congregationalists, 39, 71, 89
Conwell, Russell H., 124, 157
covenant theology, and Puritans, 23, 27–29
Coverdale, Miles, 20, 35n6
Cowper, William, 79
Crapsey, Algernon, 124
creation, 4, 93

Dante, 147
Darrow, Clarence, 9
Darwin, Charles, 84, 87, 94–95
Davis, Jefferson, 40, 42, 44
Dawson, Anthony, 49
democratic individualism, 66–67, 74, 81; and crisis of authority

in early national period, 63–66
Dewey, John, 125
Dirksen, Everett, 147
Dispensationalism, 114–15
Divino Afflante Spiritu, 176
Dixon, A. C., 113
Dixon, A. T., 113
Dorner, Isaac, 124
Douglass, Frederick, 58n91
Drum, Walter, 174, 177
Duffield, George, 99n40
Dumas, David W., 52n12
Durkheim, Emile, 42
Dwight, Timothy, 55n40, 77n20, 84–85

Education, public, and Bible, 4, 8, 16n36, 17n43; and Catholics, 165–66
Edwards, Jonathan, 10, 46–48, 61–62
Eichhorn, J. G., 179n21
Eliot, John, 6
Elizabeth I, Queen, 36n20
Elliot, Charles, 98n28
Emerson, Ralph Waldo, 79, 81, 96n9
England, as elect nation, 45
England, John, 169
Enlightenment, 62–64, 74
Erasmus, 61
Ervin, Sam, 147
Estienne, Robert, 20
Evans, William, 111–13, 116
evidences, for Christianity, 86–87
Exodus, the, 43, 49–50, 55n38

Falwell, Jerry, 156
Faulkner, William, 4, 12n7

Fillion, Louis, 174
Finney, Charles G., 75, 85, 89, 98n28
Fisher, George, 98n31
Fisher, Nathaniel, 54n34
Fitzmyer, Joseph A., 177
Forsyth, P. T., 133
Fosdick, Harry Emerson, 116, 141–42, 146, 153
Foster, George Burman, 123
Foxe, John, 35n12
Franklin, Benjamin, 40
Free-Will Baptists, 68–69
Frei, Hans W., 158n2
French Revolution, 64
Freud, Sigmund, 42
Fundamentalism, 101–4, 108–17, 144, 154; and the "Bible reading," 110; and synthetic Bible study, 112–13
Furniss, Norman, 101

Gallup, George Jr., 3, 141
Gaustad, Edwin S., 122
Geddes, A., 179n21
Genovese, Eugene, 50, 57n77
geology—see science
Gibbons, James, 173
Gilby, Anthony, 20
Ginger, Ray, 101
Gladden, Washington, 116, 122
Goodman, Christopher, 35n6
Gordon, Adoniram Judson, 112, 127–28
Gordon, George A., 124, 127–28
Gould, Ezra P., 123–24
Graham, Billy, 156
Grannan, Charles P., 173–74, 179n34
Gray, James M., 111–14, 116
Great Awakening, 62

Green, Jacob, 47
Green, L. W., 87
Green, William Henry, 119n31, 123, 133
Greene, John C., 14n17
Grimké, Sarah Moore, 79–80
Grund, Francis, 121–22
Gunn, Giles, 129

Hague, Dyson, 110
Haldeman, I. M., 113–14, 119n37
Handy, Robert T., 122
Harper, William Rainey, 123–24, 132–33
Hart, Levi, 47
Haupt, Paul, 123
Haydock, Canon, 172
Hertz, Emmanuel, 56n53
Hewitt, Augustine, 170
higher criticism, of Bible, 102–3, 105, 111, 123–24, 134n5–7
historical consciousness, 122–27, 133
historico-critical method, 173–74, 176
Hitchcock, Edward, 100n41
Hitler, Adolf, 126
Hodge, A. A., 118n21, 123
Hodge, Charles, 88, 90–91, 96n13, 99n35–38, 106, 121
Hofstadter, Richard, 101
Holley, Israel, 47
Holmes, Oliver Wendell, 125
Hopkins, Mark, 86, 91, 98n30
Hopkins, Samuel, 47–48, 51
Howard, Simeon, 62
Howlett, T. R., 55n51
Hudson, Winthrop S., 5, 122, 156–57
Hughes, John, 165
Hughes, Sarah, 14n16

Hutchinson, Anne, 31–33
hymns, 85
Hyvernat, Henri, 173

Iggers, Georg, 125
inerrancy, of Bible, 13n13, 89–90,
    97–99n26–36, 106, 124–25,
    135n13–14, 154–55
inspiration, of Bible, 104–7, 113,
    124–25
Ireland, John, 166, 173

Jackson, Andrew, 64
Jackson, Stonewall, 79
James, William, 125
Jastrow, Morris, 133
Jefferson, Thomas, 4, 12n8, 40, 64
Jesus Christ, in Bible, 23–24, 32,
    50, 108
Jews, 5, 7, 14n17, 16n29, 44
Johnson, Edward, 31
Johnson, Franklin, 118n30
Johnson, James Weldon, 55n38
Johnson, Lyndon, 5, 14n16

Kant, Immanuel, 81
Keane, John, 173
Keith, George, 37n25
Kelsey, David, 139, 143, 155
Kempis, Thomas à, 172
Kennedy, John F., 5
Kenrick, Francis Patrick, 9, 165,
    169–72, 175
Kenrick, Peter R., 170–72
King, Henry Churchill, 123
Kleist, James, 176
Knox, John, 35n6
Kuhn, Thomas, 103–4, 117
Kuyper, Abraham, 159n10

Lagrange, Marie-Joseph, 174
Lamar, J. S., 84
Lattey, C., 175–76
Leo XIII, Pope, 173
Levine, Lawrence, 49, 57n77
Lewis, C. S., 8
Liberalism, Protestant, 105–8,
    122–24, 155
Liberation Theology, 149
Lilly, Joseph, 176
Lincoln, Abraham, 4–5, 10, 39–
    40, 42–45, 52n3, 55n44, 59–
    60, 75, 79
Lindsell, Harold, 119n39
literacy, 30, 49, 150–51
literature in America, and Bible,
    4, 16n34–35, 147, 154,
    161n45
Lockridge, Kenneth A., 34n2
Loisy, Alfred, 173–74
Luther, Martin, 20, 22–23, 35n13,
    36n16, 61, 71
Lutheran Church—Missouri Synod,
    4, 155
Lutherans, 141
Lynd, Robert and Helen, 122

McGiffert, A. C., 123–24
McKim, Donald, 97n26, 98n28,
    135n13
McLoughlin, William G., 77n20
McNemar, Richard, 73
Maas, Anthony J., 174
Machen, J. Gresham, 133
Madison, Bishop James, 56n55
Mahan, Asa, 85
Mannheim, Karl, 125
Maring, Norman H., 98n32, 104
Marsden, George M., 35n3,
    102–3, 115
Marsh, James, 82

Marshall, Robert, 78n40
Martin, Paulin, 174
Marx, Karl, 42
Mary Tudor, Queen, 20
Mather, Cotton, 45
Mathews, Donald, 51
Mauro, Philip, 144
May, Henry, 76n9, 125
Mead, Sidney, 158n4
Melville, Herman, 4, 12n7, 79
Mennonites, 155
Methodists, 62, 71, 141
millennialism, 31, 44, 75, 114
Miller, Perry, 5, 29, 35n3
Miller, William, 75
Mitchell, Henry H., 151–52
Mitchell, Hinckley, 124
Modernism, in Catholic church,
    174; see also Liberalism,
    Protestant
Moody, Dwight L., 112, 145
Moody Bible Institute, 113
Moore, George Foote, 123
Morgan, Edmund S., 70
Mormons, 73
Mott, Lucretia, 77n13
Mullins, E. Y., 133
Munger, Theodore T., 124
Munhall, Leander, 118n30

Nevin, John W., 60, 71, 73–74
New Testament, 44, 71–72
Newman, John Henry, 171
Newton, Isaac, 81
Newton, William L., 175–76
Niebuhr, H. Richard, 101, 149
Norton, Andrews, 81
Noyes, John Humphrey, 70–71

Oaks, Urian, 30
O'Brien, Larry, 5

O'Connell, Denis J., 172–74,
    179n34
Oden, Thomas, 145
O'Hara, Edwin Vincent, 175–76,
    179n41
O'Kelly, James, 71
Old Testament, 5–6, 23–24, 29,
    43, 45, 47, 49–50, 71
Olivetan, 21
Oneida Community, 70
Orr, James, 119n31
Osgood, David, 55n39

Paley, William, 86
Palmer, Benjamin, 39, 82
Park, Edwards A., 88
Parker, Joseph, 111, 119n40
Parker, Theodore, 88, 122
Peake, A. S., 133
Peale, Norman Vincent, 156
Pelikan, Jaroslav, 36n16
Pells, Richard H., 122
Penn, William, 26
Pierson, A. T., 111, 119n30
Pilgrims, 28
Pius, XI, Pope, 174–75, 179n34
Pius XII, Pope, 176
Poels, Henri, 174, 179n34
politics, and Bible, 8–9, 24–25,
    147–49, 156
Powell, John Wesley, 133
Presbyterians, 13n12, 71–72, 89
Prince, John, 55n55
Princeton Theology, 88, 90,
    105–6, 143
printing, of Bible, 6–7, 39
Protestantism, and biblical author-
    ity, 20, 61–62, 80
Providentissimus Deus, 173
Purcell, John Baptist, 171
Puritanism, 19–34, 45, 156

Quakers, 26–27, 37n25, 155

Raboteau, Albert, 150–51
Rampolla, Mariano, 173
Ramsay, David, 53n23
Rasmussen, Larry, 140
Rauschenbusch, Walter, 123, 148–49, 160n28
Reid, Thomas, 82, 96n10–11
Rennie, Ian, 97n26
Reynolds, John, 26
Riceour, Paul, 133
Rogers, Jack B., 97n26, 98n28, 135n13
Roman Catholics, 9–10, 17n43, 80, 141, 163–78
Russell, William, 173

Sampson, Thomas, 35n6
Sandeen, Ernest, 98n28, 102, 135n13, 136n24
Sargent, Abel, 78n39
Schaeffer, Francis, 154
Schmidt, Nathaniel, 123–24
Schroeder, Joseph, 173
Schuller, Robert, 156
Schwarz, W., 35n13
science, and Bible, 86–95, 106–7; geology, 87
Scofield, C. I., 114
Scottish Common Sense Philosophy, 82–83, 85, 90–95, 115
Scripture—see Bible
Seabrook, Whitemarsh, 49
Second Great Awakening, 74–75, 84
Shakers, 73
Sheldon, Charles M., 146, 159n19
Shepard, Thomas, 11

slavery, and Bible, 8–9, 47–48, 54n30
slaves, and religion, 48–51, 57n73, 150–51
Smith, Elias, 66–68, 71–72, 75, 77n20, 77n23–24
Smith, Henry B., 89, 97n22
Smith, Henry Preserved, 124
Smith, Joseph, 69, 73, 79
Smith, Lucy Mack, 69, 71, 73
Smith, William Robertson, 121, 124
Smyth, Newman, 123
Social Gospel, 148
Society of Biblical Literature, 8, 16n36, 177
Sola Scriptura, 60, 71, 86
Southern Baptist Convention, 4, 141
Spencer, Aloysius, 175
Stiles, Ezra, 44, 63
Stone, Barton, 71–75
Straton, John Roach, 116
Strong, Augustus H., 130–33
Strong, Charles Augustus, 133
Strong, John Henry, 133
Stuart, Moses, 92–93
Swing, David, 124

Taylor, John, 63, 76n9
Taylor, Kenneth, 6
Taylor, Nathaniel William, 77n20
Tennent, Gilbert, 9
Thomas, Latta R., 152
Thomas, W. H. Griffith, 109, 113
Thompson, John, 78n40
Todd, John E., 54n33
Torrey, Reuben A., 110, 112, 116
Toy, Crawford H., 123–24, 131
Transcendentalism, 81–82

Trent, Council of, 163–64, 167,
    175
Trinterud, Leonard, 26
Troeltsch, Ernst, 125
Trumbull, Benjamin, 53n22,
    54n34
Turner, Nat, 17n39, 79
Twain, Mark, 81
Tyler, Samuel, 82
Tyndale, William, 20
types—see Bible: typology

Unitarians, 63–64, 81, 88
Universalism, 63, 68

Vatican II, 176–77
Vigouroux, Fulcran Grégoire, 174

Wakefield, Samuel, 89
Walden, Treadwell, 56n52
Wallis, Jim, 148
Walther, C. F. W., 98n28
Warfield, B. B., 118n21, 123, 133,
    143, 145
Washington, George, 3, 41, 43–
    45, 53–54n25, 55n43, 56n55

Wayland, Francis, 86
Weber, Max, 125–26, 153
Webster, Daniel, 40
Webster, Noah, 4, 39
Weems, Mason, 3
Weld, Theodore Dwight, 8, 16n37
Wesley, John, 61–62, 71
West, Samuel, 33–34
Westcott, Brooke Foss, 25
Wheelwright, John, 31–32
Whitaker, Nathaniel, 55n42
White, Morton, 125
Whitefield, George, 61–62
Whittingham, William, 20, 35n5
Wilson, John F., 158n4
Wilson, Woodrow, 4, 10, 59, 132
Winchell, Alexander, 124
Winchester, Elhanan, 67, 71
Winthrop, John, 27–28, 33
Wise, Isaac, 16n29, 44
Wolterstorff, Nicholas, 142,
    159n10
Wood, Gordon S., 65
Woodbridge, John D., 97n26,
    97–98n28
Woods, Leonard, 89, 98n28
Worcester, Noah, 63–64, 76n13
Wright, Conrad, 122
Wright, George Frederick, 133
Wycliffe Bible Translators, 7